IMAGES
of America

BARTOW

ON THE COVER: Engine No. 5, possibly the Florida Southern Railway's 2-4-4T Mason locomotive, waits on the outskirts of Bartow while passengers leisurely pick and enjoy nature's bounty in an orange grove. A maintenance handcar, also known as a section car, rests beside the locomotive, while additional railroad cars concealed by citrus trees snake in the background. (Courtesy State Archives of Florida, Frisbie Collection.)

IMAGES
of America

BARTOW

William Lloyd Harris

ARCADIA
PUBLISHING

ISBN 978-0-7385-9872-7

Published by Arcadia Publishing
Charleston, South Carolina

Printed in the United States of America

Library of Congress Control Number: 2012949198

For all general information, please contact Arcadia Publishing:
Telephone 843-853-2070
Fax 843-853-0044
E-mail sales@arcadiapublishing.com
For customer service and orders:
Toll-Free 1-888-313-2665

Visit us on the Internet at www.arcadiapublishing.com

To my wife, Sharon, and family for supporting this project; and to the late Louise K. Frisbie, historian and journalist, who inspired generations to cherish the history of our city.

Contents

ACKNOWLEDGMENTS

It is my sincere wish to thank each and every one who played a part in producing this book. In particular, foremost gratitude is extended to S.L. Frisbie IV, author, publisher, editor, and fellow historical commissioner, for his encouragement and for allowing me the privilege to utilize the Louise K. Frisbie Collection and resources of his office; Tom Muir, curator of the Polk County History Center, whose assistance and advice has been invaluable; Peggy Kehoe, managing editor, Aileen Hood, general manager, and the staff of the *Polk County Democrat* for their total support; and Odell Robinson, editor of the Polk County Historical Association, for promoting this project.

In addition, my thanks go to the following friends and institutions for their assistance in providing photographs, references, and technical support: State Archives of Florida; the Georgia Historical Society; Myrtice Young, director of the Polk County History Center, and staff member Maria Trippe; director Joe Spann of the Polk County Historical and Genealogical Library and staff members Gail Seger, Dorothy Manley, and Dorinda Garrard; Brian Hinton, executive director, Bartow Community Health Care Foundation; Clifton Lewis, director, and the Historic L.B. Brown House; First Presbyterian Church of Bartow; Roxanna Tovrea, director, Bartow Public Library; Linda Chancey, Polk County Library Cooperative; Jeff Clark, executive director, Virginia Condello, and the Greater Bartow Chamber of Commerce staff; David Brewer, president, and Freddie Wright, director and editor emeritus, of the Polk County Historical Association; Sally and Dudley Putnam; George McClelland; Mollie Marion; Kenneth Laurent; Lynda Belle and David Black; Barbara and Wallace Orr; Lois Phillips; Corine Head; Mary Cromartie; Dr. Paul E. Coury; Bo Raulerson; Andy Laurent; Linda Sue and Bruce Munroe; Ron Pritchard; Corinne O'Bryan; Laquill Mason; Marion E. Wheeler, Martha "Marcie", and the late Eugene Miller; Jeanette Smith; Wayne Shelton; Jan Crawford; Geraldine Watson; Eloise Whitman; Rob Robinson; Lotis Davis; John Padgett; Keith Warren; Mike Butler; the late Dr. Medora Van Fleet; Shirley Padgett Johnson; Rev. Rick Rodriguez and Alex Harris for technical support; Dorothy Harris; Ginny and Rusty Music; and my best friend and wife, Sharon A. Harris.

INTRODUCTION

A forest of oaks and pines, rich in subtropical verdure, inhabited by wildlife and yet full of promise—this was the scene met by Bartow's first settlers. Prior to 1850, only soldiers, the first government land surveyors, native Seminoles, and hunters and cattlemen seeking game or pasture came this way, none with the intent to put up permanent dwellings and stay.

The incentive to settle resulted from the Armed Occupation Act of 1842, enacted at the conclusion of the Second Seminole Indian War. The act granted, under certain conditions, 160 acres of land to homesteaders willing to clear and cultivate at least 5 acres, erect a dwelling, and take part in armed protection of the area.

A hardy pioneer named James D. Green arrived in 1850 and cleared 4 of the 160 acres he claimed under the act. He built a small log cabin just northwest of the present Polk County History Center (old county courthouse). Green willingly sold his "improvement" a year later to Riley R. Blount, one of the four sons of Readding Blount, who arrived in the area in October 1851 and moved onto the Green claim, having relocated from Alligator (Lake City).

Readding Blount's party included his two married sons and their families; two younger sons; a son-in-law, Streaty Parker, with his wife and two children; and John Davidson with his wife and child. In addition, there were 12 slaves whose families were noted as pioneers of the African American community. Other settlers soon followed the Blounts into this area. Circuit-riding Baptist minister Rev. Jeremiah Hayman provided spiritual comfort and laid the foundations for many churches. Tension with the Indians resumed, and a log blockhouse built in 1853 by the Blounts became a place of refuge and gave the community its first name, Fort Blount. The settlement was also known as Peace Creek.

The Third Seminole Indian War began in 1855 and ended in 1858. There were no attacks upon Fort Blount, but a military presence was at hand. Capt. Leroy Leslie's Company of Florida Mounted Militia was mustered into service at Fort Blount on March 12, 1856.

Settlement continued in the area, but was again hampered by war clouds when Florida seceded from the Union on January 10, 1861. On February 8, Polk County was created from Hillsborough and Brevard Counties. The county's name, suggested by Readding Blount, honored former US president James K. Polk, who was sworn in as president the day after Florida achieved statehood. Pioneer conditions and the instability of wartime stalled a permanent site for the county government. First located at Mud Lake, then at Jefferson, a townsite never developed.

The first major battle of the Civil War took place at Manassas, Virginia, on July 21, 1861. A popular southern lawyer turned soldier, Col. (Bvt. Brig. Gen.) Francis Stebbins Bartow, of Savannah, Georgia, was the first general officer to die in combat, and communities throughout the South sought to honor this hero. Two towns in Florida changed their names to venerate Bartow. The Confederate Post Office Department settled the issue, as reported in a government publication, *A List of Establishments, Discontinuances and Changes in Names of the Post Offices in the Confederate States since 1861*. Polk County's community would retain the name Bartow, and Jackson County's town would be named Beauregard. Fort Blount officially became Bartow.

It would seem that the earliest record of the town of Bartow is in the *Register of Accounts Current of Post Offices in the State of Florida, 1862* for January to March, listing W.P. Brown's accounts as the postmaster for Bartow. The same period witnessed much activity and zeal.

With the onset of the Civil War, Bartow's men had quickly organized under Capt. William B. Varn and met at regular intervals to conduct military drills. The unit was reorganized with a new commander, Capt. Nathan Snow Blount, and on March 8, 1862, the community gathered to honor the "South Florida Bulldogs" with a sumptuous feast before the unit marched to Gainesville to tender its services to the Confederate army. On April 10, 1862, the men were assigned to the state's newest regiment as Company E, 7th Florida Infantry Regiment. They fought in the western theater of the war as part of the Confederate Army of Tennessee and surrendered on April 26, 1865.

Many other local men served in Capt. Francis A. Hendry's Independent Cavalry Company, or "Cow Cavalry," so called because of its unique assignment in the quartermaster department. These soldiers were tasked to drive Summerlin's and others' herds of cattle to north Florida for shipment to Savannah, Georgia, to feed the Southern armies. On the home front, spinning wheels were distributed to women to turn raw cotton into cloth for the war effort.

There were some who sympathized with the North and trekked to Union-held Fort Myers. Hardship for all was commonplace. William Watkins, a wealthy planter escaping from war-torn Virginia, arrived in the community with a large number of slaves, which served to bolster the African American community.

In 1862, wealthy cattle baron Jacob Summerlin purchased the Blount property for $3,000, moved his family to Bartow, and engaged in blockade-running and driving vast herds of cattle to feed the Confederate armies. Florida's final surrender came on May 20, 1865, and hard times continued. There were only about 150 souls in the community at the time, and Summerlin donated cows from his herd to insure the locals would not starve. It was then that he made his most profound gift. Jacob Summerlin gave to the people 120 acres of land to be divided three ways: 40 acres each to establish a county seat of government, churches, and a school. With this gift, he could rightly be called "the father of Bartow."

Summerlin had oxteams haul a sawmill to the site to turn the wilderness into homes. He paid for and gifted the area's first two-story building, to be used as a Masonic lodge and a school, the Summerlin Institute. The building was also used by the county court and the Baptist and Methodist churches until they sold their lands and acquired funds to erect their respective houses of justice and worship.

The area was not much more than wilderness when the founding fathers took the necessary steps to incorporate the City of Bartow on July 1, 1882. By 1884, the young city could only boast a thousand people, yet industry and change hovered on the horizon. Henry B. Plant's railroad reached the city in 1885. The door had been opened, and with it the first boom in population and growth.

The area's cattle, citrus, and phosphate attracted major players, and, with the town's prosperity, artisans and those of special talent followed. Among such individuals was one George P. Freeman, photographer, the first in a line of men and women who recorded the images that make up the historical chronicle seen by future generations. These are the stories of life, the stories of our city, the story of Bartow.

One

Pioneers 1851–1884

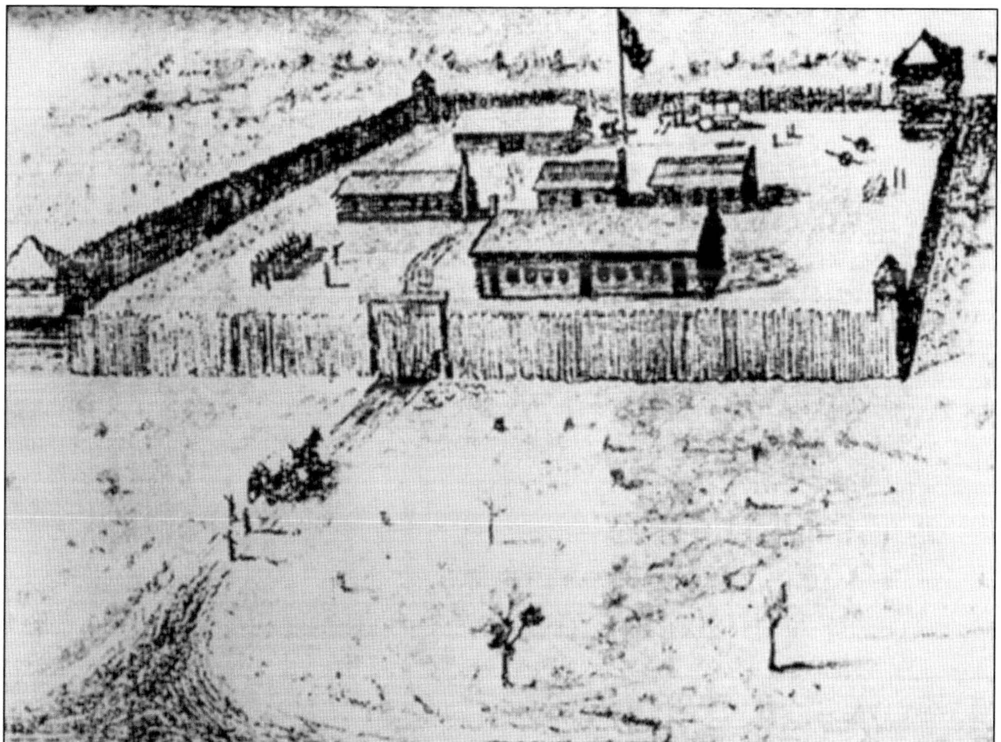

Fort Fraser, north of Bartow, was established in 1837 during Col. Zachary Taylor's Second Seminole Indian War campaign. The stockade consisted of pine poles, towers, and interior cabins for barracks and the storage of supplies. It played a major role in Taylor's victory at the Battle of Okeechobee. Deactivated in May 1838, the fort saw service again in the Third Seminole Indian War. (Courtesy State Archives of Florida.)

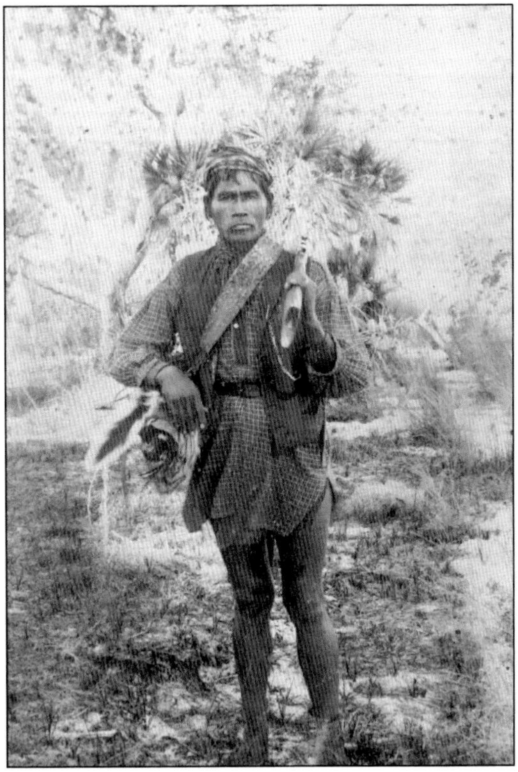

The Blount party found remains of a Seminole hunting camp in 1851, and hostilities prompted the building of a civilian fort. After the Civil War, visiting Seminoles bartering for goods were treated with an air of celebrity. This warrior is thought to be a son of Chief Chipco, who resided at Lake Pierce, east of Bartow, until that site was abandoned about 1896. (Courtesy State Archives of Florida.)

Fort Blount was erected in 1853 and served as a community refuge through the end of the Third Seminole War in 1858. It was not an active military post and was never attacked. The 1858 Davis map of Florida recorded it as a blockhouse. The present marker and Fort Blount Park are east of the fort's actual location. (Courtesy State Archives of Florida, Frisbie Collection.)

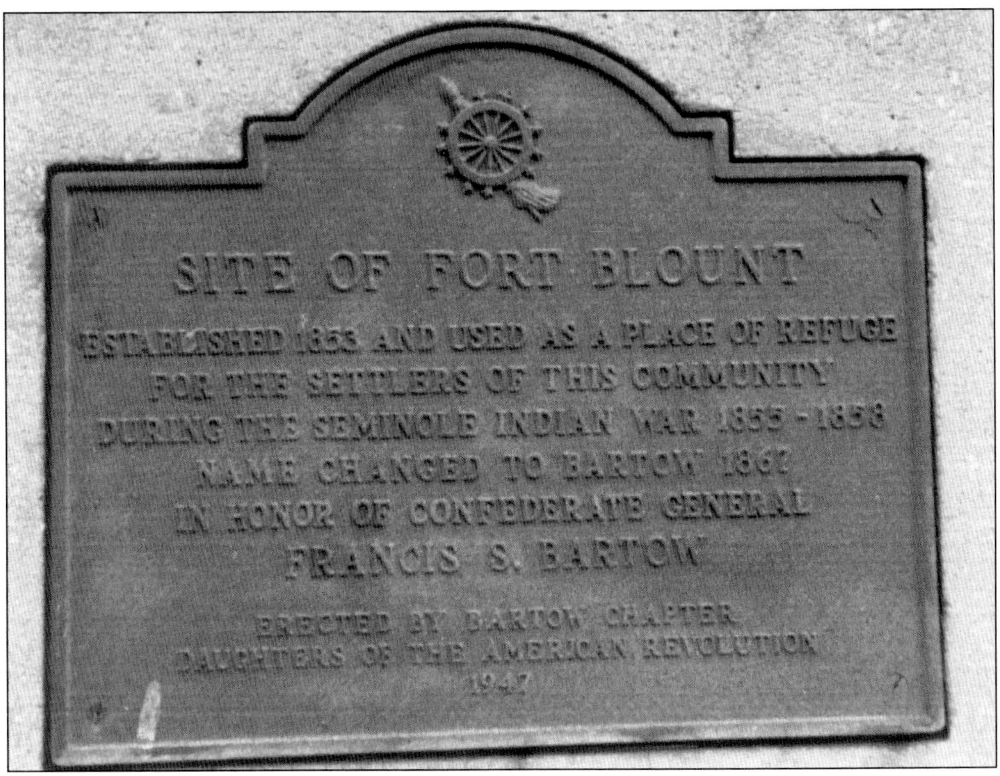

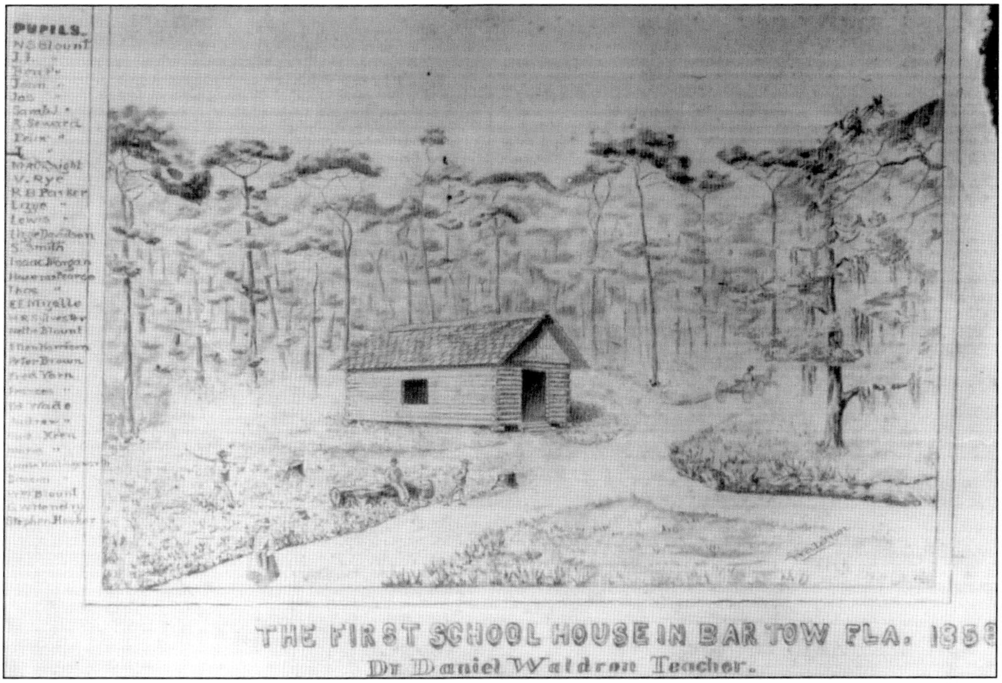

This 1858 image of Bartow's first school, known as the Peas Creek or Fort Blount School, was sketched by the first teacher, Dr. Daniel Waldron. A potbellied stove, two windows for light, and rough-hewn logs for seats provided the atmosphere for daily lessons. The building was also used as a court, church, and post office. (Courtesy State Archives of Florida, Frisbie Collection.)

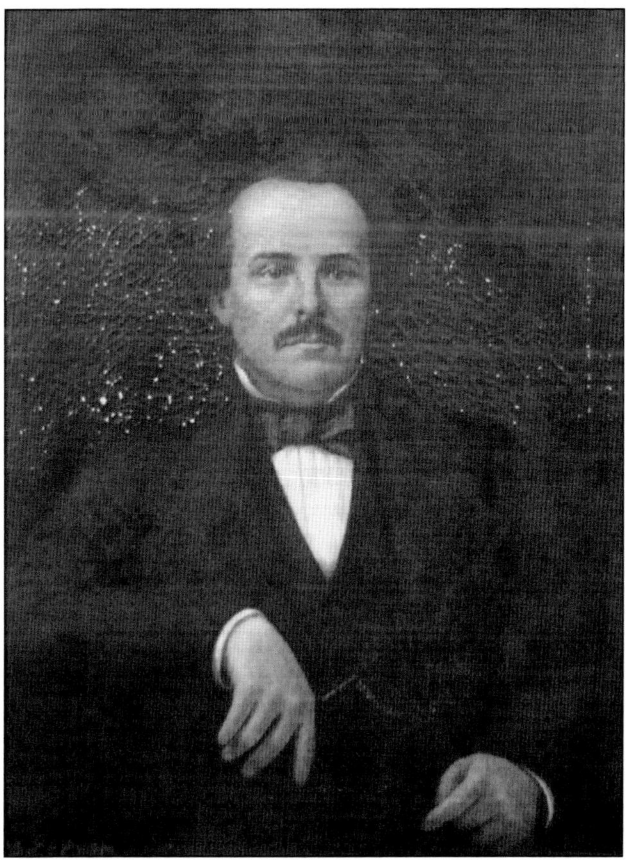

Francis Stebbins Bartow, a lawyer and politician, of Savannah, Georgia, rose to prominence early in the Civil War. He resigned a congressional seat to command a brigade in Virginia and was killed in action on July 21, 1861, at the First Battle of Manassas. He was the first general officer to fall in battle and communities including Fort Blount were renamed to honor the brevet brigadier general. (Courtesy Georgia Historical Society.)

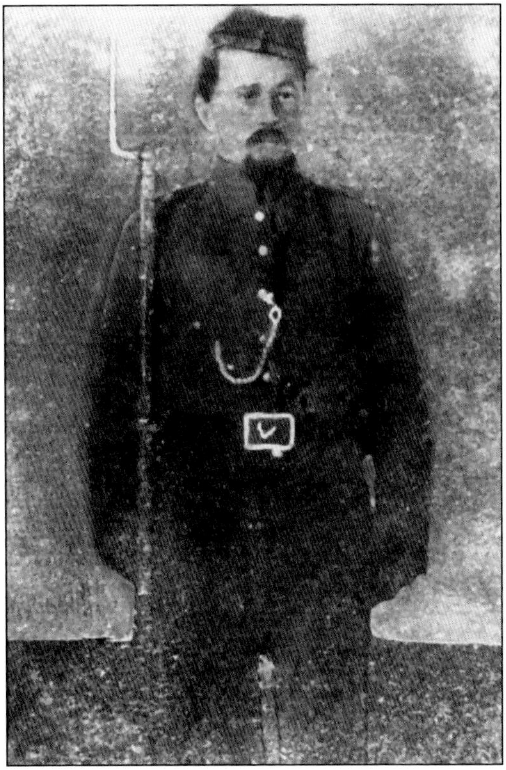

Streaty Parker served in two Polk County units in the Civil War. He is shown here in the uniform of the Confederate 1st Florida Special Cavalry Battalion, assigned to guard and herd cattle for the quartermaster corps within the state. The "South Florida Bulldogs," commanded by Capt. Nathan S. Blount, departed Bartow to serve in the 7th Florida Infantry, CSA, in the war's western theater. (Courtesy State Archives of Florida.)

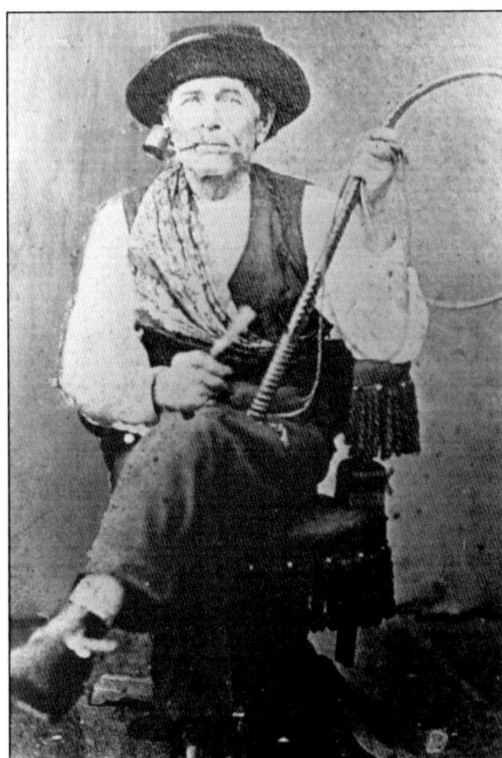

In 1862, Jacob Summerlin, a cattle baron and philanthropist, purchased the Blount homestead for $3,000. The Civil War found him engaged in blockade-running and providing cattle for the Southern forces in Georgia and the Carolinas. In 1866, he made his famous grant of 120 acres to establish Bartow as the county seat, with 40 acres each for court, school, and churches. (Courtesy State Archives of Florida, Frisbie Collection.)

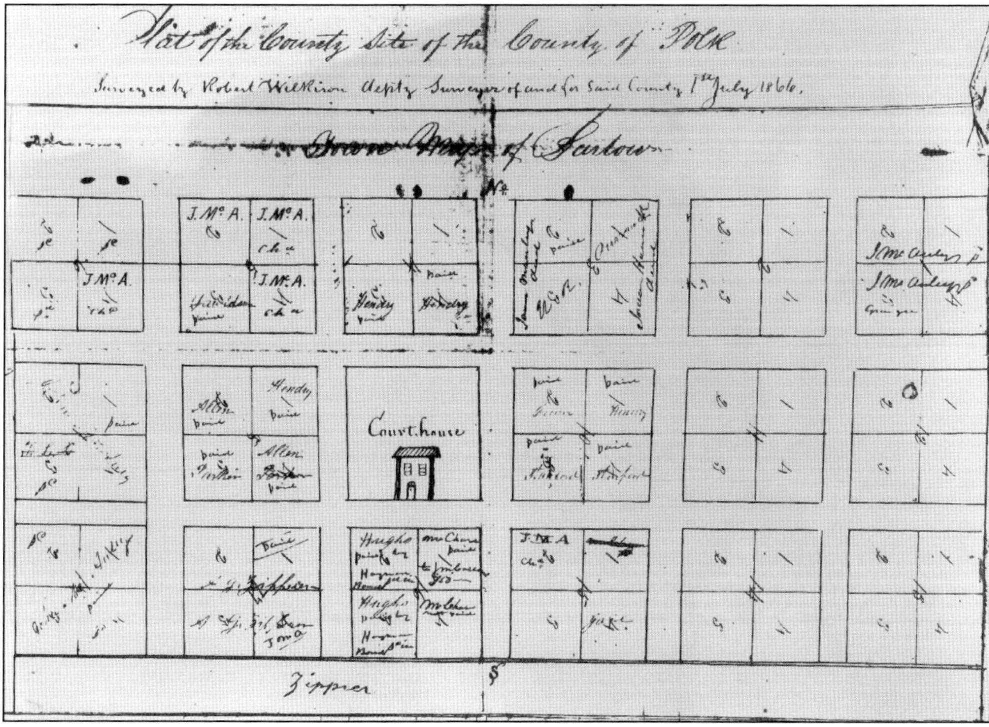

Following Summerlin's grant came Robert Wilkison's survey and Bartow's first map, dated July 1, 1866. The courthouse is seen at center, and the names of pioneers appear, including McAuley, Davidson, Allen, Hendry, Zipperer, Hughes, Crum, Stanford, and Hayman. Summerlin built and gifted the first two-story building, a Masonic lodge and school, on Zipperer Street, prompting a name change to Summerlin Street. (Courtesy State Archives of Florida, Frisbie Collection.)

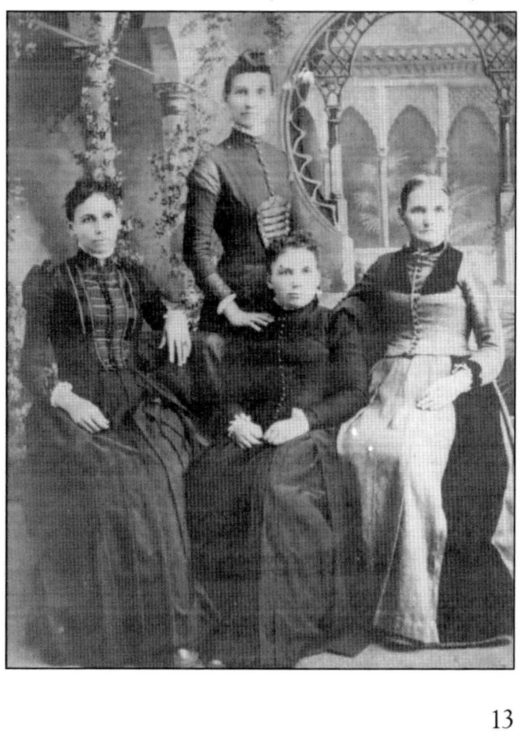

Riley Blount's daughters appear in the fashion of the day. Shown in this c. 1875 photograph are, from left to right, (seated) Mary Elizabeth (Oeland), Ada Ula (Selvidge), and Martha Ann Knight, a stepdaughter married to Nathan Blount, the youngest brother of her stepfather; (standing) Sarah Louisa (Parker). Riley Blount and his father were pioneers of the Fort Blount settlement and headed Bartow's "first family." (Courtesy State Archives of Florida, Frisbie Collection.)

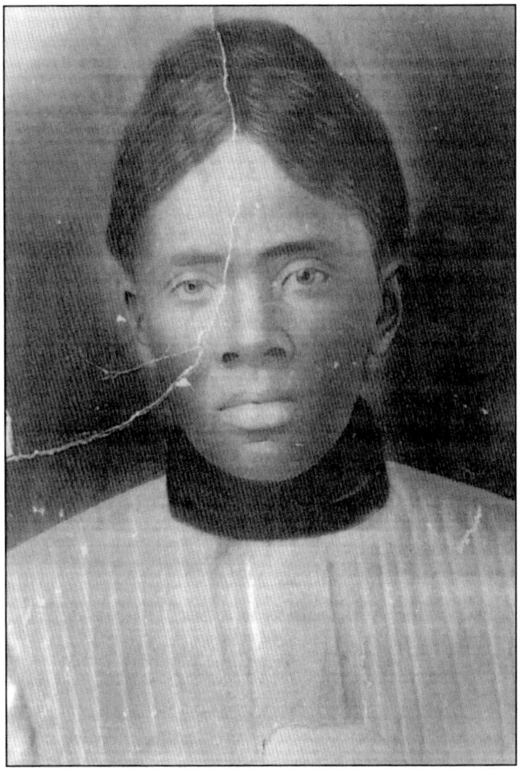

Elizabeth Moore, an African American pioneer, was the daughter of Andy Moore and Tanner Reid. She married Thomas Waldon of Virginia in 1882 and homesteaded 160 acres south of Bartow. Her father, an accomplished fiddler, arrived with refugee Virginia planter William J. Watkins in 1862 and was present when community blacks were notified of their freedom at the conclusion of the Civil War. (Courtesy Clifton Lewis, Historic L.B. Brown House.)

The Fortner family is seen here in front of their home, built just after the Civil War. The central breezeway, often called a dogtrot, divides the cooking area on one side and the bedrooms opposite, and was typical of pioneer living. Additions were made to accommodate family growth. Note the log construction, wood shingles, chimney, and picket fence to deter livestock. (Courtesy State Archives of Florida, Frisbie Collection.)

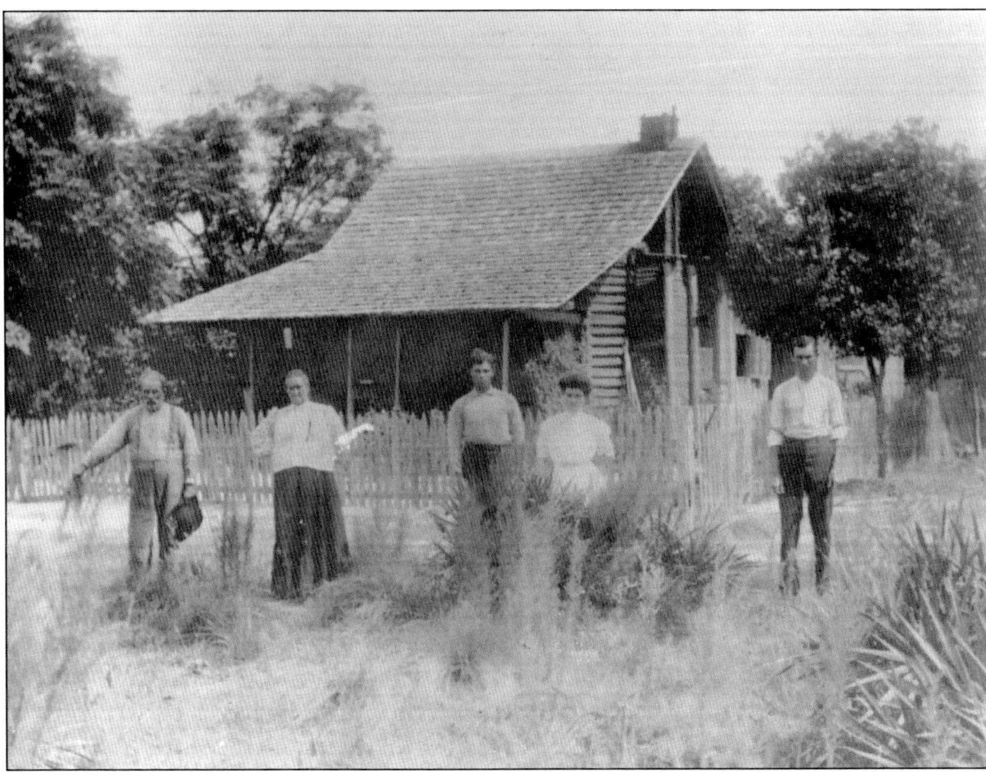

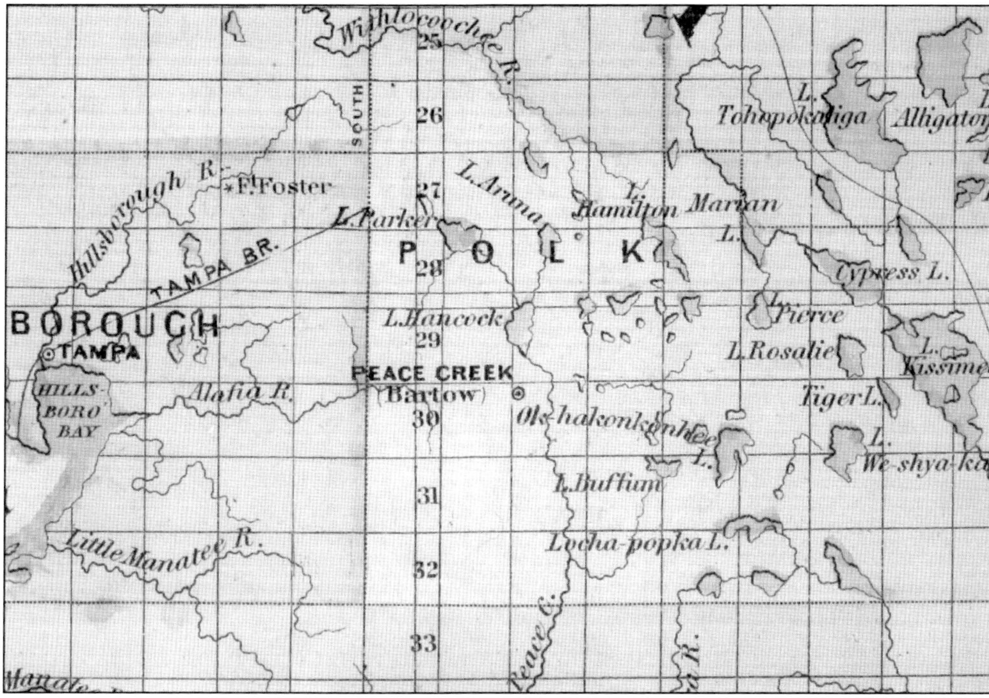

This 1873 Asher & Adams map, printed during Reconstruction, imparts a dilemma: Peace Creek or Bartow? Fort Blount was named Bartow as early as January 1862, and postwar townsmen retained the name in 1867. Two years later, disregarding Southern sentiment, the government reestablished the post office as Peace Creek, provoking old rebels to address their mail "to Bartow at Peace Creek" until 1879, when the name Bartow was restored. (Courtesy W.L. Harris collection.)

Bartow's first church building, the First Methodist Episcopal Church South, was dedicated on March 11, 1883. Rev. William C. Jordan had served in the area since 1858, and in 1867 was appointed to Bartow as the pastor of a young congregation. The 1866 Summerlin grant of 20 acres was sold as lots, and monies collected enabled construction of the church and parsonage, situated on West Church Street. (Courtesy State Archives of Florida, Frisbie Collection.)

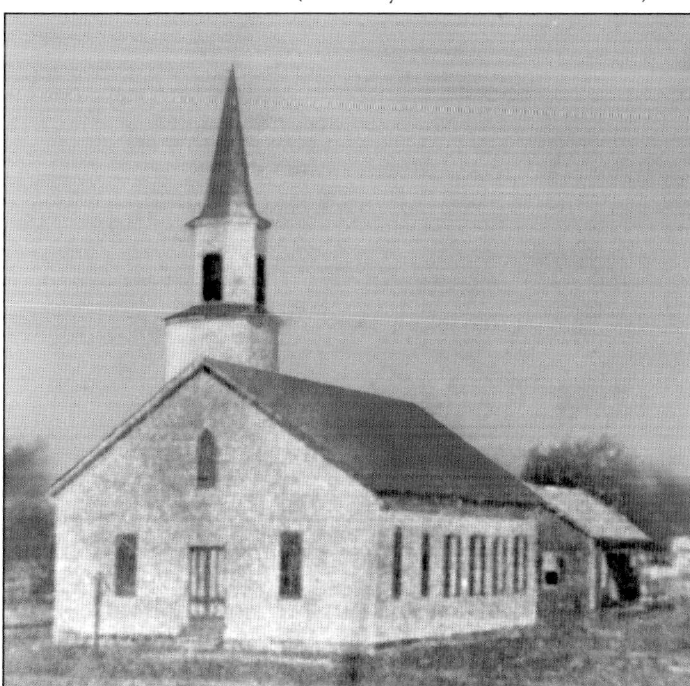

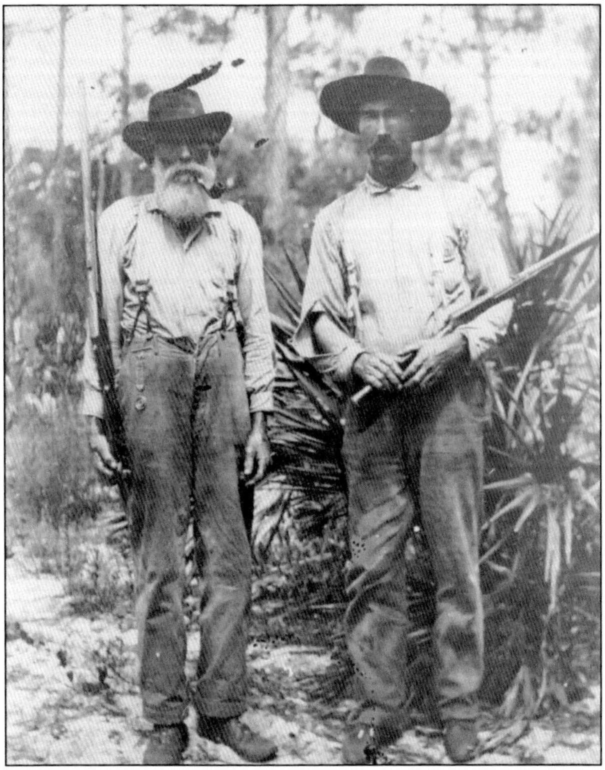

These two pioneers among the pines and palmettos are identified as Noah Whidden (left) and "brother." It isn't clear who "brother" actually is; he may be a son or other relative. They are armed with rifles, and Noah has a watch fob suspended from his right pocket. He was a veteran of the Third Seminole Indian War of 1856. (Courtesy State Archives of Florida, Frisbie Collection.)

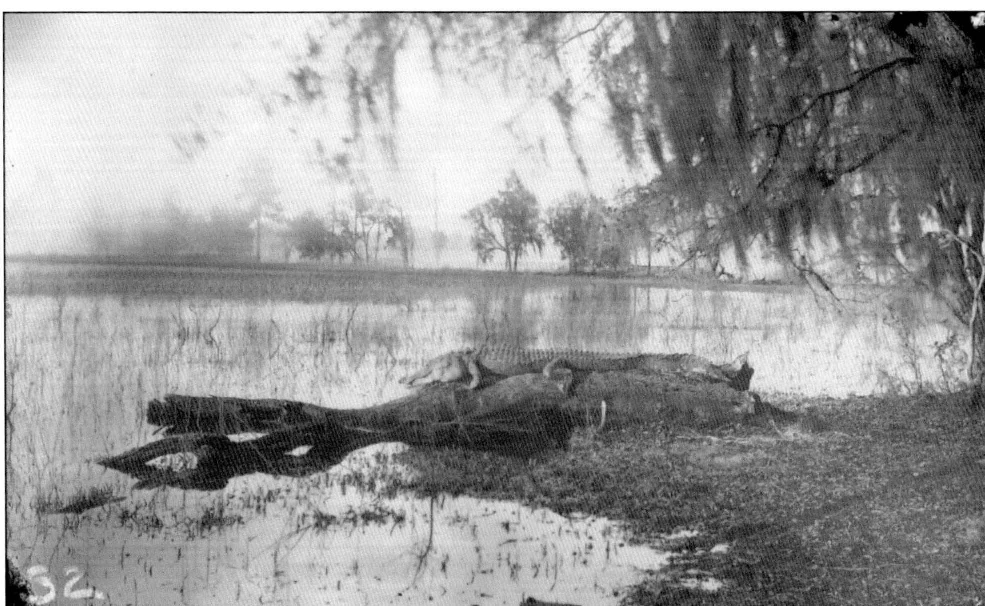

The large alligator photographed near Bartow in the 1880s illustrates just one of the many hazards facing pioneers. Ben and James Blount reported killing a panther near the present-day high school while hunting in 1866. Bears were so numerous that as late as 1887 the county offered a $5 bounty each for the roving carnivores. Bears' prevalence sheds light on the origin of Bartow's Bear Creek, or Bear Branch. (Courtesy State Archives of Florida, Frisbie Collection.)

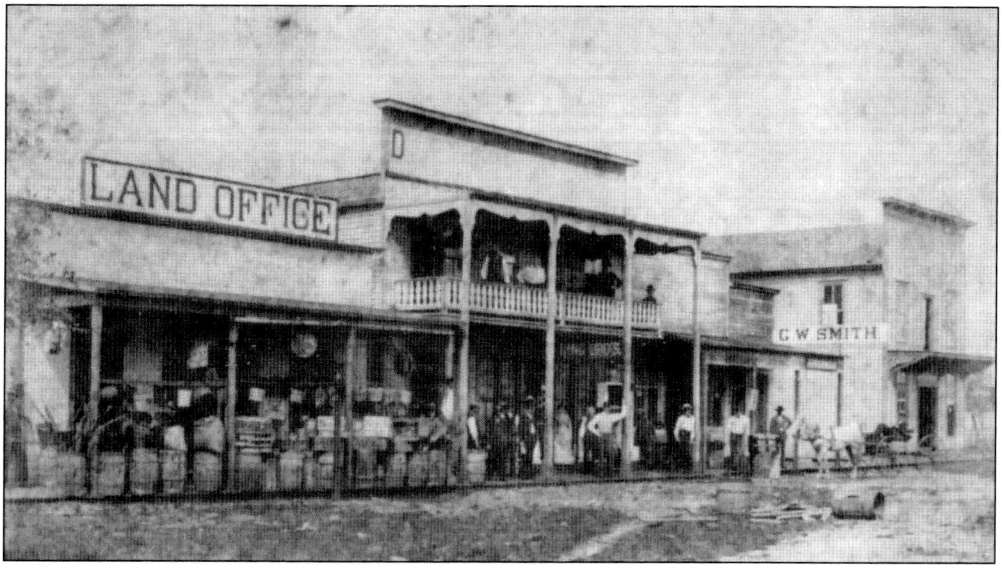

The 100 block of North Broadway, presently Fort Blount Park, is seen in this 1885 photograph. William T. Carpenter's Mercantile Store and Land Office, at left, displays a profusion of goods; sugarcane, barrels, buckets, and brooms line the street. Further north on the block are Lang Brothers dry goods, G.W. Smith's, and Lyle's store. (Courtesy State Archives of Florida, Frisbie Collection.)

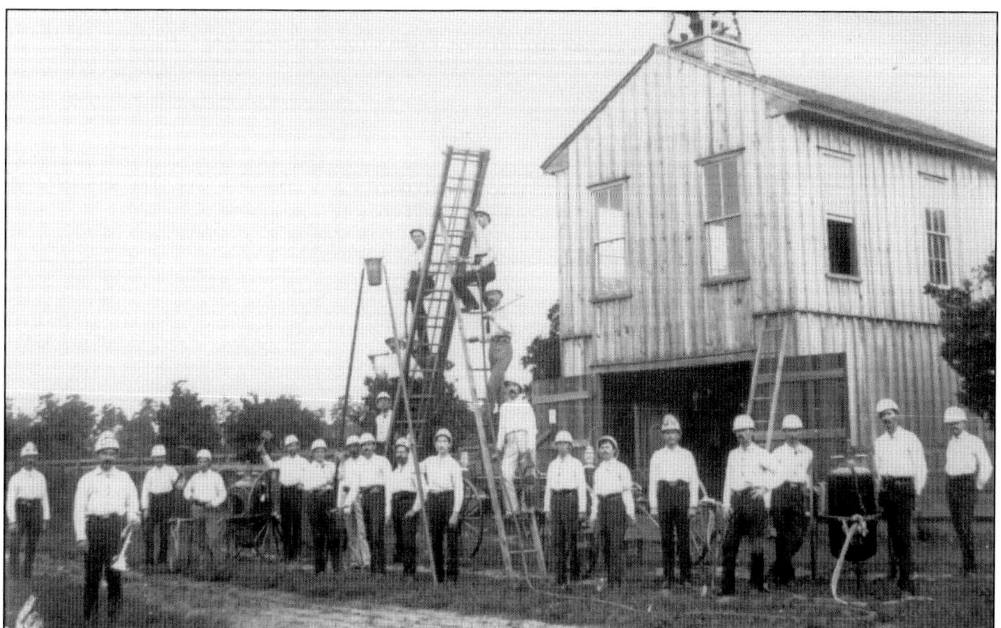

The Bartow Volunteer Fire Company poses for the photographer in front of the city hall and firehouse, built in 1887 on Church Street. The firemen display their equipment, including two 30-gallon chemical hose carts, axes, hammer, buckets, prying bars, and poles. Three ladders and an equipment wagon round out the department's tools. The chief holds a trumpet, used for communication during fires. (Courtesy State Archives of Florida, Frisbie Collection.)

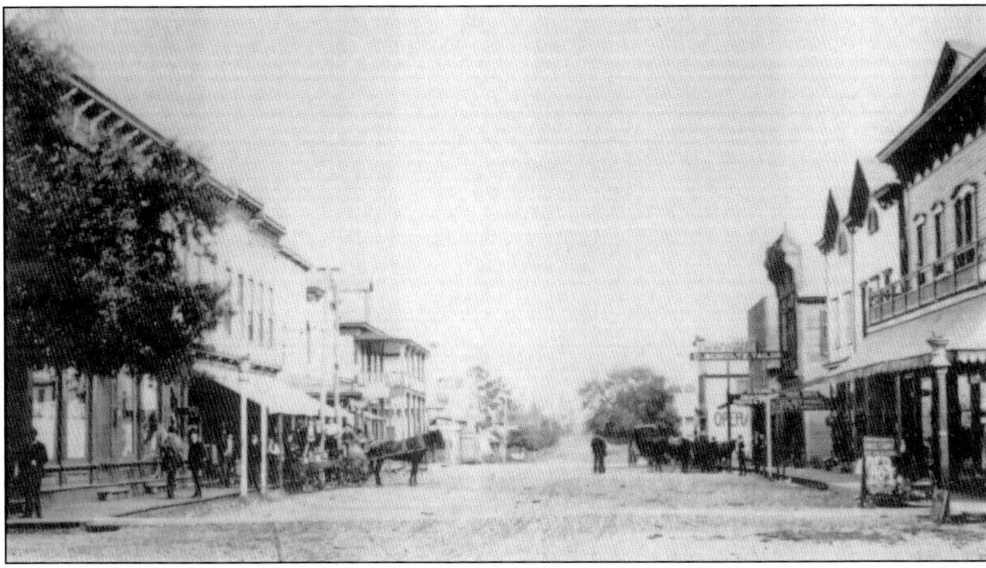

In this 1880s photograph of East Main Street, Dr. Oppenheimer's drugstore, at far right, advertises ice-cold soda and red-hot coffee. A clothing store, tailor shop, grocery, livery stable, and Bartow's first opera house round out the south side. A drugstore is at left, with the post office and the St. Mark Hotel, with its two-story veranda, to the right. (Courtesy State Archives of Florida, Frisbie Collection.)

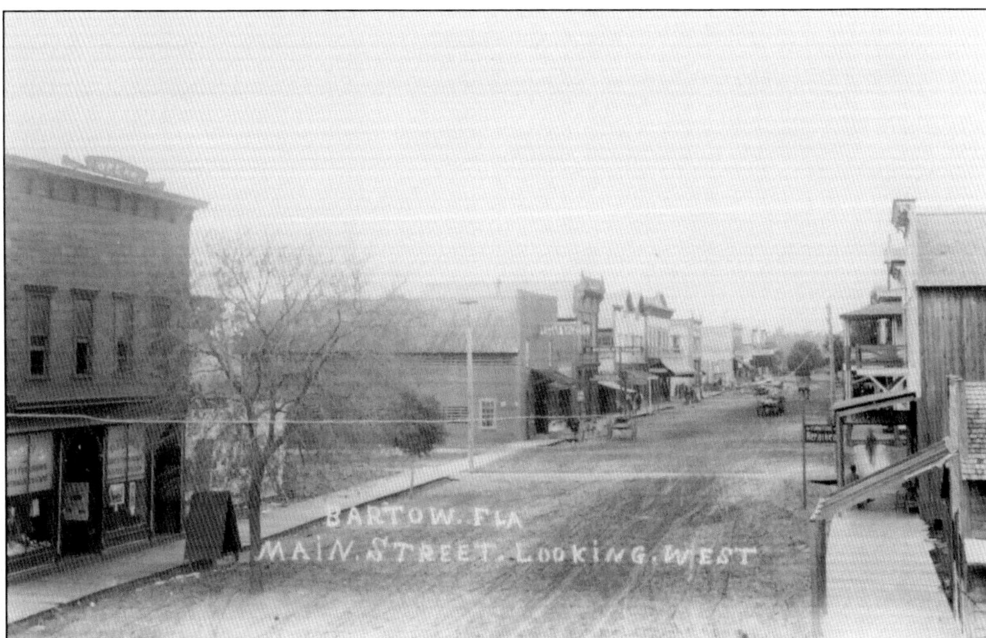

The Bartow Opera House and Gent's clothing are seen on the left in this 1887 view of West Main Street from Florida Avenue. In 1886, fire destroyed the 100 block in front of the courthouse; reconstruction activity is noticeable beyond the wagon in the middle of the street. The entire block would be reconstructed with brick. (Courtesy State Archives of Florida, Frisbie Collection.)

Two

Urbs in Rure
1885–1890

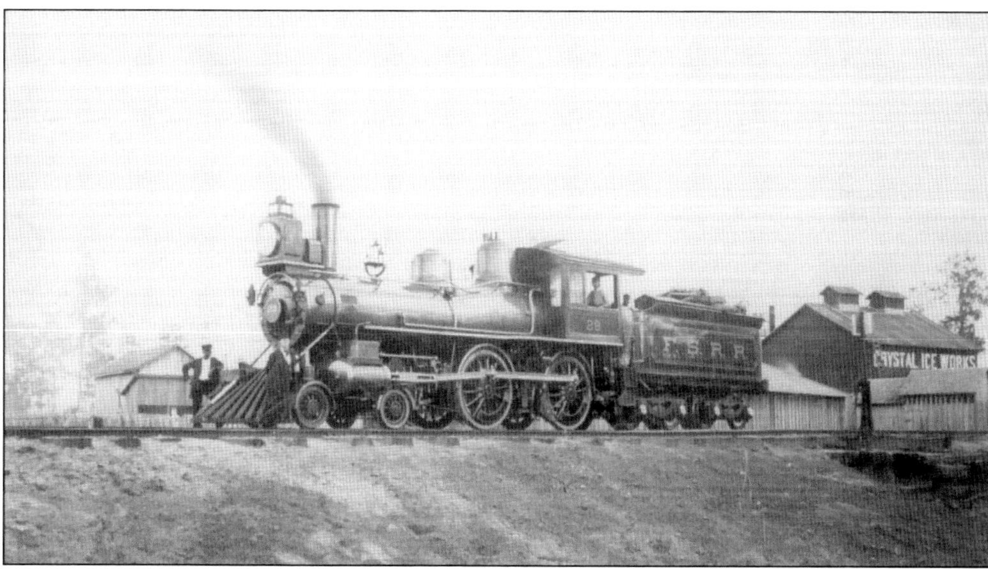

Florida Southern Railroad's locomotive No. 28 faces north on the line below Bartow's first depot, located on the northwest corner of the intersection of present-day West Parker Street and South Mill Avenue. Crystal Ice Works appears in the background. The railroad was one of many owned by Henry B. Plant, and its arrival in 1885 was the catalyst for growth. (Courtesy George McClelland.)

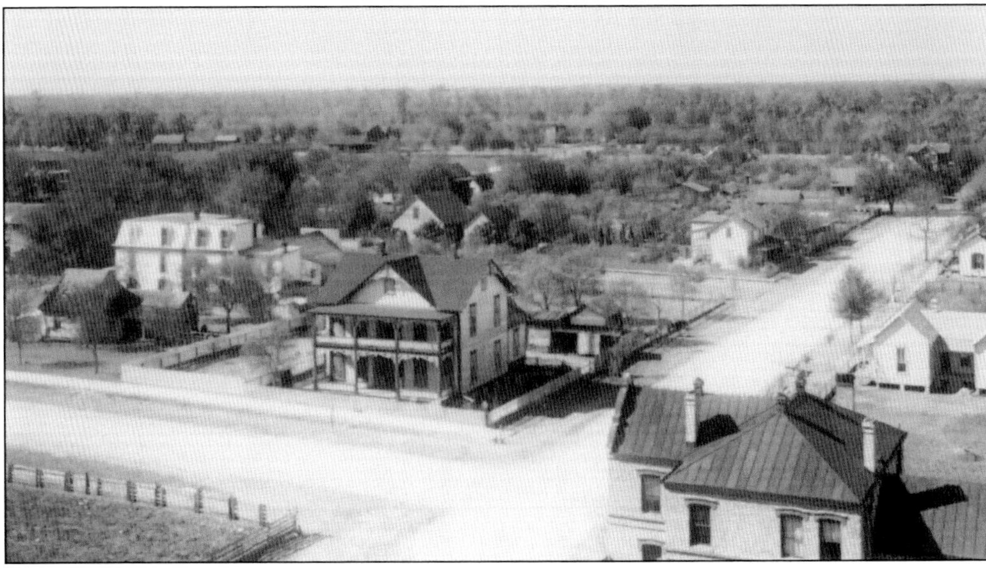

This southwest-facing photograph, taken from the water tower, shows the 1887 county jail in the right foreground. The intersection is North Broadway Avenue and Church Street, and the three-story building at center is an early hotel, the Bartow House. The forested area at upper left surrounds headstones in Oak Hill Cemetery, left of Bartow's first railroad depot on West Main Street. (Courtesy State Archives of Florida, Frisbie Collection.)

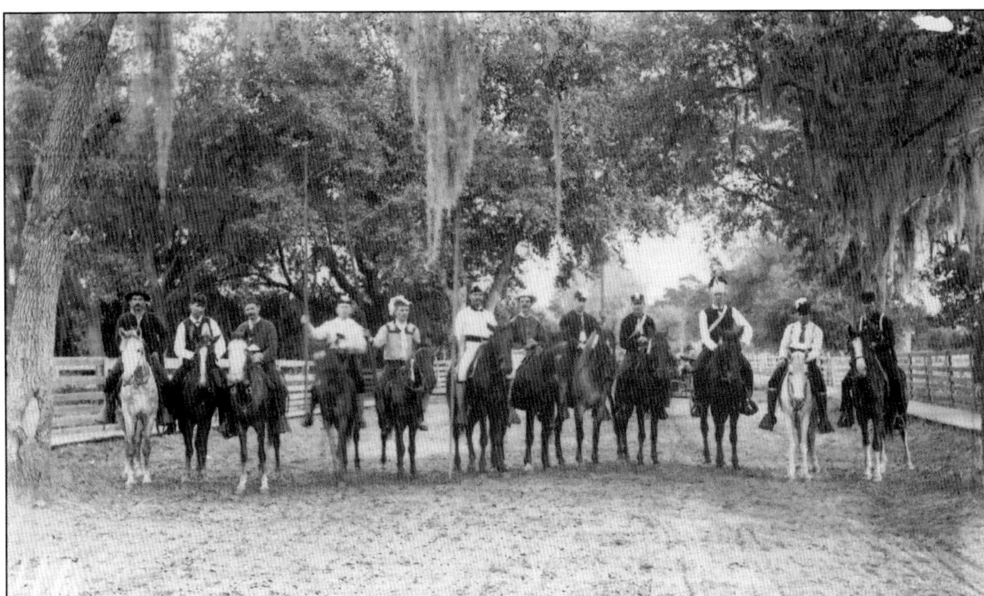

Chivalry was not dead, as shown in this 1880s photograph of plumed horsemen holding lances. Before 1890, Bartow held "ring tournaments" in conjunction with May Day activities. Reflecting the glamour of knighthood, the elaborate ceremony involved "knights" riding full speed to impale suspended rings of varying sizes. The knight securing the greatest number would have the honor of crowning the "Queen of Beauty." (Courtesy State Archives of Florida, Frisbie Collection.)

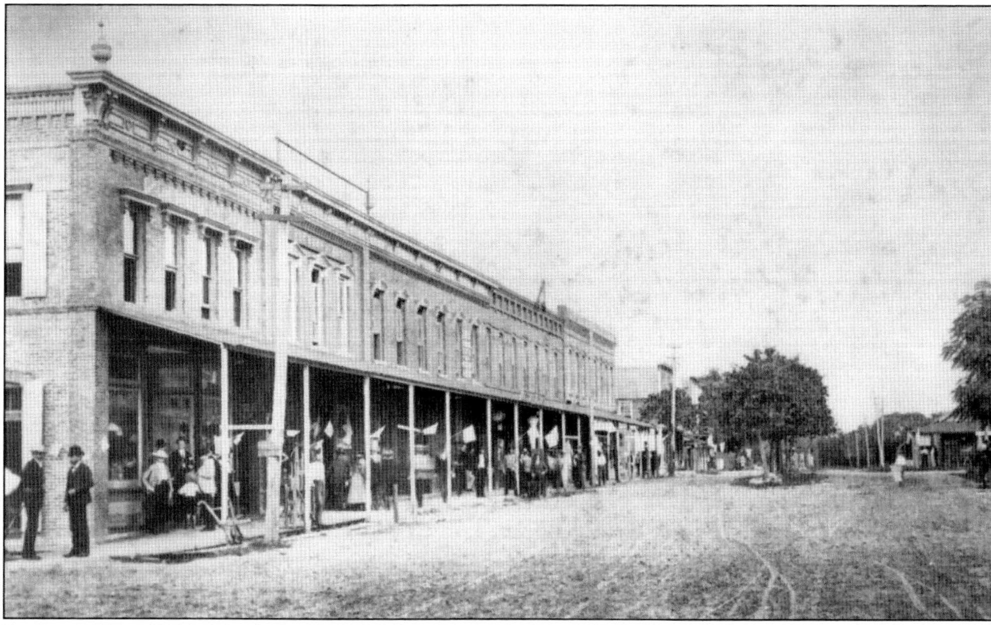

Bartow's first brick block on Main Street, across from the courthouse, is festooned with flags celebrating Independence Day. The brick buildings replaced the wooden block destroyed by fire in 1886. The first building on the left is the only store with a boardwalk landing extending to the street. Wagon tracks lead to sour orange trees lining the center of the street. (Courtesy State Archives of Florida, Frisbie Collection.)

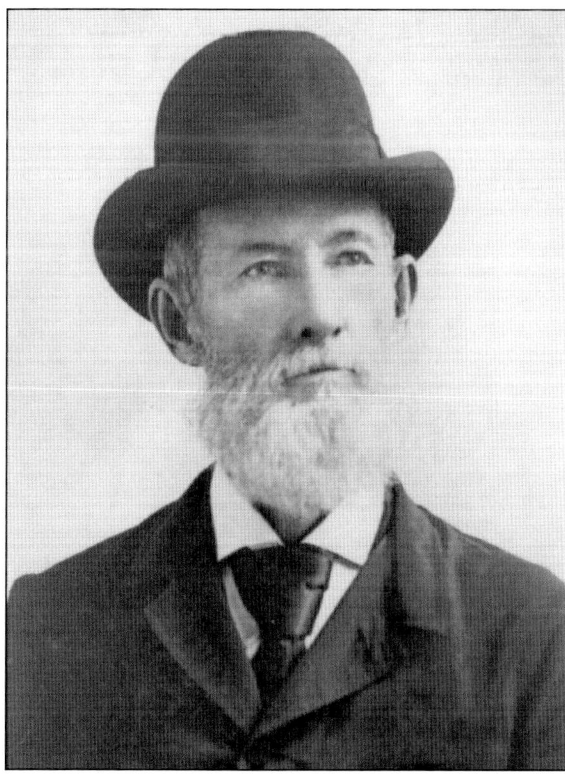

Baptist minister Rev. Jeremiah Hayman arrived in the community in 1852. As a circuit-riding preacher, he laid the foundation for congregations throughout central Florida, in particular Peace Creek Baptist, founded in 1854. African American church First Providence Missionary Baptist traces its heritage to 1856 baptisms in Bear Branch. Reverend Hayman was the first pastor of First Baptist Church, from 1875 to 1883. (Courtesy State Archives of Florida, Frisbie Collection.)

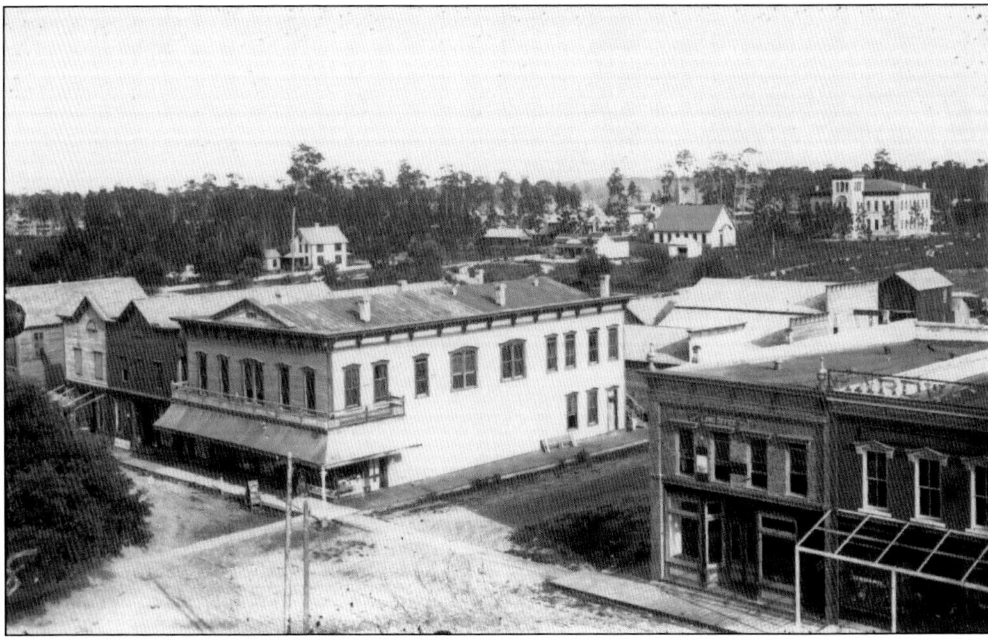

This southeast view from the courthouse reveals a growing town. The First Presbyterian Church, Bartow's third church building, and Summerlin Institute are seen in the upper right. The 1886 Gold Building, on the southeast corner of Central Avenue and Main Street, housed a drugstore on the ground floor and boarding rooms upstairs. It would later become Bartow's second opera house. (Courtesy State Archives of Florida, Frisbie Collection.)

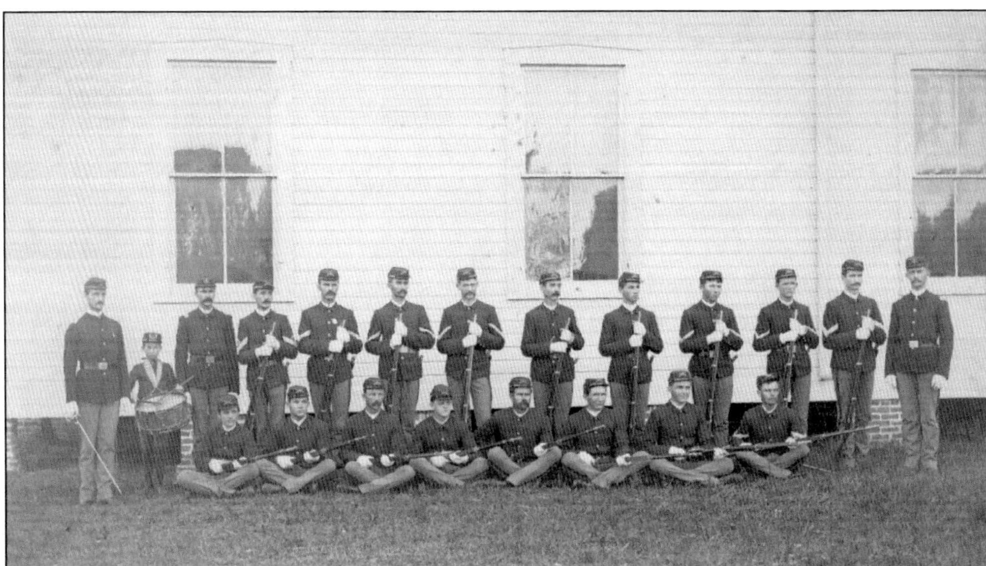

The Bartow Rifles first appeared in uniform on June 10, 1888, at a special service of the First Presbyterian Church. An earlier attempt to form a military company, in 1878, was short-lived, making the Bartow Rifles the second company formed in the city since the Civil War. The Rifles were officially part of the Florida State Troops, a forerunner of the National Guard, and disbanded by 1892. (Courtesy W.L. Harris collection.)

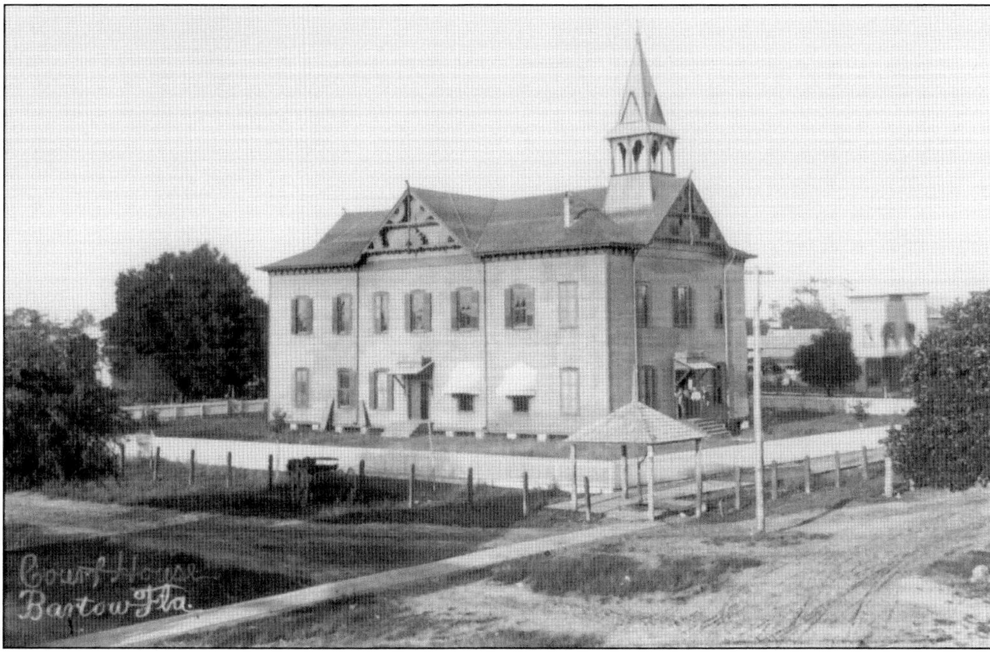

This image of the 1884 county courthouse depicts efforts to beautify the grounds with a picket fence enclosure and newly planted oaks. The small structure on the corner of Main Street and Broadway Avenue was a water pump with a tin can attached for public drinking. A spittoon for tobacco chewers sits to the right of the pump. (Courtesy State Archives of Florida, Frisbie Collection.)

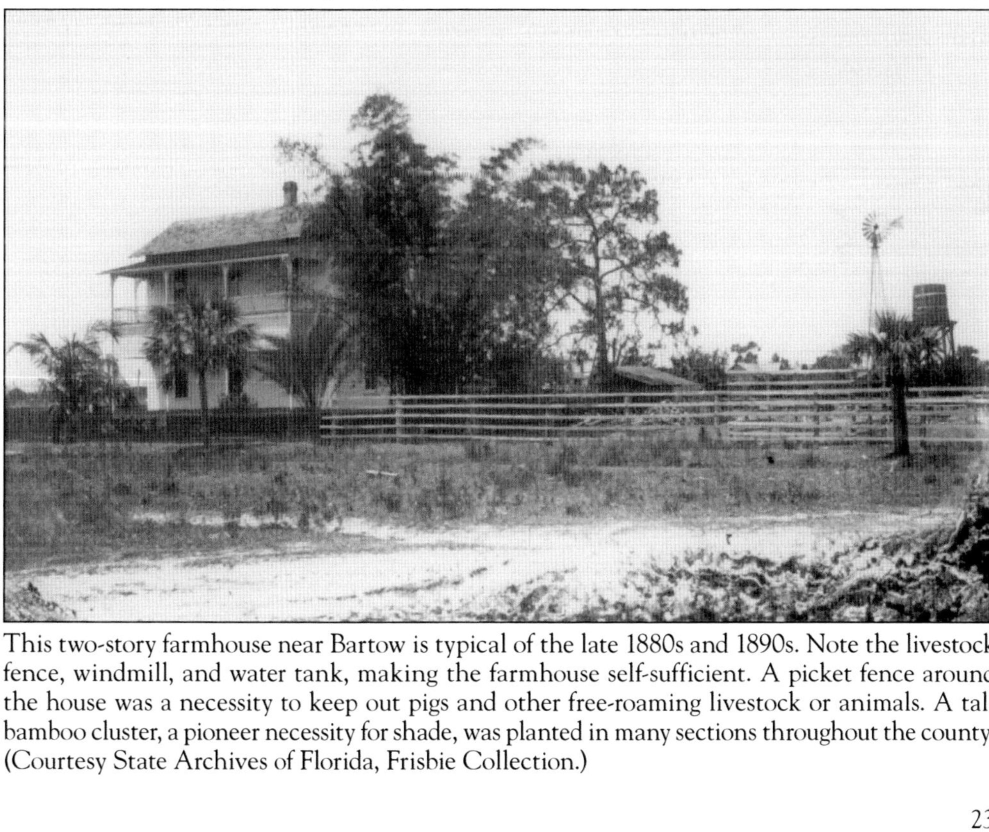

This two-story farmhouse near Bartow is typical of the late 1880s and 1890s. Note the livestock fence, windmill, and water tank, making the farmhouse self-sufficient. A picket fence around the house was a necessity to keep out pigs and other free-roaming livestock or animals. A tall bamboo cluster, a pioneer necessity for shade, was planted in many sections throughout the county. (Courtesy State Archives of Florida, Frisbie Collection.)

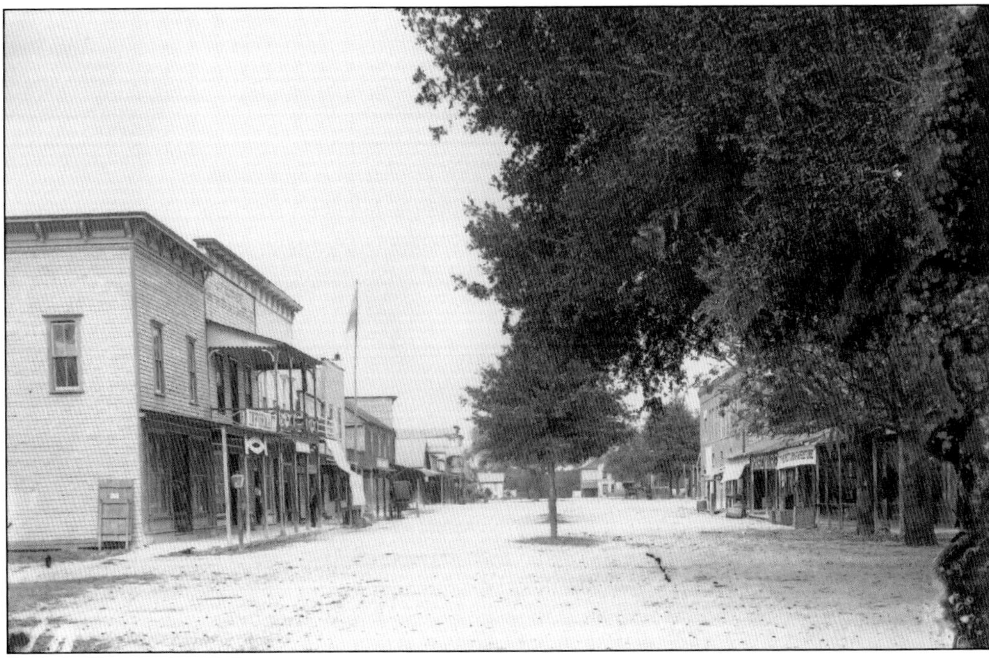

This view of Broadway Avenue, looking north from Summerlin Street, shows a profusion of oaks. The location of the post office is indicated by the flagpole. The *Informant* newspaper office, the second building on the left, stands across from furniture and hardware stores. The courthouse square can be seen past the brick building on the right. (Courtesy State Archives of Florida, Frisbie Collection.)

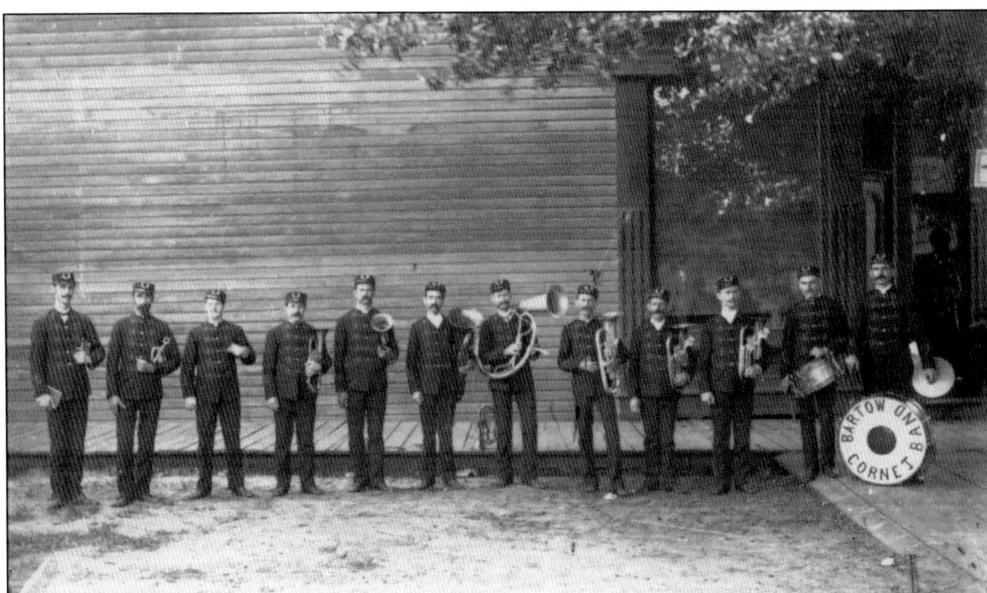

Resplendent in their uniforms, 12 members of the Bartow Cornet Band pose for a group photograph. The brass-and-drums group was composed of 13 members; one man's absence is noted by his instrument and music on the boardwalk. The band presented concerts every Sunday afternoon and appeared at social events and parades. (Courtesy State Archives of Florida, Frisbie Collection.)

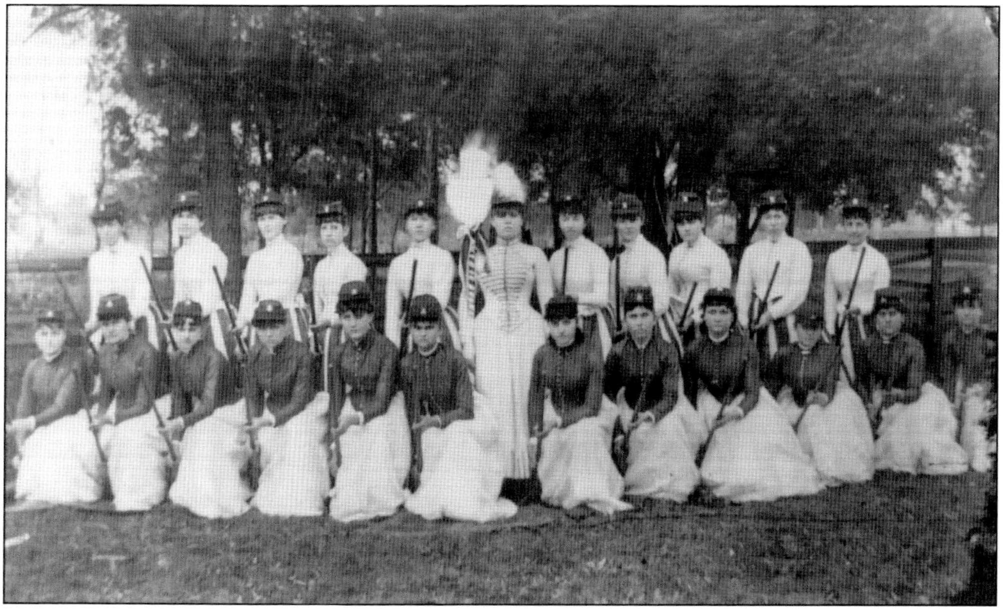

The Bartow Belles drill team assumes the infantry square, a 19th-century bayonet formation designed to repel charging cavalry. The Belles, armed with brooms, were divided into two detachments, A and B. They are wearing kepis (French-inspired caps), gray-and-white jackets, and white, striped skirts. The commander has added a plume and a tunic adorned with tracings of braid. (Courtesy State Archives of Florida, Frisbie Collection.)

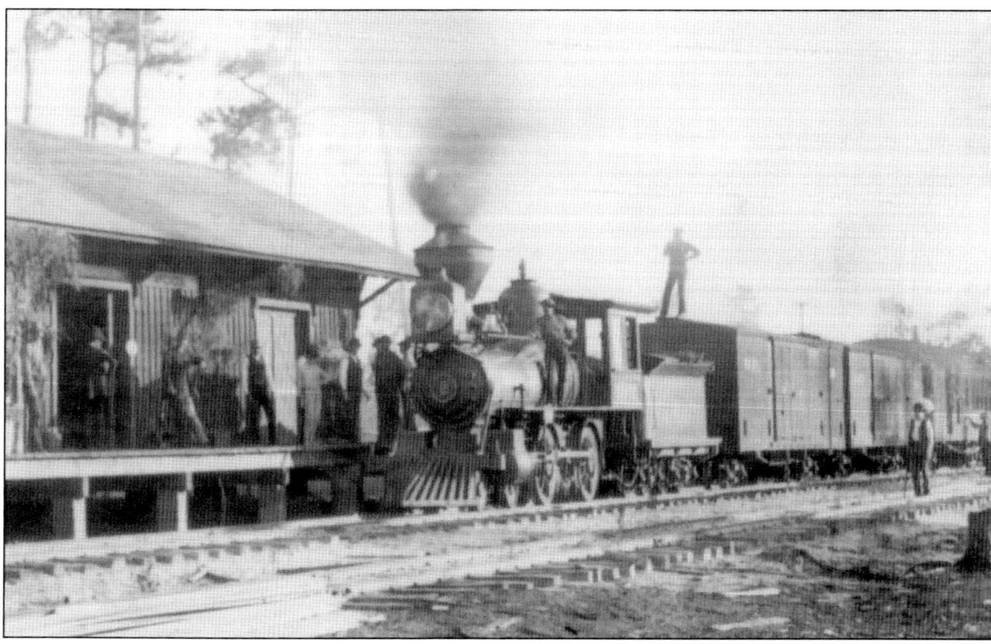

Florida Southern Railway's engine No. 8 pulls the first train to Arcadia from Bartow. Two ventilated boxcars and passenger cars follow the wood-laden tender. The railway, built jointly with the South Florida Railroad, reached Punta Gorda in 1886. The South Florida operated north of the Bartow depot, and the Florida Southern Railway operated south of it. Both railroads were part of the Plant System. (Courtesy State Archives of Florida, Frisbie Collection.)

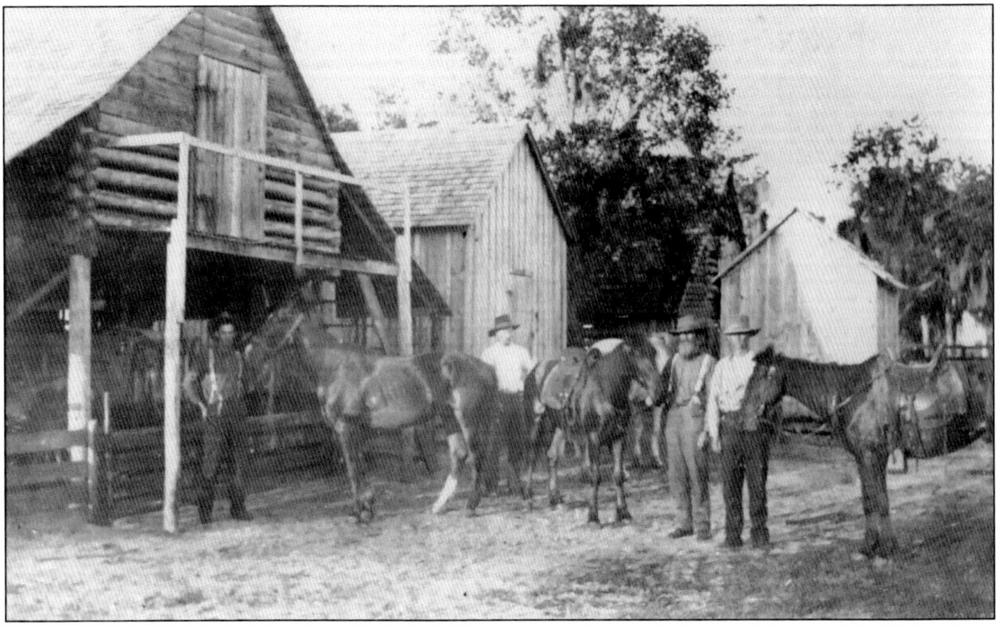

This unidentified livery stable and the structure right of center were built using logs. Two other buildings were constructed with finished lumber produced by the sawmill, located near present-day South Mill Avenue. A livery stable kept horses and vehicles for hire; in 1889, Bartow had four livery stables and a wagon works. The horses are saddled with the widely used McClellan saddles. (Courtesy State Archives of Florida, Frisbie Collection.)

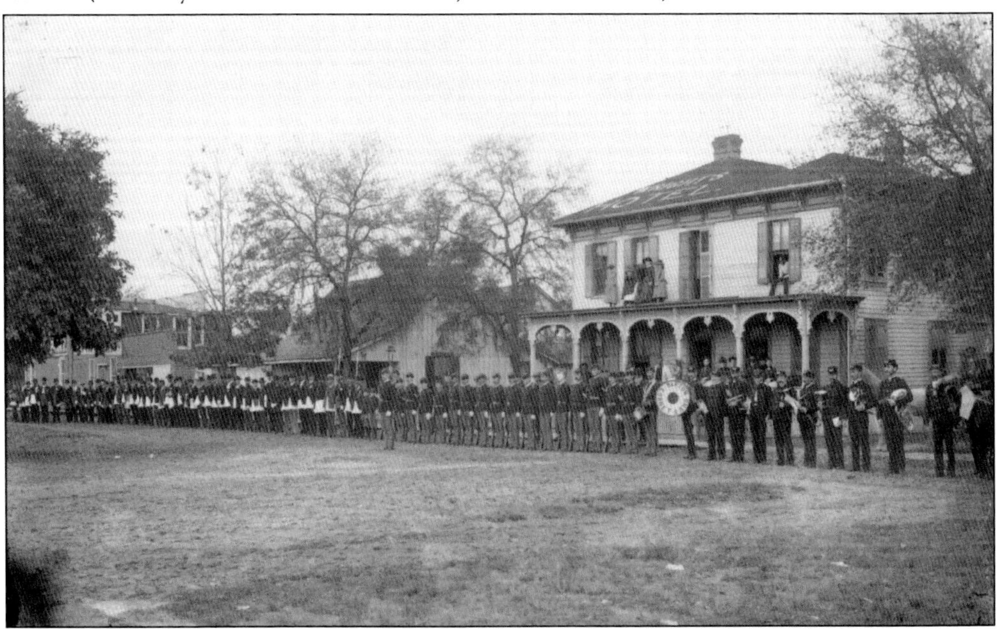

Wright's Hotel provides the backdrop for this early parade lineup on Davidson Street. Shown assembled are, from left to right, the members of Tuscan Lodge No. 6, the Free and Accepted Masons; the Bartow Rifles of the Florida State Troops; and the Bartow Cornet Band. The occasion may have been the grand opening of Summerlin Institute, on January 2, 1889. (Courtesy State Archives of Florida, Frisbie Collection.)

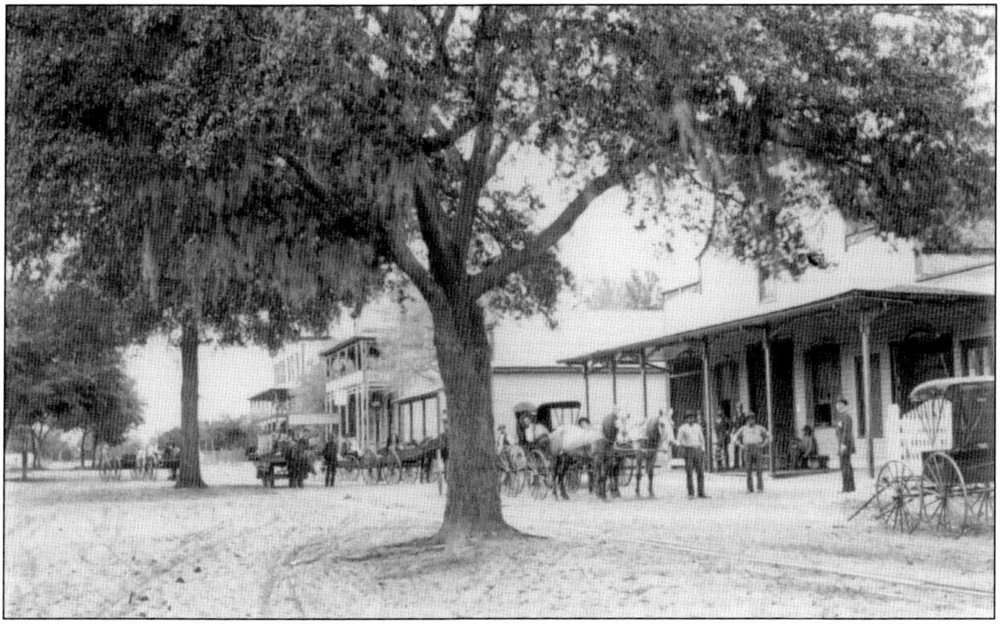

The center of activity on the right has been identified as the Lightsey and Lewis livery stable. This early scene represents a typical sandy street before the addition of so-called Bartow Macadam clay dug from the city's pit. The clay pit, located north of Polk Street and west of Broadway Avenue, was sought after for paving material before the advent of asphalt. (Courtesy State Archives of Florida, Frisbie Collection.)

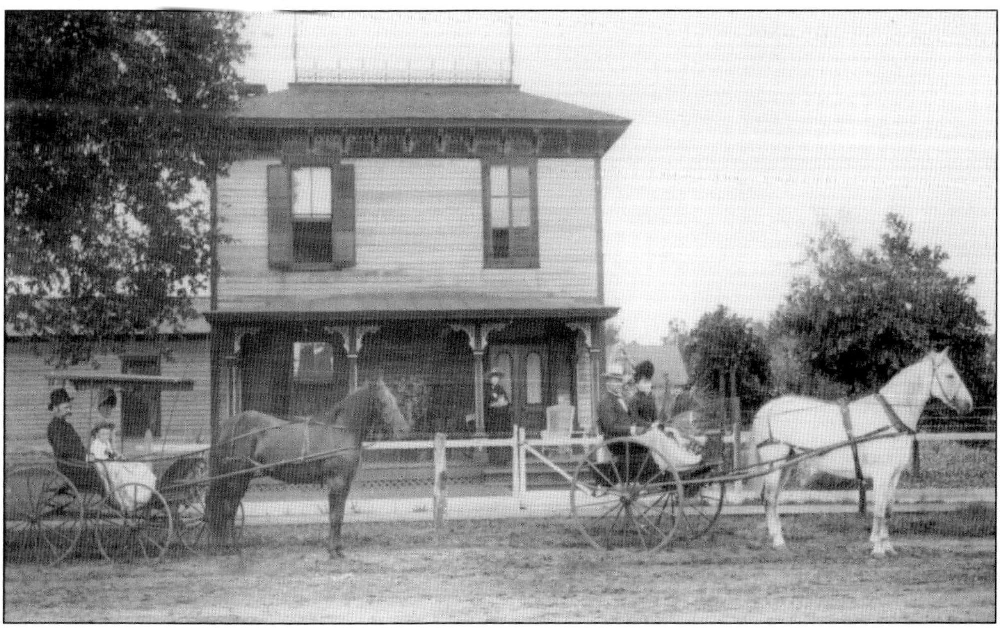

Horses and buggies were common sights and the dominant means of local transportation until automobiles became available. The two families are sporting their Sunday best and have their laps covered, suggesting a cool day. The lightning rod system across the roofline offers a path for a direct or "jumping" strike, insuring that the bolt's current will flow to the ground without causing damage or sparking a fire. (Courtesy State Archives of Florida, Frisbie Collection.)

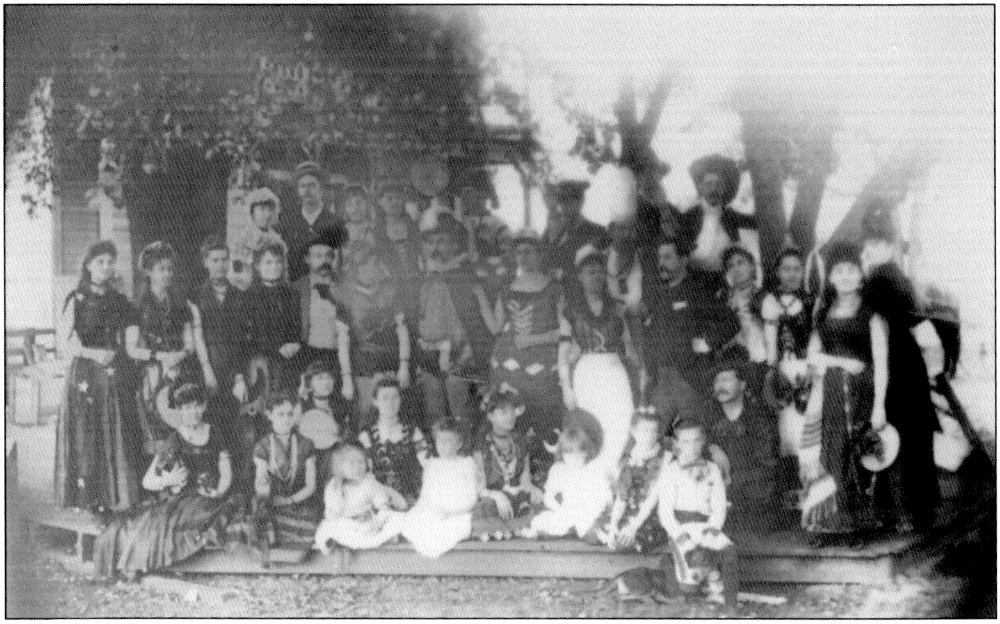

In this photograph, 33 costumed thespians pose for *The Gypsy Opera*, performed on April 26, 1888, at the courthouse. The musical production offered over four-dozen costumed characters, a gypsy camp, 12 scenes, and a concert. The proceeds were used to pay for a county promotional pamphlet, and the event was lauded as "the most artistic performance ever given in south Florida." (Courtesy State Archives of Florida, Frisbie Collection.)

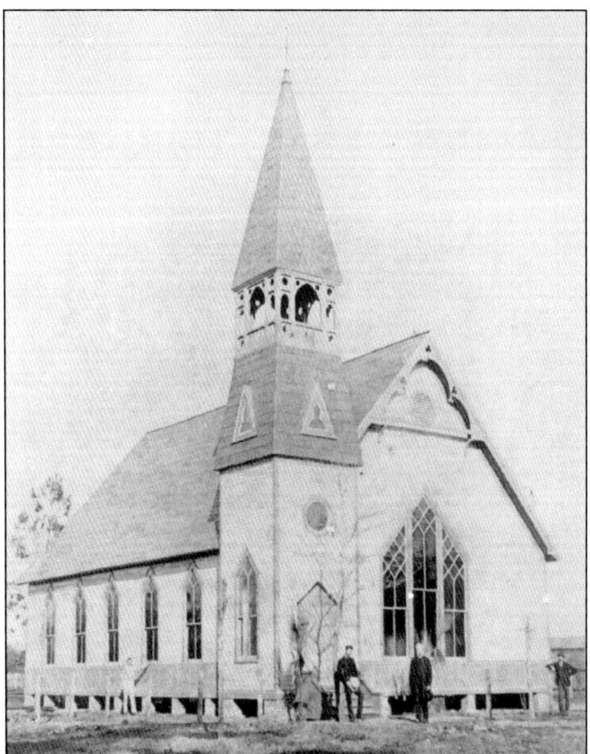

Architect McKenzie Dunlope (left), Rev. Samuel Hair (center), and an unidentified man stand in front of the newly built First Presbyterian Church in 1887. Facing east on the northwest corner of Florida Avenue and Stanford Street, it was the third church in Bartow. The congregation, formed in 1882, held its first service in the new church on Christmas Day 1887 and formally dedicated the grounds on May 20, 1888. (Courtesy First Presbyterian Church of Bartow.)

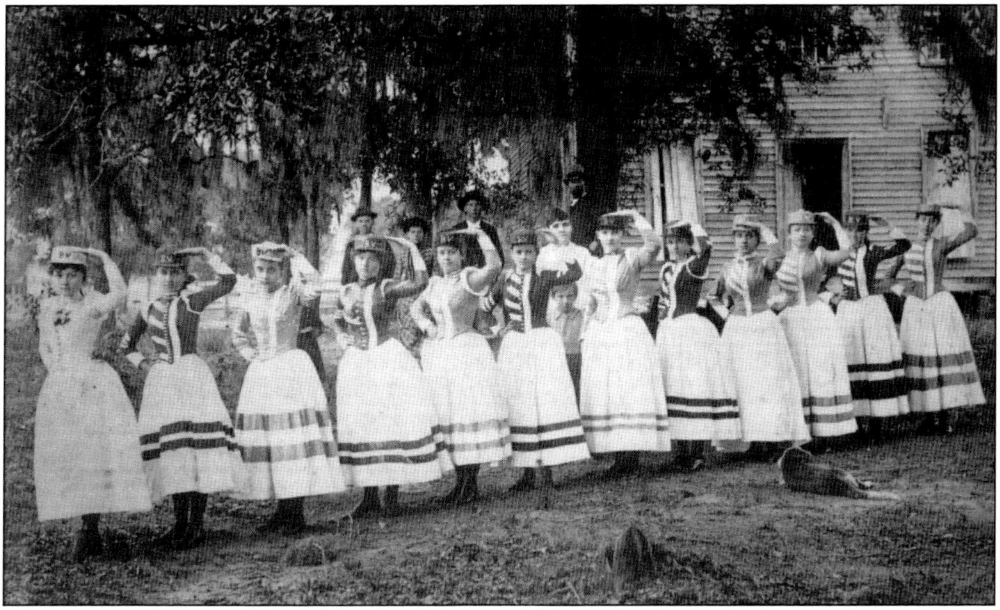

The Bartow Vivandières, or "Belles," salute in front of the first Summerlin Institute, built in 1867. Inspired by the formation of the Bartow Rifles in the late 1880s, the female group was a paramilitary drill team composed of two squads and a captain. In lieu of weapons, they used decorative brooms. Traditional vivandières were based on a Napoleonic army organization of women in uniform providing services and nursing. (Courtesy Polk County History Center.)

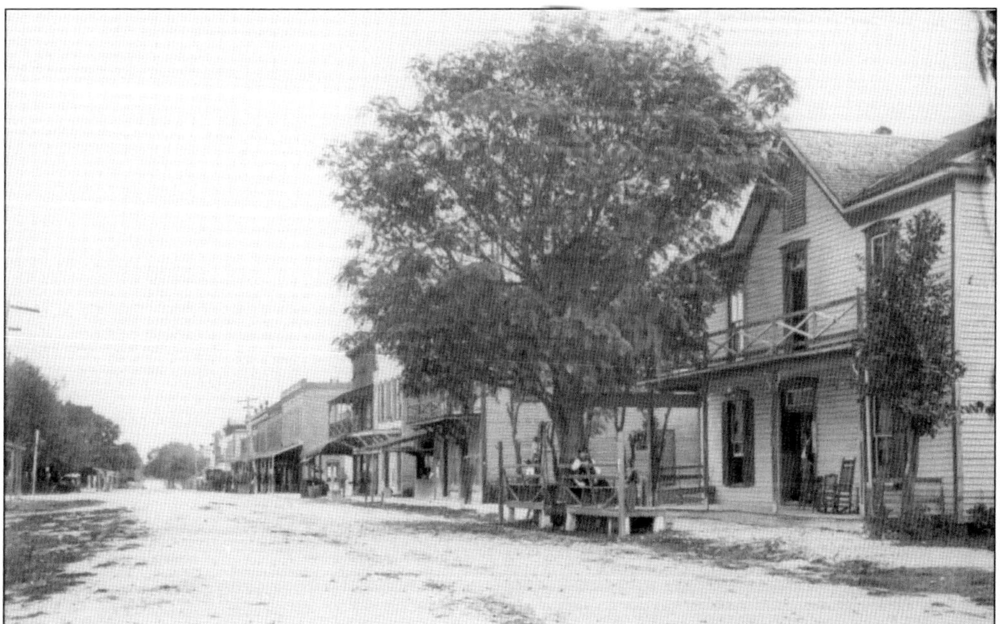

The building on the right is the Orange Grove Hotel, located at the southeast corner of Main Street and Carpenter Avenue. It was the first hotel in Bartow, known successively as the Bartow House, the Blount House, and, by 1887, the Orange Grove Hotel. Rates were $30 per month, $10 per week, and $2 per day. (Courtesy State Archives of Florida, Frisbie Collection.)

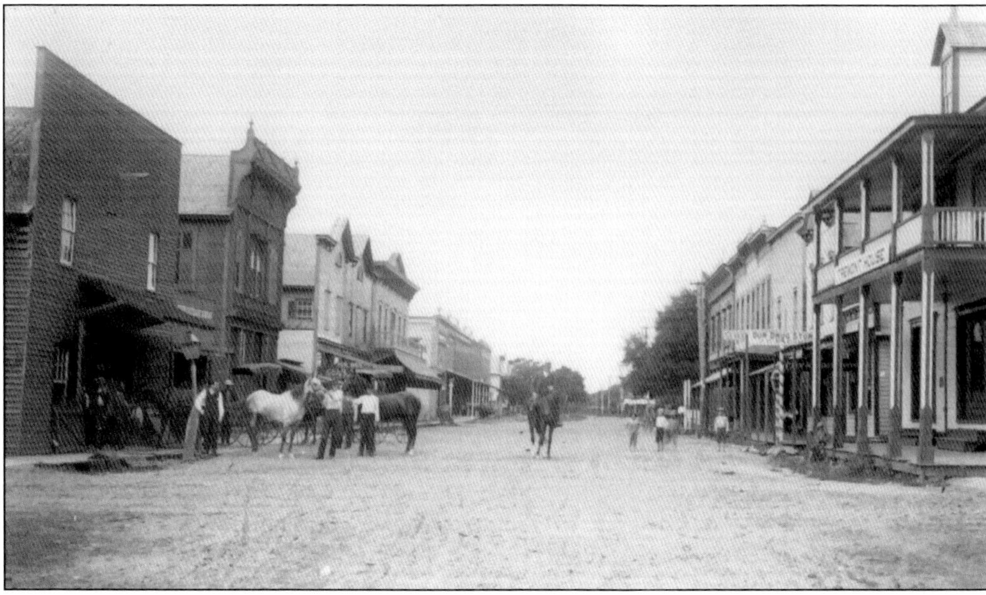

This view of Main Street, looking west from Wilson Avenue, shows the Lytle livery stable on the left and Bartow's second opera house at left center. The vested man, badge on chest, could be the town marshal or sheriff. The Tremont House, formerly the St. Mark Hotel, is on the right, adjacent to the City Barber Shop and Beaumel's drugstore. Wilson Avenue was formerly St. Mark Avenue. (Courtesy State Archives of Florida, Frisbie Collection.)

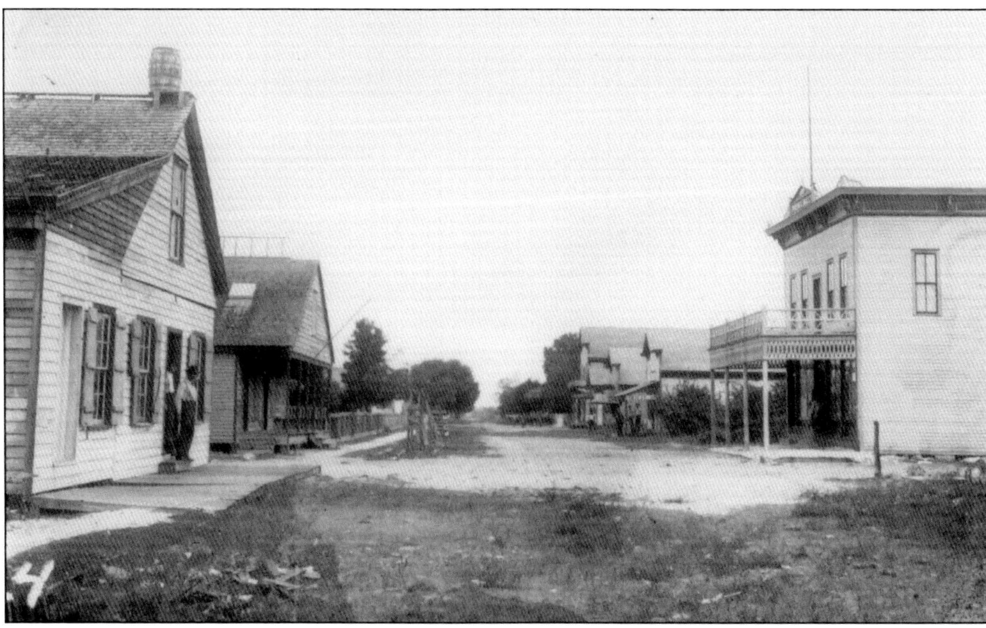

This 1880s photograph illustrates an unusual form of fire prevention; note the water barrel on the peak of the roof at left. There is a small variety store located on the right, midway in the block. The sign atop the large building on the far right reads "Phenix Hotel." There was a Phoenix Hotel in Bartow on West Church Street, originally the Carpenter House. Later photographs show the building's ornamental fretwork. (Courtesy State Archives of Florida, Frisbie Collection.)

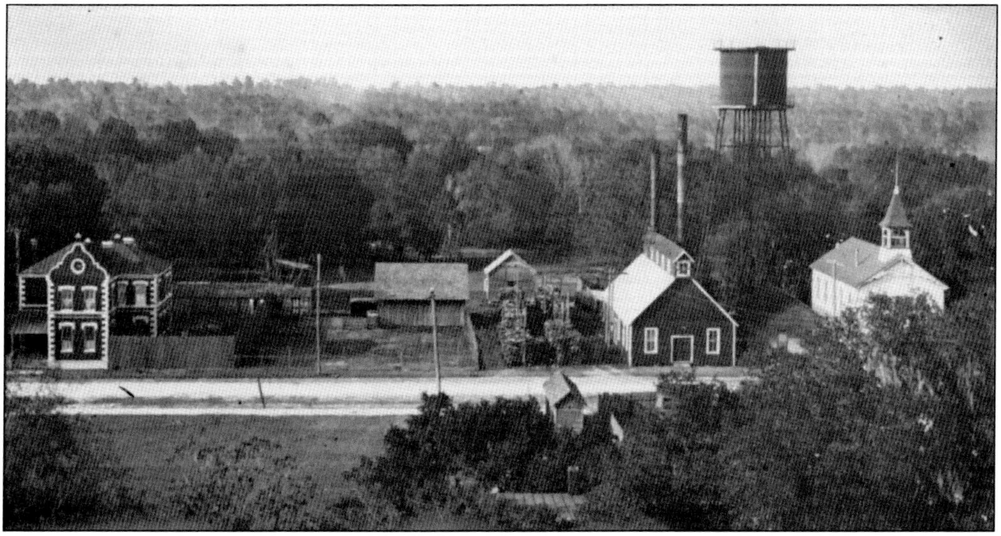

County and municipal buildings line East Church Street, which fronts the edge of a forest. Shown are, from left to right, the county jail (the present-day fire station), a storage building, a woodyard, the electric power plant, a 65-foot steel water tower, and a repair shop. Resembling a church, the fire station and city council room, complete with a bell, finishes the block. The calaboose behind the woodyard was the first jail, built in 1867. (Courtesy State Archives of Florida, Frisbie Collection.)

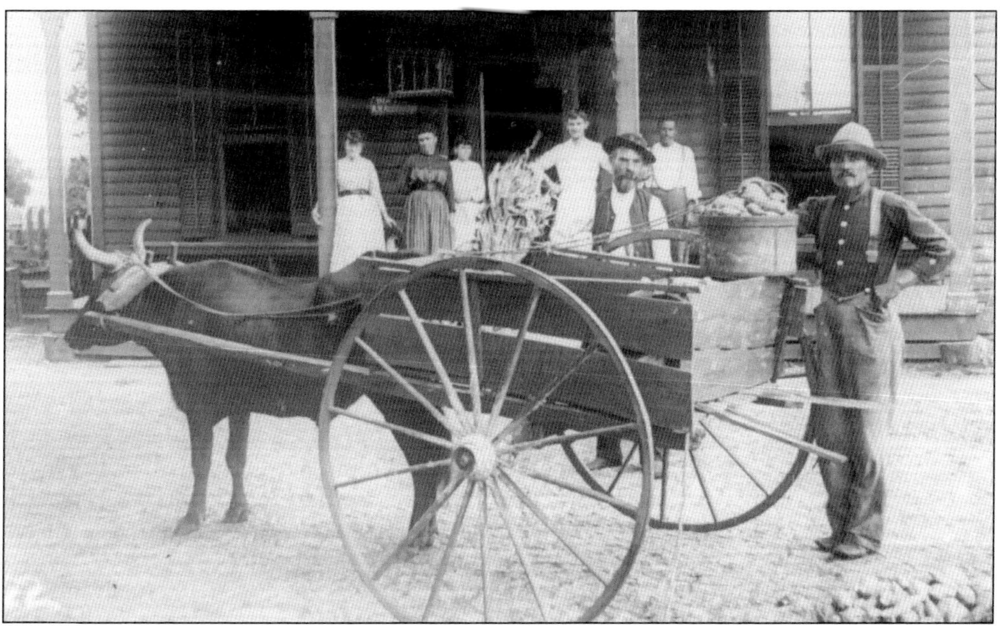

A farmer identified as E.R. Lee, shown standing by his oxcart, delivers corn and sweet potatoes to Dr. Ruben H. Huddleston's home. Lee, a truck farmer, owned an 80-acre farm two miles northwest of Bartow. He marketed sweet potatoes, corn, beans, cabbage, and squash. Dr. Huddleston, along with many Bartowans, moved to Miami between 1895 and 1900. (Courtesy State Archives of Florida, Frisbie Collection.)

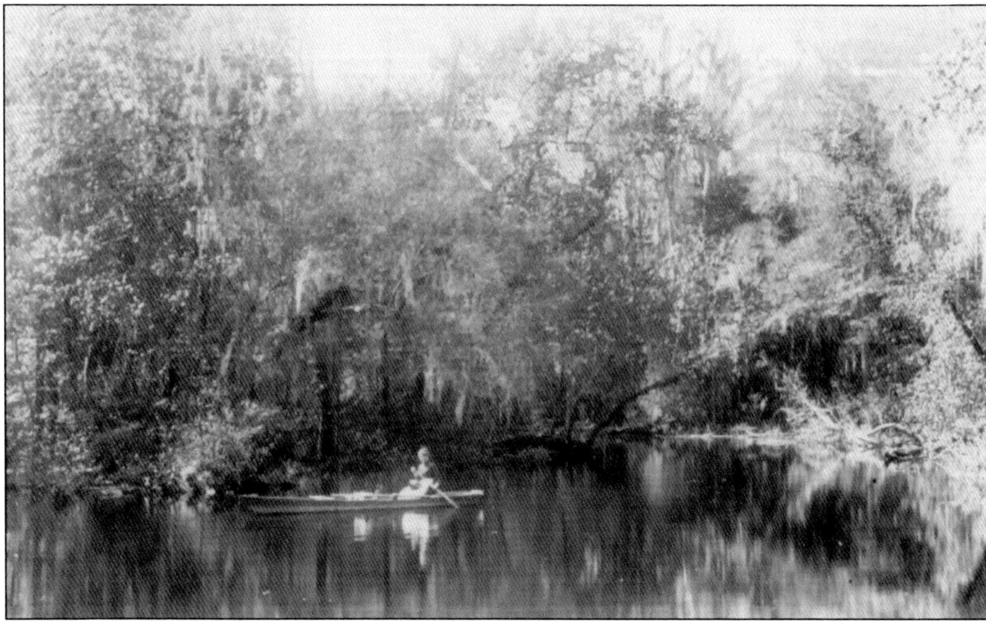

A young lady paddles a boat at Kissengen Springs, originally called De Leon Springs, a few miles south of Bartow. In 1883, a local doctor planning to create a health spa and invalid resort renamed it for the famous baths at Kissengen, Germany. The grandiose plan was never realized, and the spring continued as a popular swimming and picnic attraction until it ceased flowing about 1950. (Courtesy State Archives of Florida, Frisbie Collection.)

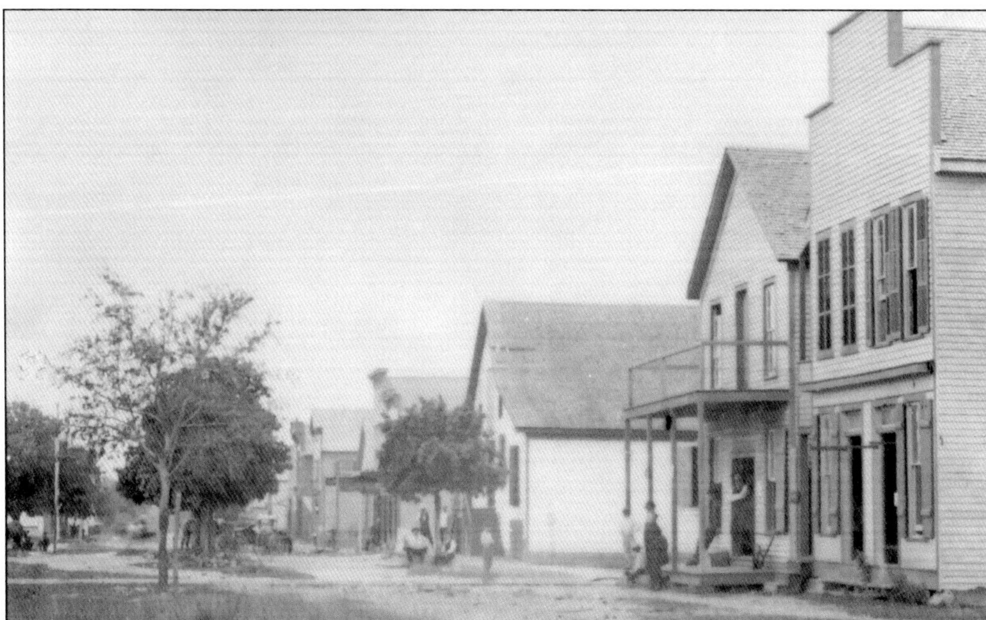

Main Street in the 1880s is seen in this photograph. The two north-facing buildings on the right are a harness shop and a grocery store. The large white building across a sandy Broadway Avenue was one of the first stores in the community owned by Capt. David Hughes. The trees in front of Hughes's store are sour orange trees. (Courtesy State Archives of Florida, Frisbie Collection.)

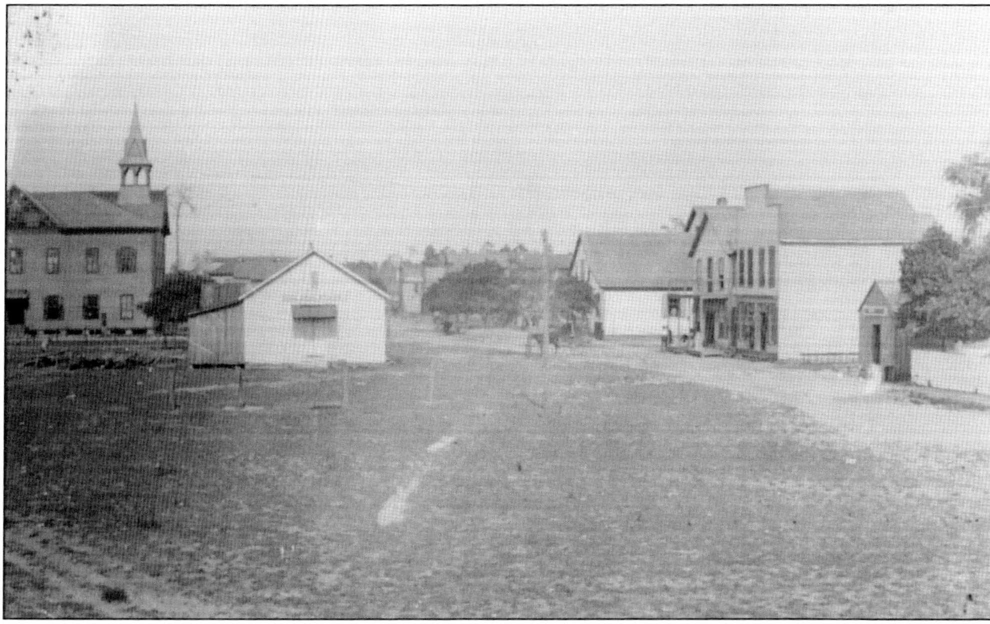

The large building on the left is the 1884 courthouse, seen behind a small drugstore in the center of an empty field. On the south side of the street are the Orange Grove Hotel's fence (far right), a millinery store, a harness shop (with ladder against the wall), and a grocery store. A horse and wagon are tethered at the base of International Ocean Telegraph's 1866 telegraph line, which linked the United States to Cuba. (Courtesy State Archives of Florida, Frisbie Collection.)

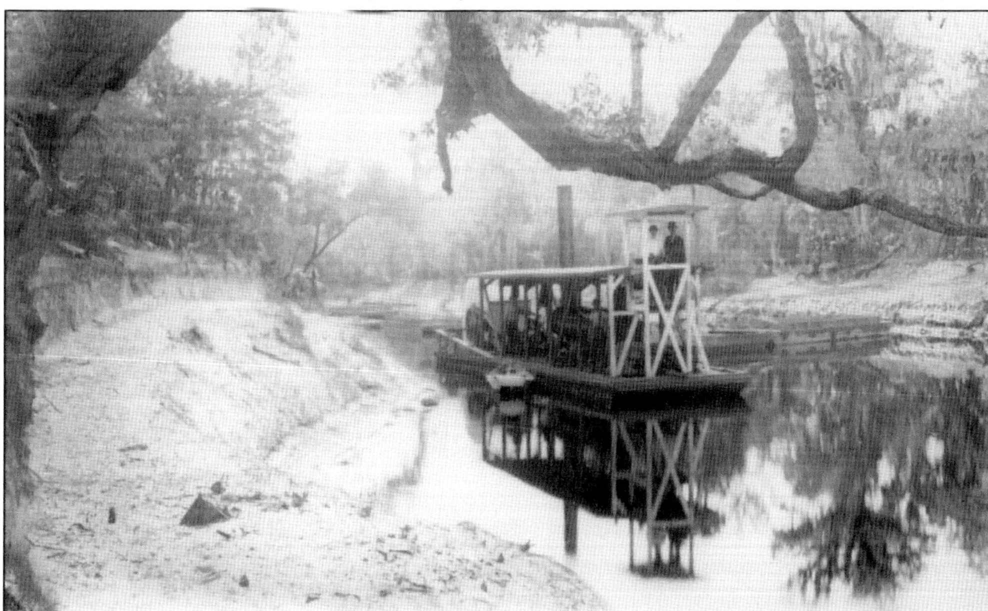

Mining of "river pebble" phosphate began in the Peace River in 1888. Seven years earlier, Capt. J. Francis LeBaron, of the Army Corps of Engineers, discovered the "white gold" while surveying for a canal, sparking a new industry and a boost to the economy. River mining operations ceased in 1908 as richer yields of land pebble and hard rock phosphate in the "bone valley" proved more profitable. (Courtesy State Archives of Florida, Frisbie Collection.)

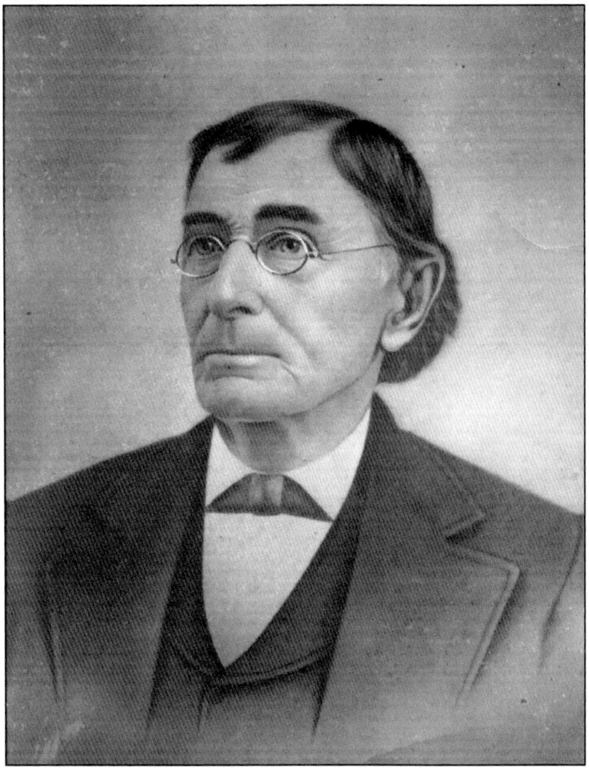

Jacob Summerlin, a cattle baron, pioneer, and philanthropist, could easily be called the "father of Bartow." His gifts established Bartow's churches, schools, and government. His munificence touched communities and the lives of future generations throughout the state. Arguably the greatest Floridian of the 19th century, he considered Summerlin Institute, the school he founded, to be his greatest achievement. (Courtesy State Archives of Florida.)

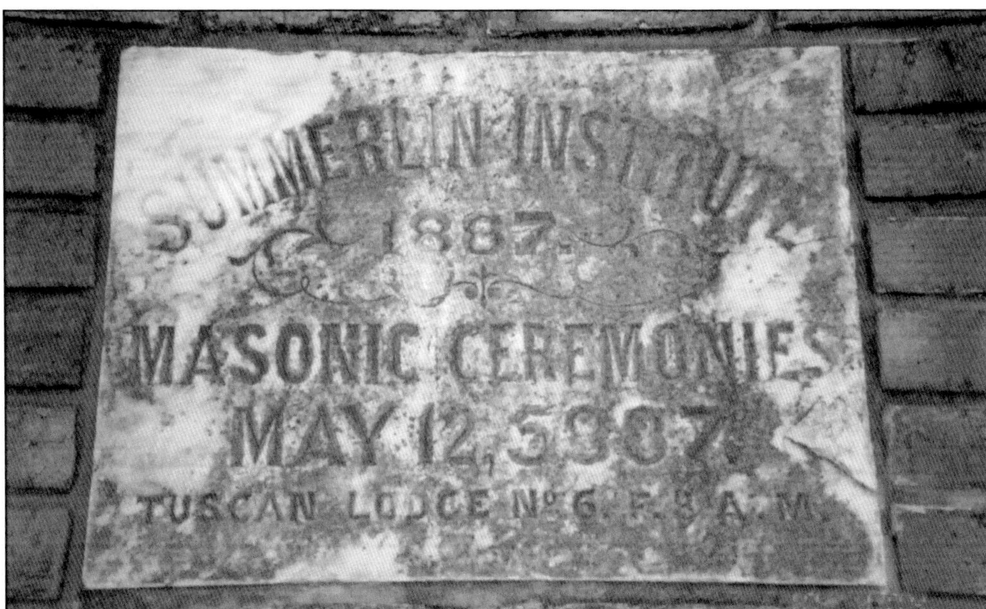

Original bricks flank Summerlin Institute's historic cornerstone, laid in 1887. The monument, at the corner of South Wilson Avenue and Stanford Street, is topped by a school bell and holds a time capsule. The marble cornerstone reads: "Summerlin Institute, 1887, Masonic Ceremonies, May 12, 5887, Tuscan Lodge No. 6, F. & A.M." The year 5887 refers to Anno Lucis, the "year of light," which references the creation. (Courtesy W.L. Harris collection.)

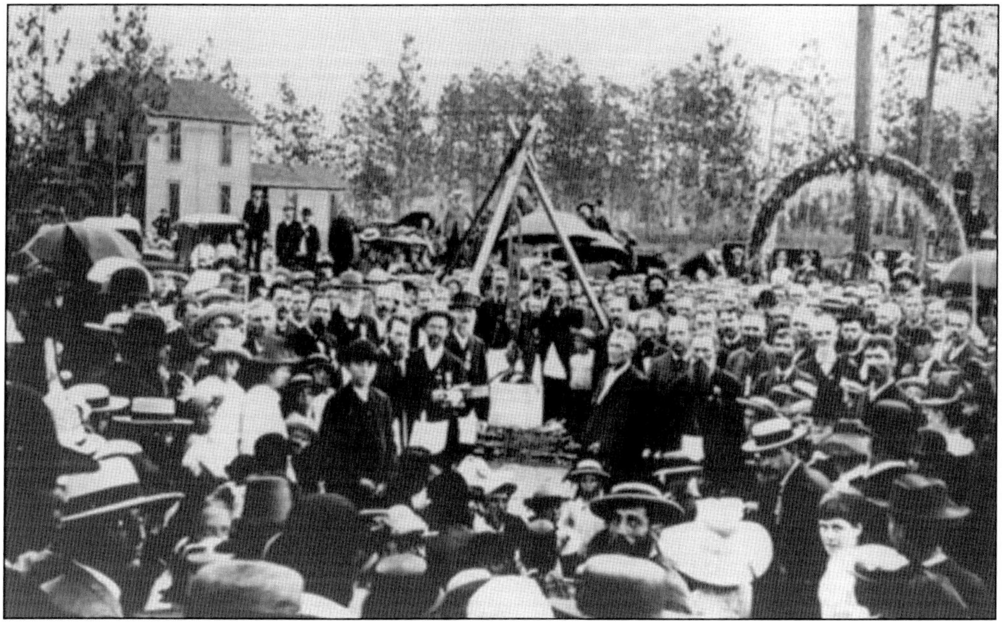

On May 12, 1887, Jacob Summerlin laid the cornerstone of Bartow's prestigious school, named for its benefactor. With Masonic solemnity, Summerlin and his lodge conducted the ceremony commencing the school's construction, which was completed in 1889. Today, the cornerstone is incorporated into a monument at the site of the school, located on the corner of Wilson Avenue and Stanford Street. (Courtesy State Archives of Florida.)

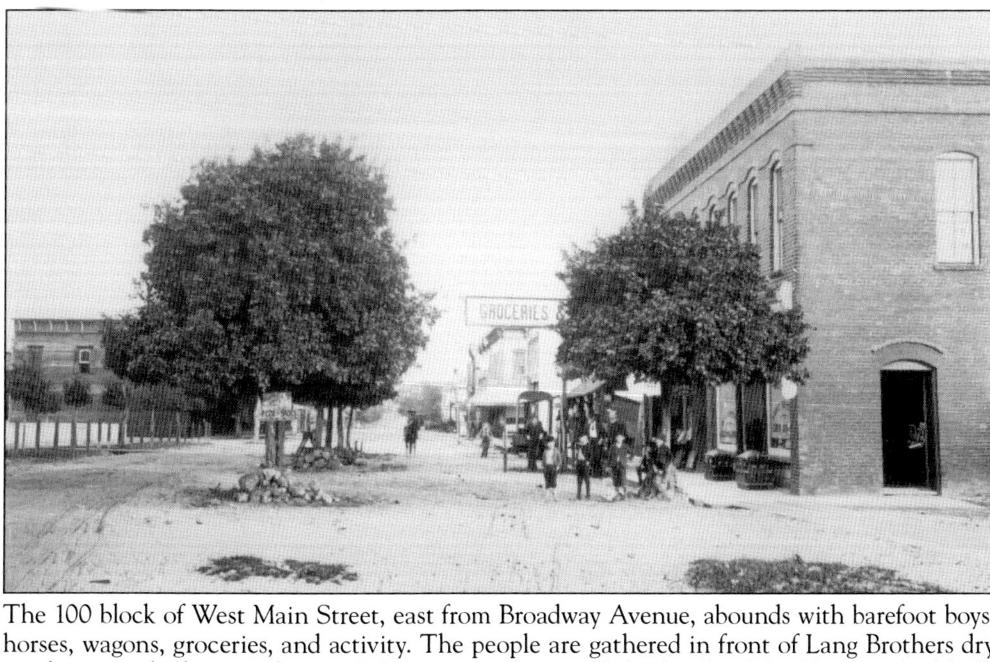

The 100 block of West Main Street, east from Broadway Avenue, abounds with barefoot boys, horses, wagons, groceries, and activity. The people are gathered in front of Lang Brothers dry goods store, which opened in 1887. The company opened the first brick building on the block. Note steamer trunks in front of Lang's and the sign advertising P. Cox Shoes on the orange tree in the street. The courthouse fence can be seen in the lower left. (Courtesy State Archives of Florida, Frisbie Collection.)

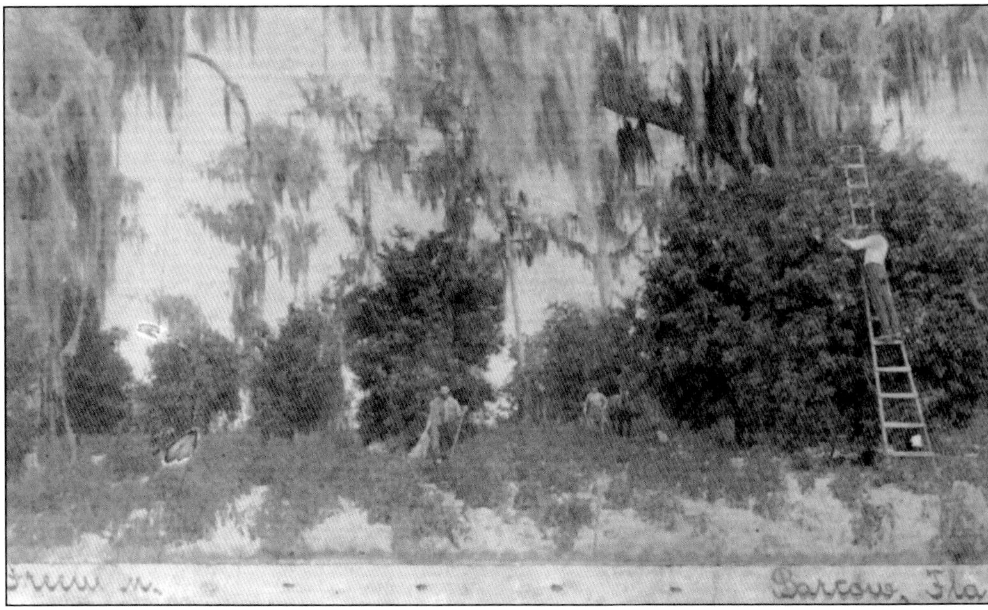

The new endeavor of harvesting fruit was destined to become one of the major industries in the county. In this photograph, a man ascends a crude ladder, one man carries a pick sack, and another attends a plow among oaks, pines, and peas. Citrus culture began in the 1880s, when farmers counted holdings by the number of trees rather than acres, and shipments went by wagon to market. (Courtesy State Archives of Florida, Frisbie Collection.)

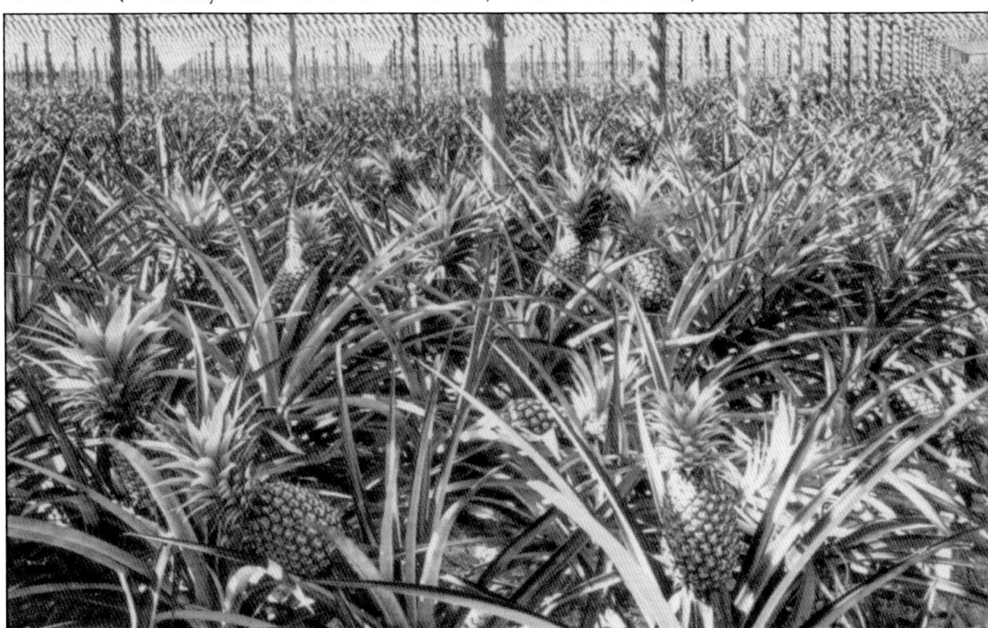

This photograph shows pineapples in the present-day Meadovista area, where extensive fields were planted to replace the tobacco crops that failed after Cuban workers departed at the end of the Spanish-American War. The pineapple, a symbol of hospitality, and the Latin motto *Urbs in Rure* (City in the Country) make up the official seal of Bartow, which was chartered on July 1, 1882. (Courtesy State Archives of Florida, Frisbie Collection.)

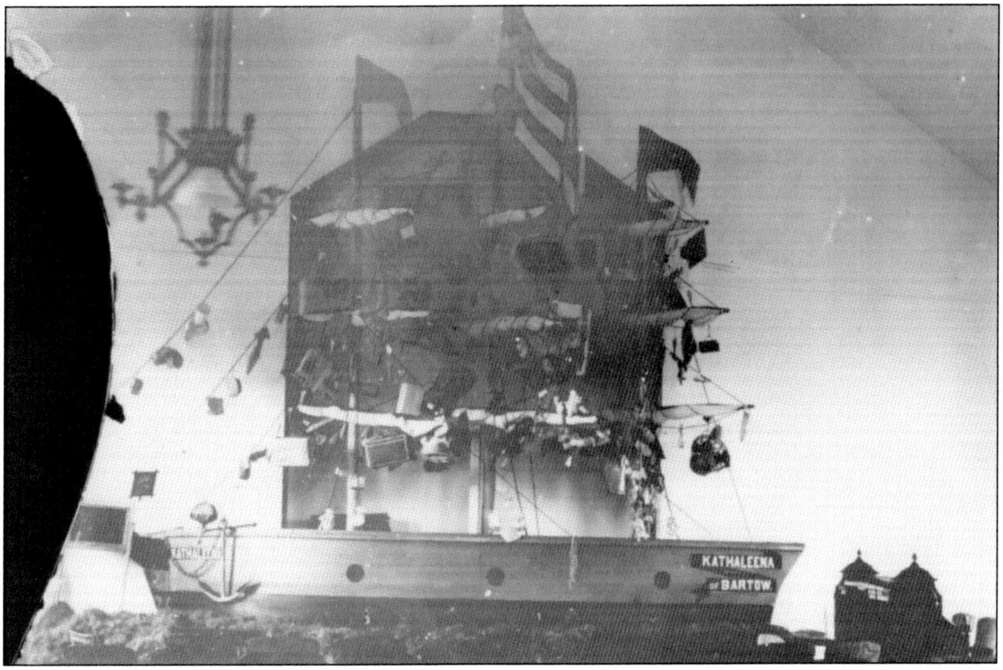

First Presbyterian Church's new sanctuary was graced with a 26-foot, fully rigged ship, christened *Kathaleena of Bartow*, for the celebration of Christmas in 1887. Rev. Samuel Hair gave the nod for builder M.M. Dunlope and congregants to moor the ship on a sea of moss between the pulpit and organ. The biblical message of hope, coupled with the distribution of gifts draping the rigging, made the holiday memorable and spiritual. (Courtesy George McClelland.)

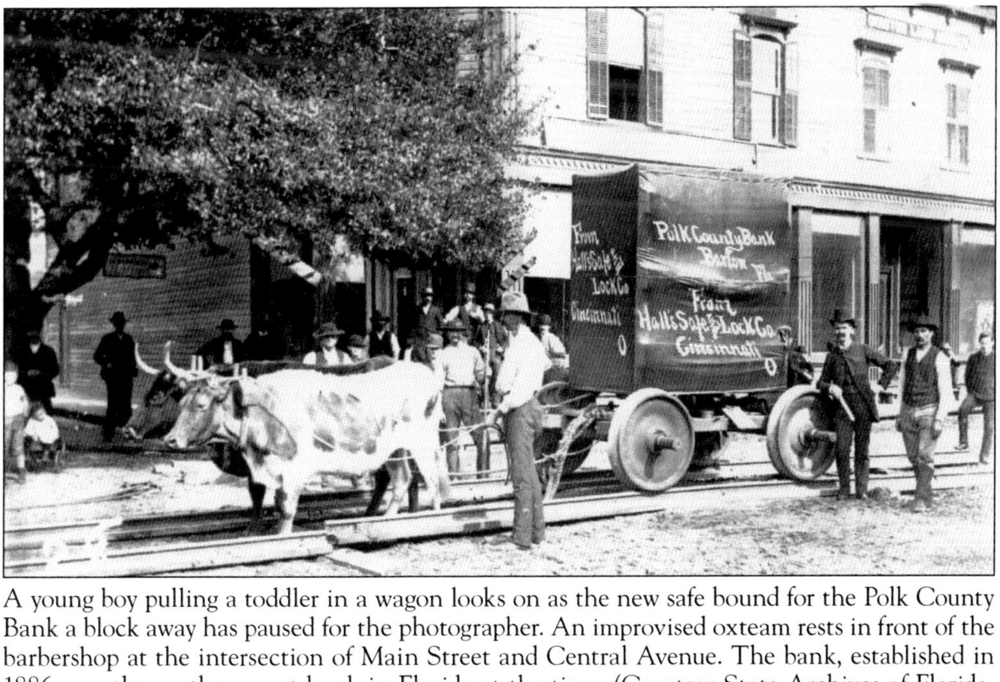

A young boy pulling a toddler in a wagon looks on as the new safe bound for the Polk County Bank a block away has paused for the photographer. An improvised oxteam rests in front of the barbershop at the intersection of Main Street and Central Avenue. The bank, established in 1886, was the southernmost bank in Florida at the time. (Courtesy State Archives of Florida, Frisbie Collection.)

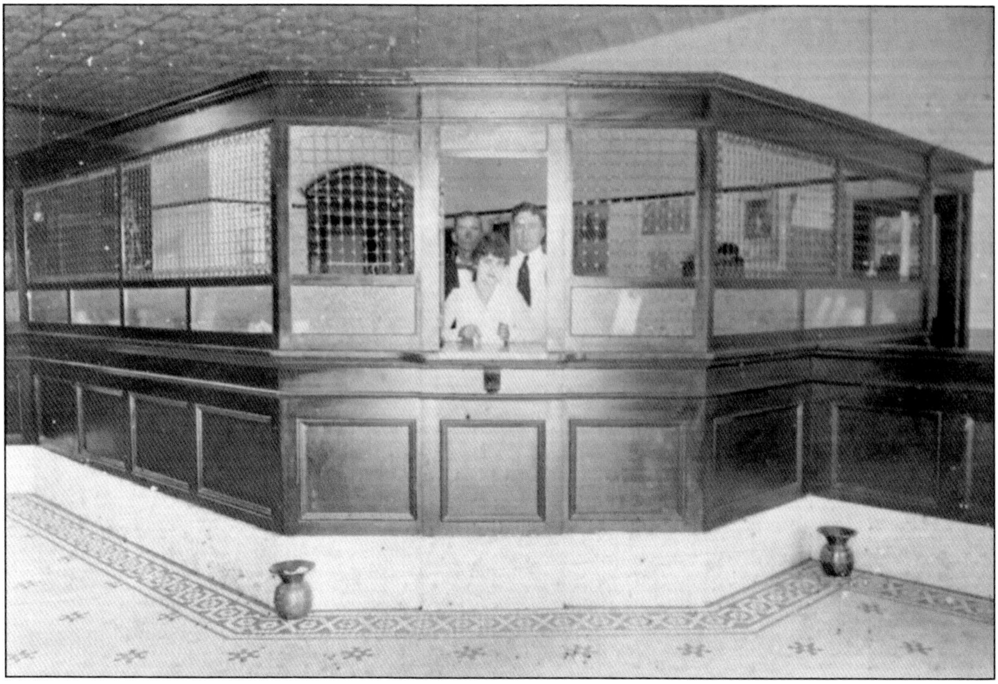

Spittoons for ubiquitous tobacco chewers stand amid the ornate tile work of the Polk County Bank, located on the northwest corner of Main Street and Broadway Avenue. The bank was Bartow's first financial institution, chartered in 1886 with $25,000 of capital. In 1891, it met the requirements to become a national bank. The Polk County National Bank was a victim of the Depression and closed in 1929. (Courtesy State Archives of Florida, Frisbie Collection.)

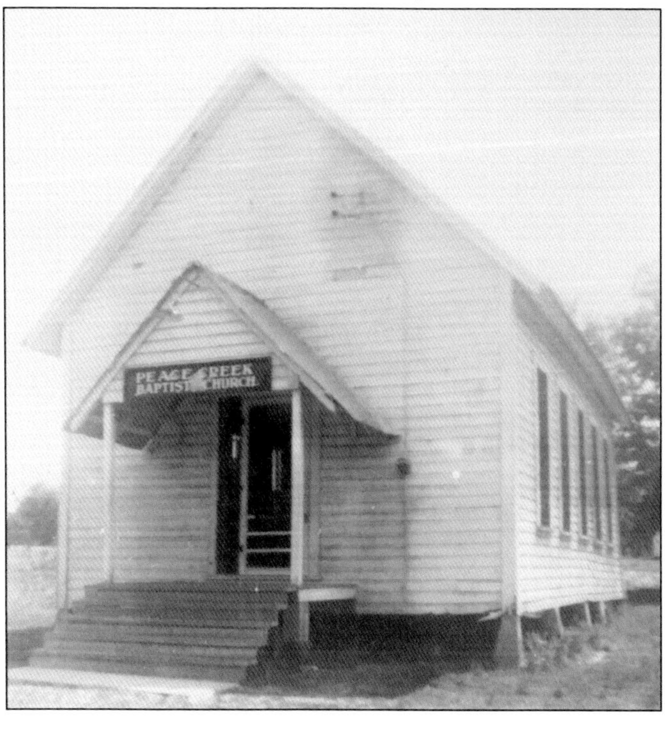

Peace Creek Baptist Church is seen here in the 1930s after 50 years of service. In 1854, minister Rev. Jeremiah Hayman established the church, comprising eight members of the Zachariah Seward and William Rogers families and an African American named Jim. It was Bartow's first church. The following year, Reverend Hayman became the first pastor, serving through 1892. The building was replaced in 1973. (Courtesy State Archives of Florida, Frisbie Collection.)

Three

PROGRESS 1891–1899

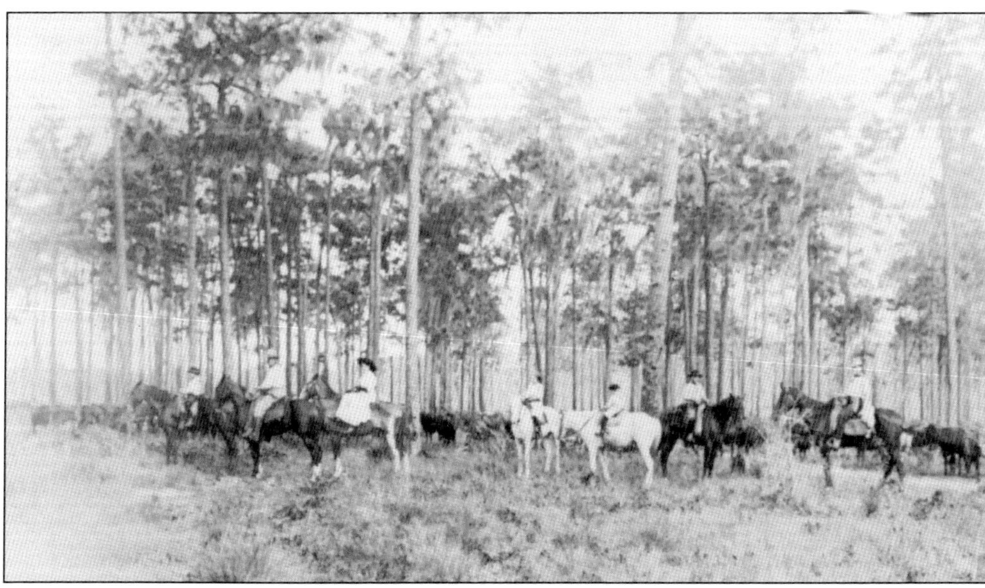

Unlike the days when thousands of cattle were herded by Jacob Summerlin, the "King of the Crackers," this photograph shows a modest herd driven by a family through the pine woods south of Bartow, at present-day Noralyn Mine Road. Cowmen were called "crackers," a term not of derision but descriptive of the popping of whips used to control boisterous bovines. (Courtesy State Archives of Florida, Frisbie Collection.)

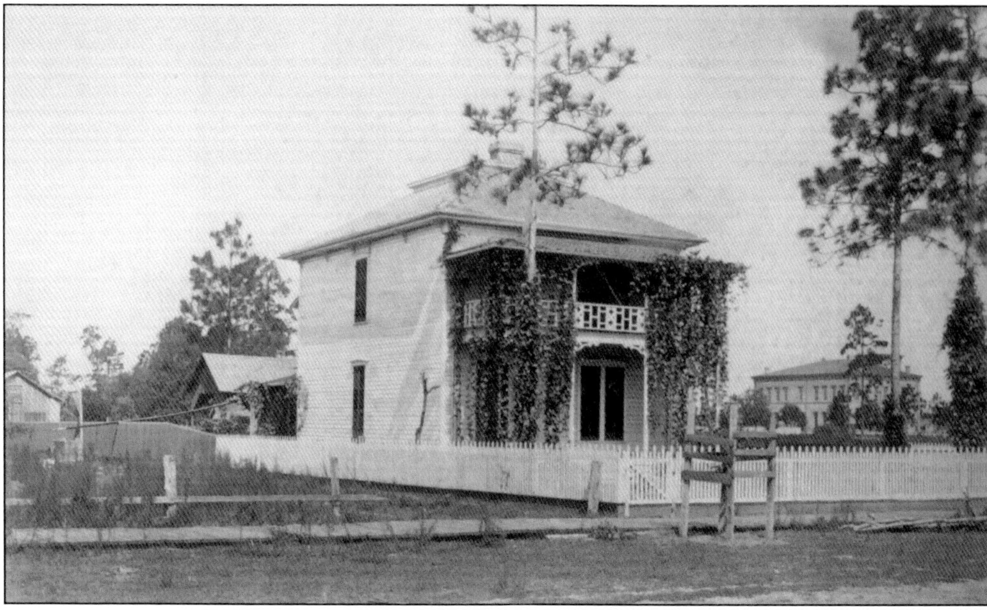

The William B. Lyle home, on Jackson Avenue, was built in 1887 of local heart pine. Lyle was a prominent buyer and shipper of citrus and vegetables. Hanging vines provided shade and beauty. Note the well on the left, with bucket line and lowering arm, and the boardwalk along the dirt street. The back of Summerlin Institute can be seen to the right. (Courtesy State Archives of Florida, Frisbie Collection.)

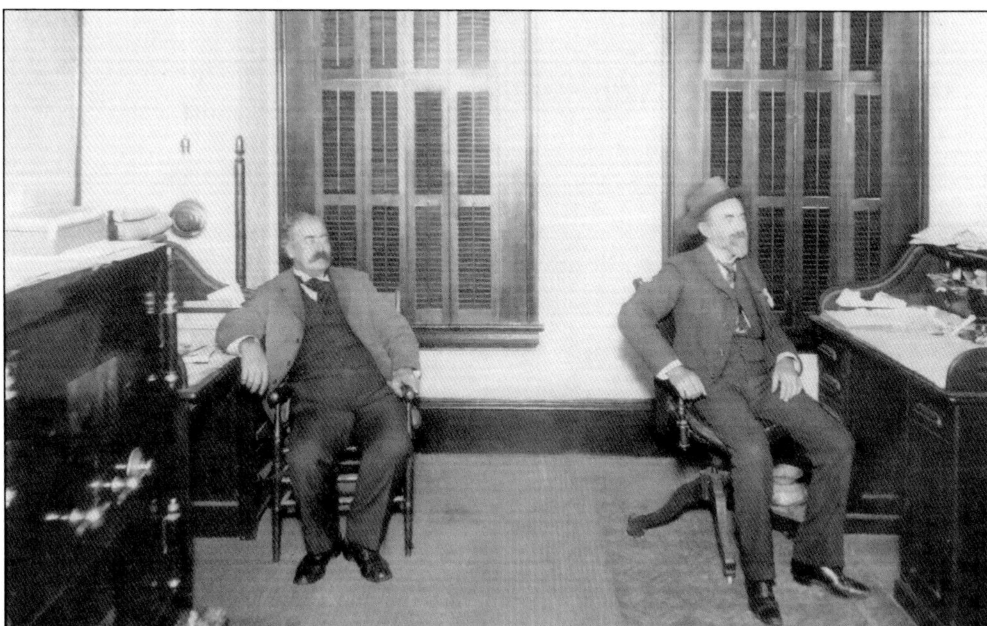

William Van Fleet (left) and Alfred Parslow, pioneer railroad, real estate, and phosphate developers, relax in their office in the 1890s. Van Fleet's efforts brought the railroad into the heart of Polk County, sparking growth and the first land boom. He organized several phosphate companies and, following major commercial losses, managed a small business in Bartow. He was the father of Gen. James A. Van Fleet. (Courtesy State Archives of Florida, Frisbie Collection.)

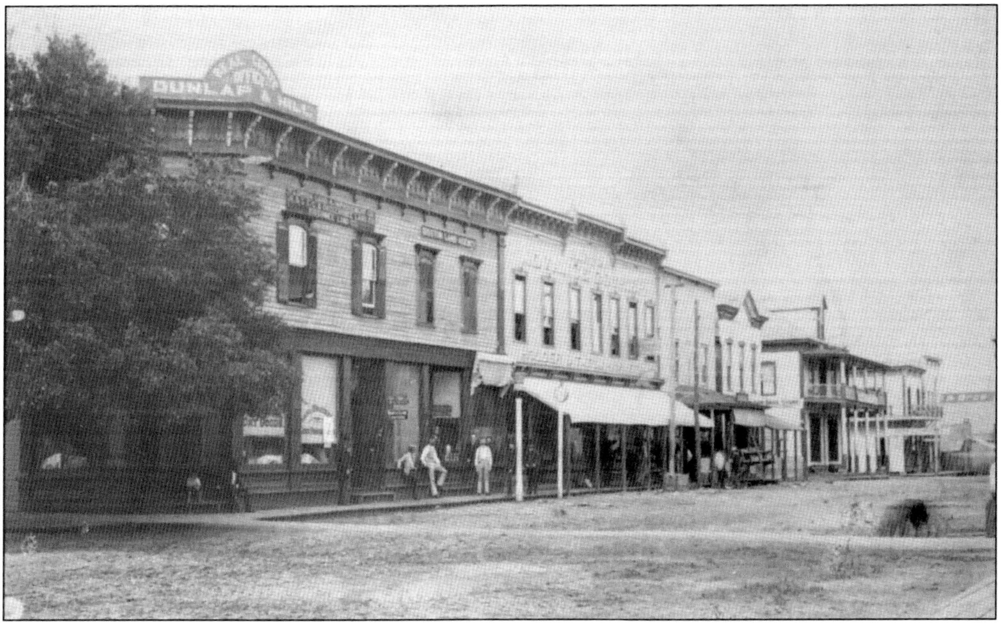

The image of a blurred free-roaming hog shows Main Street's sandy expanse in the 1890s. A wooden crosswalk kept pedestrians from bogging down in the sand. The block was occupied by Dunlap & Hill real estate, Disston Land Agency, Lang Brothers dry goods, Oppenheimer's Drugs (note the apothecary sign and watch), the *Advance Courier* newspaper office, City drugstore, and the Tremont House. (Courtesy State Archives of Florida, Frisbie Collection.)

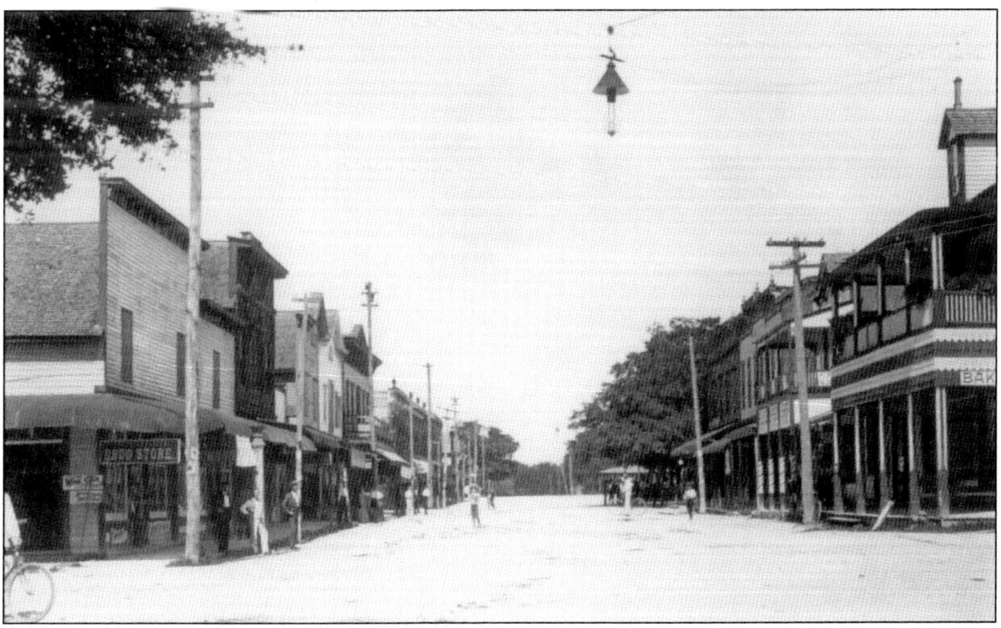

Two arc lights are seen above the thoroughfare in this turn-of-the-century photograph of Main Street. On April 13, 1897, the switch was thrown at Bartow's new power plant, dispelling the darkness. Initially, seven arc lights were installed: two at the courthouse, and one each at the jail, express office, Wilson Avenue, Oak Avenue, and Summerlin Institute. (Courtesy State Archives of Florida, Frisbie Collection.)

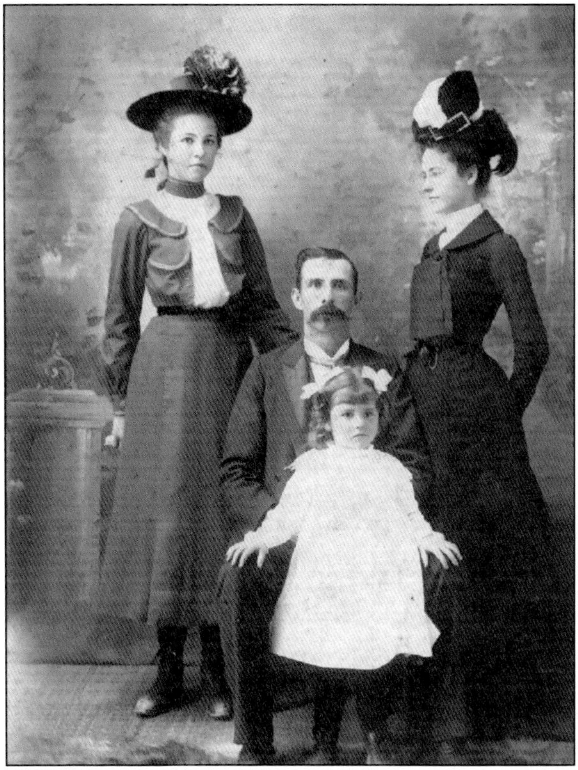

The Silas Lee Caldwell family posed for this formal portrait in the 1890s before coming to Bartow. Silas was the owner of an extensive farm between present-day Highway 17 and the Peace River and, later, was proprietor of Florida Realty Company. Shown here are, from left to right, daughter Jessie, Silas Lee, daughter Clarinda, and wife, Lenora. (Courtesy Barbara and Wallace Orr, Lynda Belle and David Black family.)

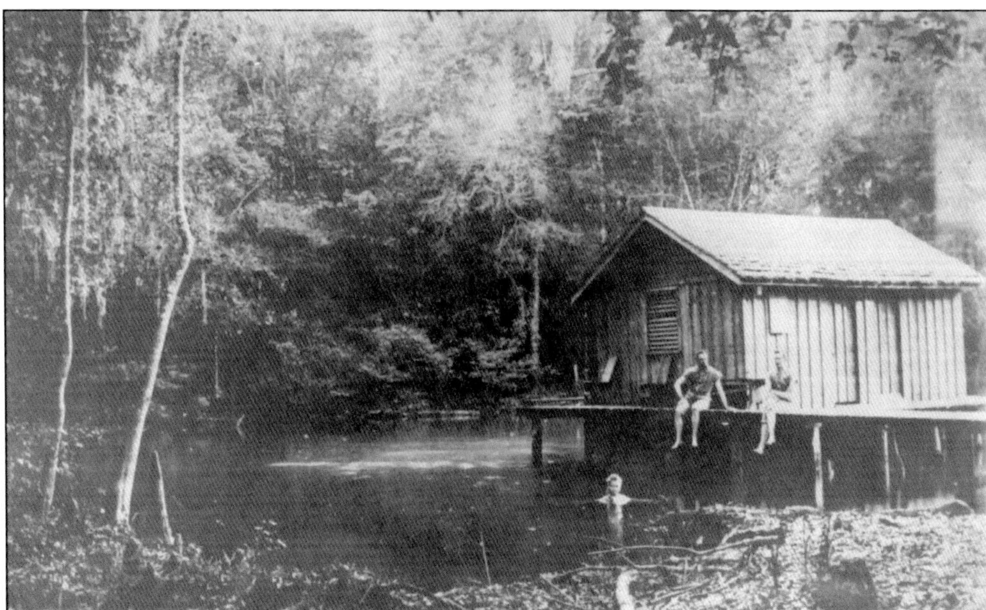

Swimmers relax at Kissengen Springs, south of Bartow, in the early 1890s. The bathhouse was the first attempt to make the springs a tourist destination after two local doctors purchased the site and planned a spa and hotel. The dream never materialized, and the site was later developed into a recreational establishment that lasted until the spring ceased flowing in the 1950s. (Courtesy State Archives of Florida.)

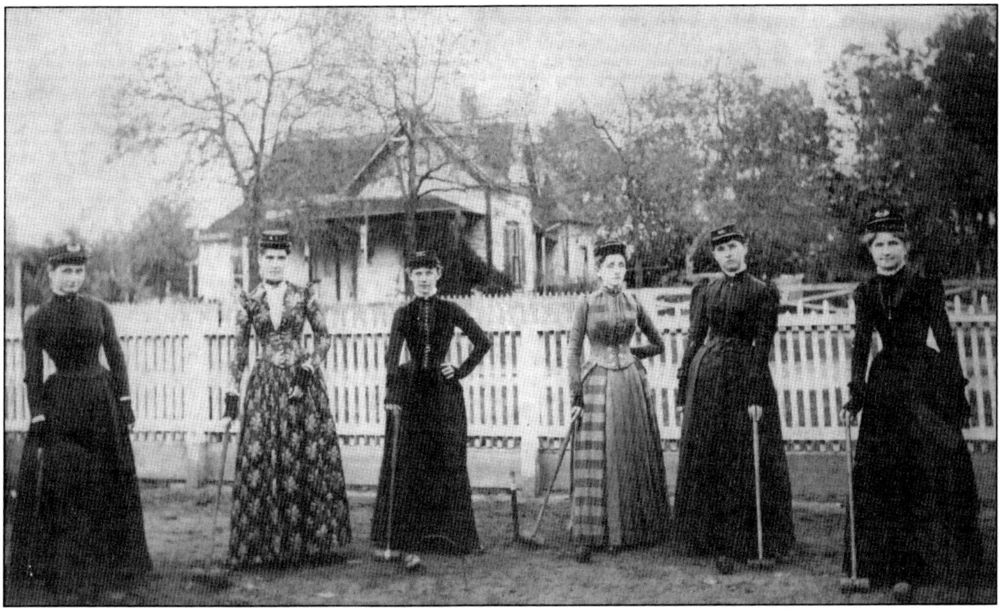

Croquet had been around for 40 years when this photograph was taken in the late 1890s. The game was initially most popular among women and gave them the chance to play outdoors in the company of men. At the time, outdoor parties were called croquet parties. Pictured here are, from left to right, Minnie Granger, Fannie Brown, Ida Snell, Sallie Snell, and May Harrell. (Courtesy State Archives of Florida, Frisbie Collection.)

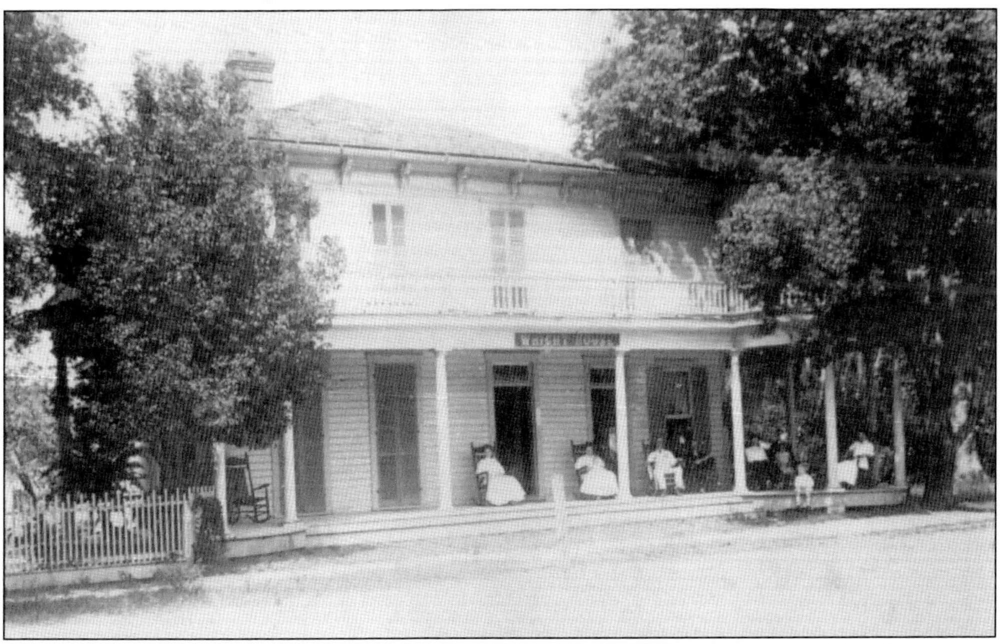

Guests in rocking chairs relax at the Wright House, on the northwest corner of Davidson Street and Wilson Avenue. It was famed for "a most excellent table" and hosted inventor Thomas A. Edison and a company of friends for a week in May 1887. Edison amazed locals, encouraging them to "speak into his phonograph" and recording their voices on tinfoil. This photograph is from the early 1890s. (Courtesy State Archives of Florida, Frisbie Collection.)

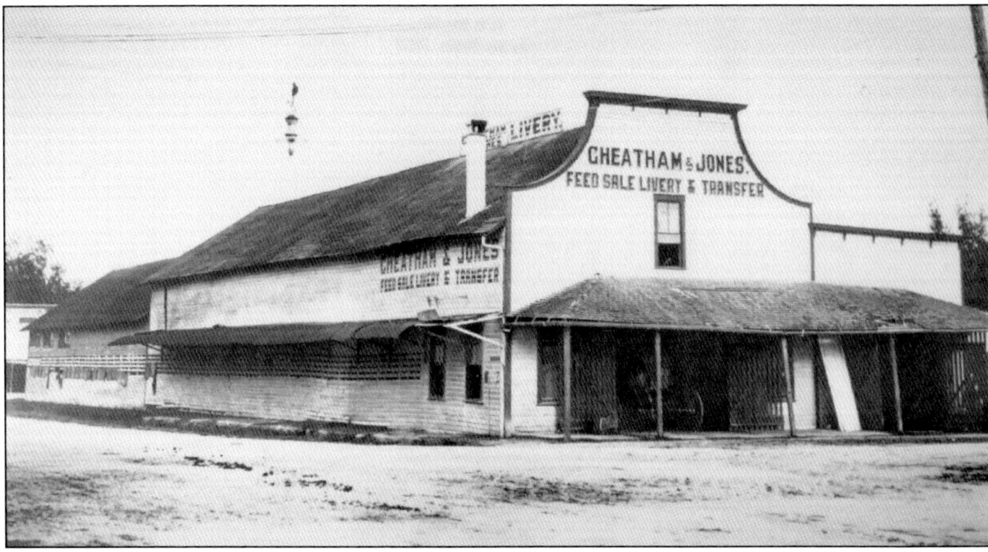

Cheatham & Jones Livery Stable, on the northwest corner of Central Avenue and Summerlin Street, was one of the town's most valued business centers. The livery stable offered full transportation services, renting wagons, buggies, horses and harnesses. Also available were 40 stables, and feed and water for horses. Cheatham & Jones offered transfer services akin to modern moving and delivery. (Courtesy State Archives of Florida, Frisbie Collection.)

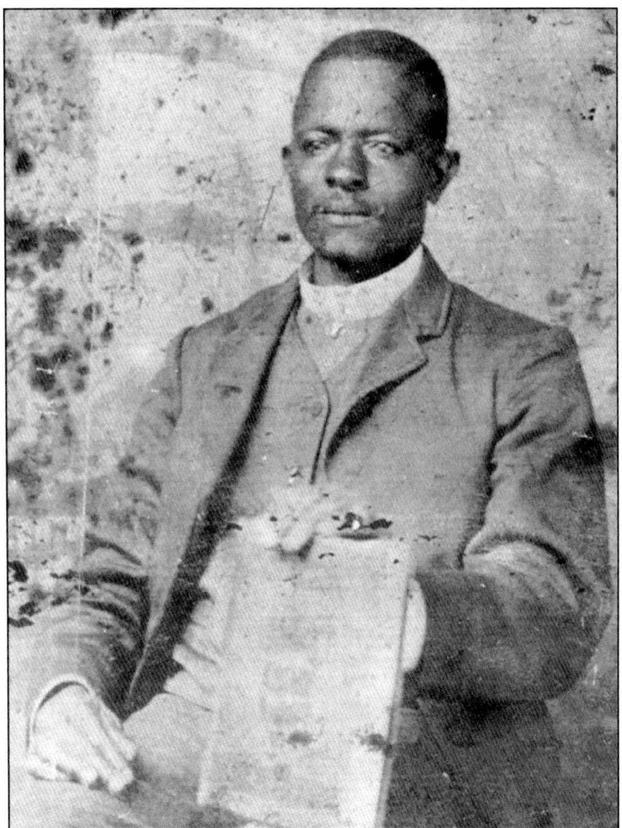

Lawrence Bernard Brown, a former slave, was an entrepreneur who came to Bartow after 1885. He was self-educated, a master carpenter, and a prosperous businessman. Acquiring land and building rental properties led to his becoming a foremost citizen. He sold Bibles and was a church clerk for many years. His restored 1892 home is now a museum and hosts an annual African American cultural festival. (Courtesy Historic L.B. Brown House.)

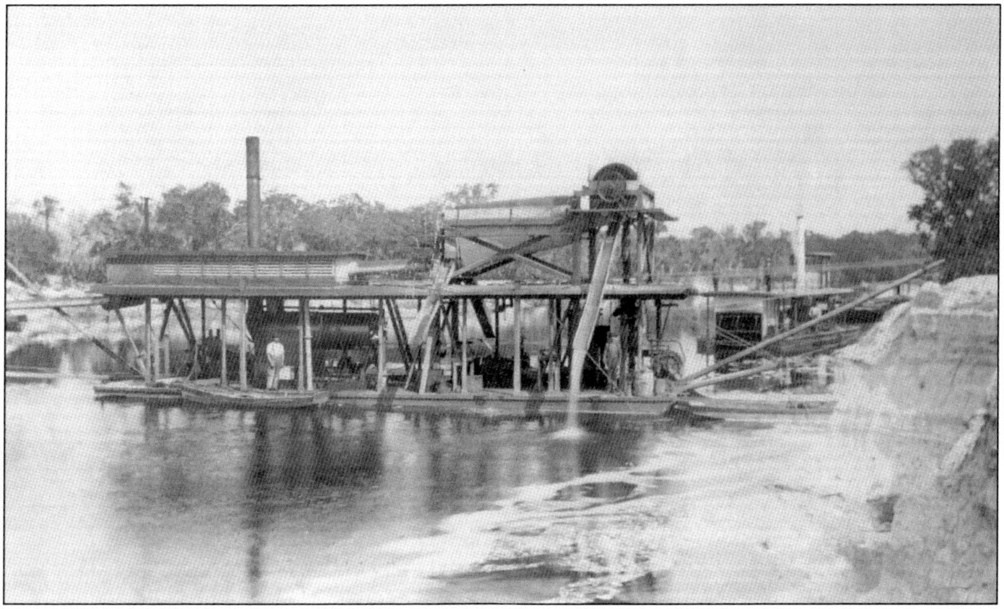

Steam dredges mine phosphate in Peace River south of Bartow. After the discovery of phosphate in 1881, Bartow became a hub in the rush for the "white gold" found in the surrounding Bone Valley. Today, huge draglines feed the plants that process chemicals and fertilizers and extract uranium from phosphate, which continues to play a vital role in the local economy. (Courtesy State Archives of Florida.)

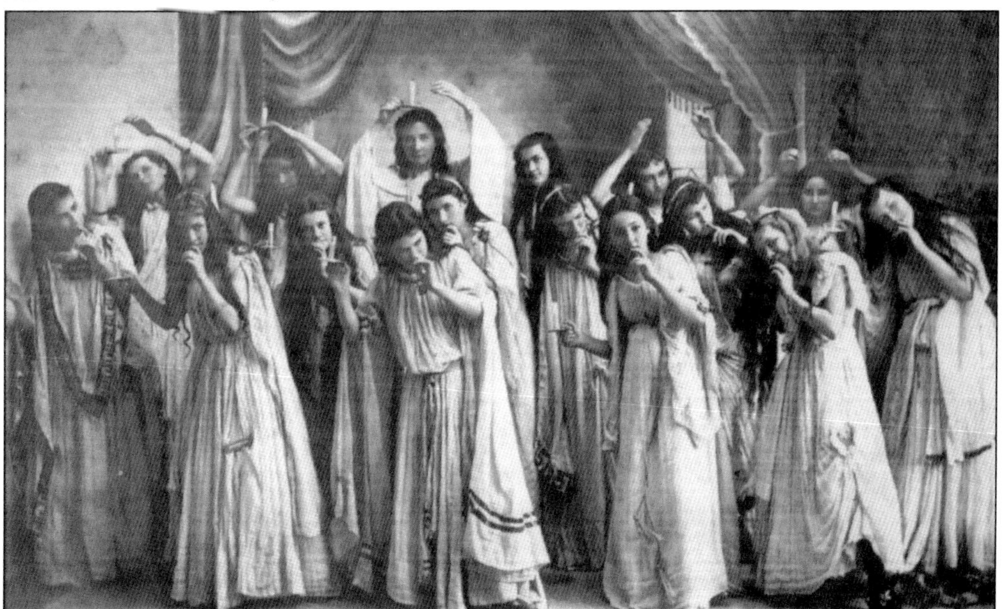

A "living tableau" is the description given this to photograph taken at the Opera House. It exhibits 16 girls in classical costumes. A *tableau vivant*, a depiction of a scene formed by persons posed in static attitudes, was sometimes used at the ends of acts in 19th-century melodramas. Bartow was home to two opera houses providing arts and entertainment to the community. (Courtesy State Archives of Florida, Frisbie Collection.)

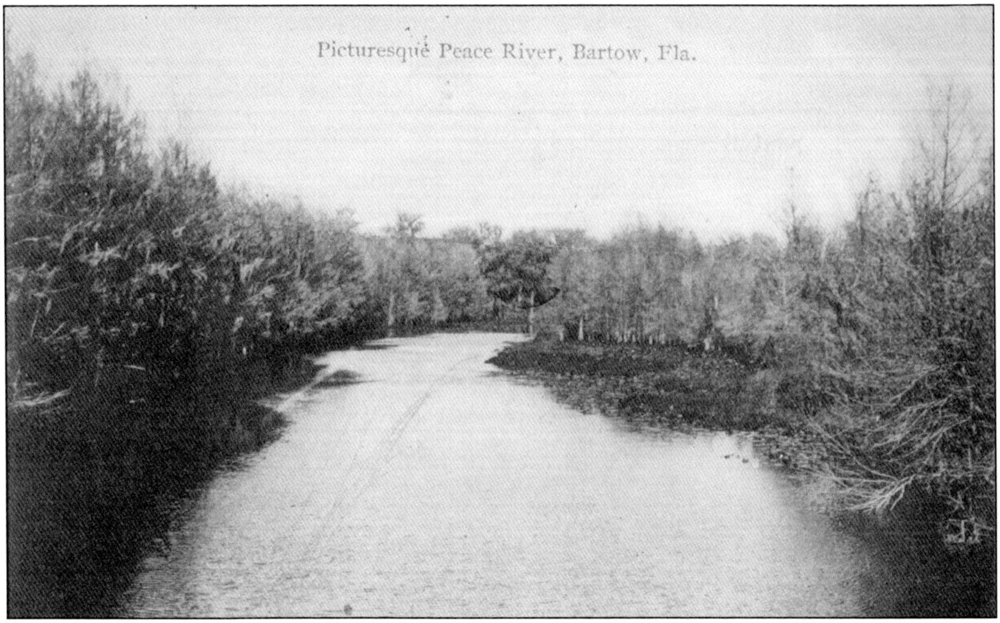

This postcard image of wide water and cypress trees depicts the Peace River near Bartow. Until 1879, the community shared its name with the river—spelled as Pease River or Peas River, and interchanging the words *river* and *creek*. The name dates to the Spanish conquistadors. The Indian name Talakchopko Hatchee (River of the Long Peas) is suggested, but a 1527 map by Hernando Colón has the name Rio de la Pas (River of Peace). (Courtesy State Archives of Florida, Frisbie Collection.)

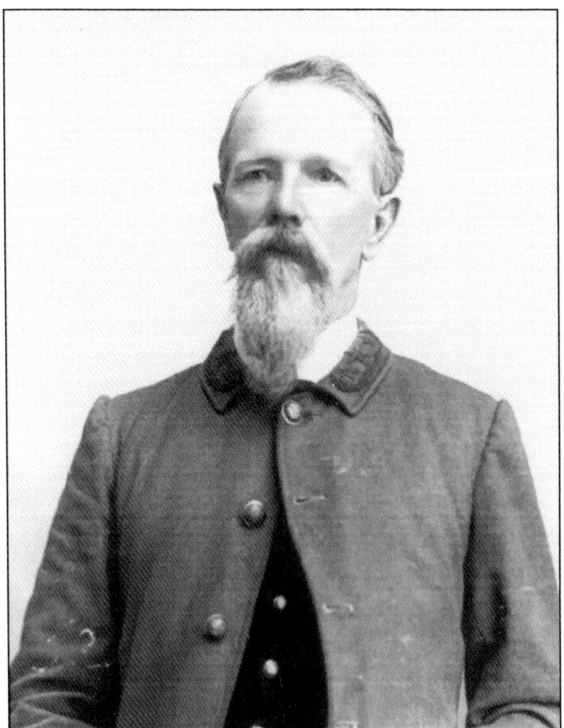

Maj. Gen. Evander M. Law, Confederate soldier and educator, was the founder in 1894 of the South Florida Military Institute (later College), located southeast of the intersection of Broadway Avenue and Stuart Street. The college (1895–1905) was consolidated with other state colleges to form the University of Florida at Gainesville. Law resigned in 1903 to become an editor and school board trustee. (Courtesy State Archives of Florida, Frisbie Collection.)

William Hampton Johnson wears the uniform of the Francis Bartow Camp, United Confederate Veterans. Born in Georgia, Johnson moved to Florida and joined Bartow's Confederate contingent as its first sergeant. He served as justice of the peace, tax assessor, clerk of the court, and mayor of Bartow. In his honor, every Bartow business closed during his funeral in 1915. (Courtesy State Archives of Florida.)

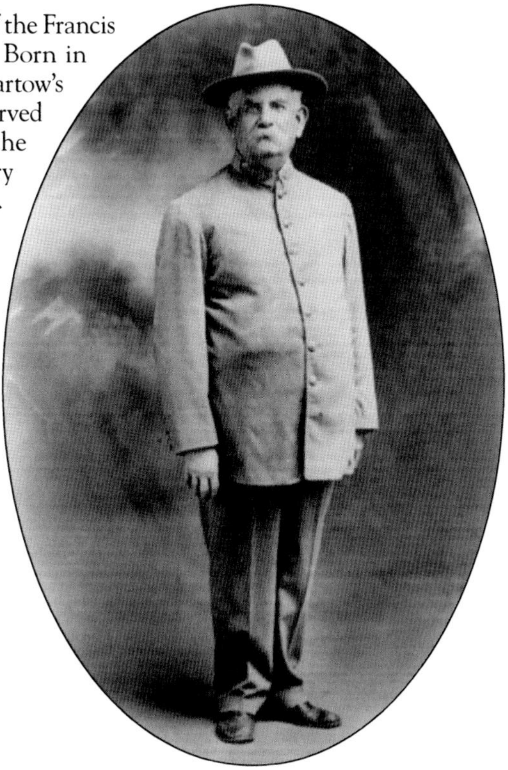

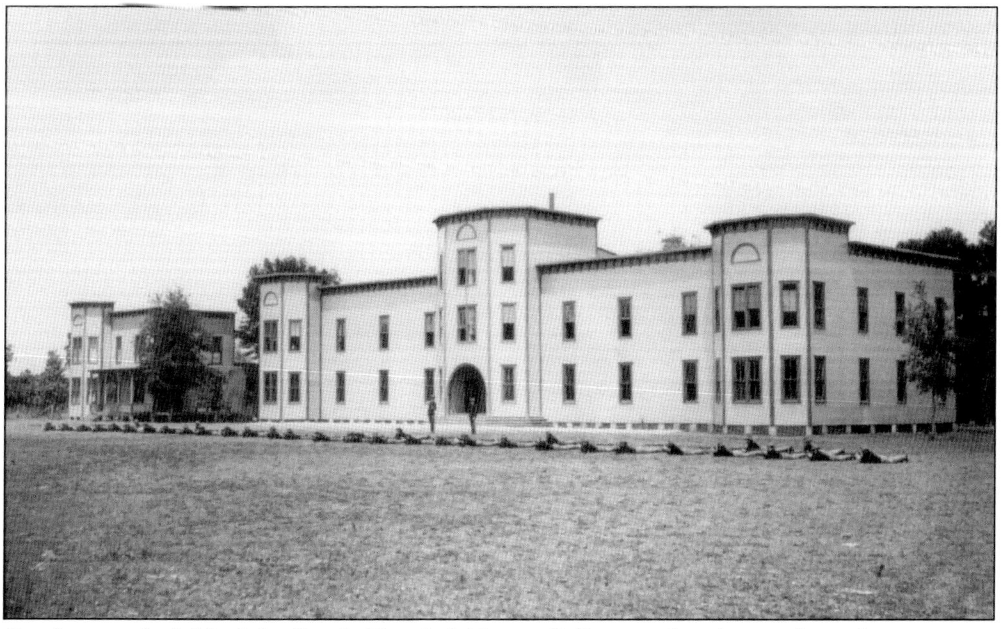

On the parade field of the South Florida Military College, cadets form a firing line in prone positions. Located between present-day Stuart and Tharp Streets, the school, built in 1894, was modeled after West Point. The bachelor officers' quarters and educational building were painted white with barn red trim. The education building consisted of classrooms, barracks, sick room, and chapel. (Courtesy State Archives of Florida, Frisbie Collection.)

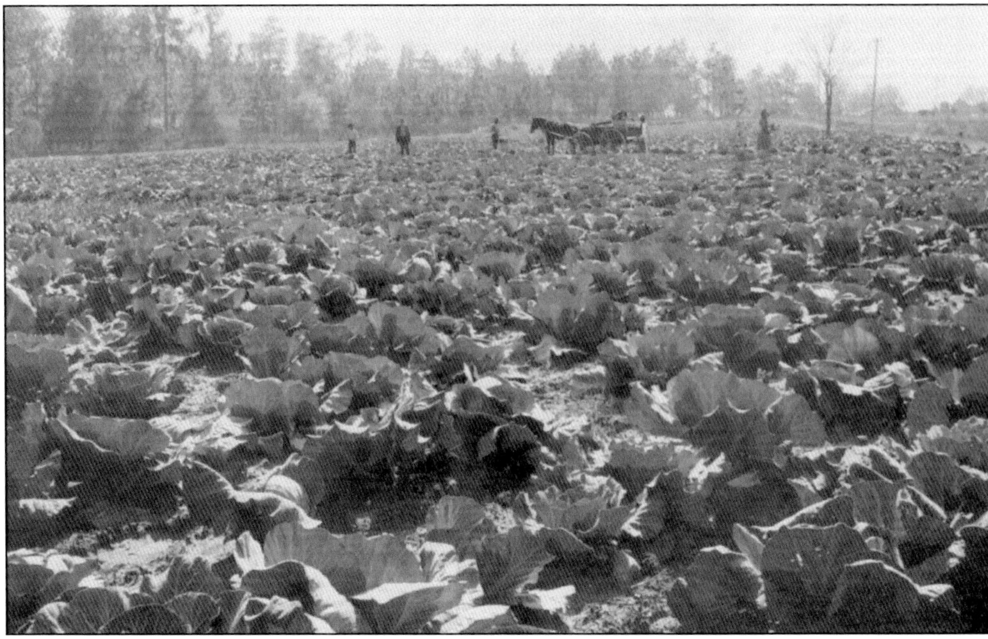

This photograph shows a cabbage field owned by W.B. Lyle. A man is loading cabbage on the wagon while a woman wearing a sunbonnet inspects a cabbage head. Bartow growers produced a variety of crops, and records indicate that cabbages, strawberries, and tomatoes were the leading items. Lyle shipped vegetables by rail to Northern markets. (Courtesy State Archives of Florida, Frisbie Collection.)

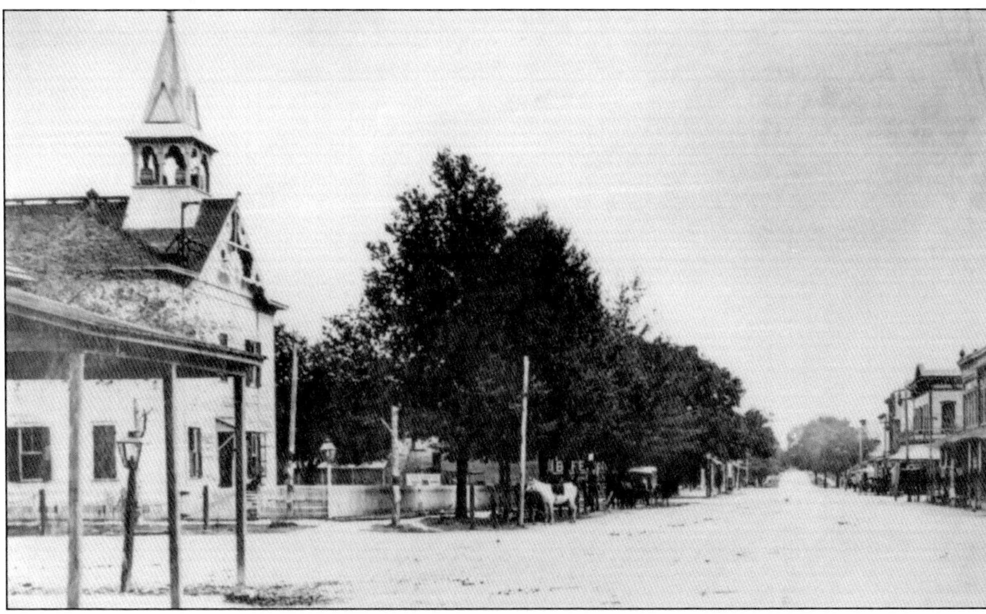

This photograph of Main Street is looking east from Broadway Avenue. On the left, the courthouse, just over 20 years old, shows itself to be in need of paint, new shutters, and roof work, as indicated by the hoist. Note the water barrels in the bell tower for fire protection, the large streetlamps, a tethered horse, oak trees, and the business block on the right. (Courtesy State Archives of Florida, Frisbie Collection.)

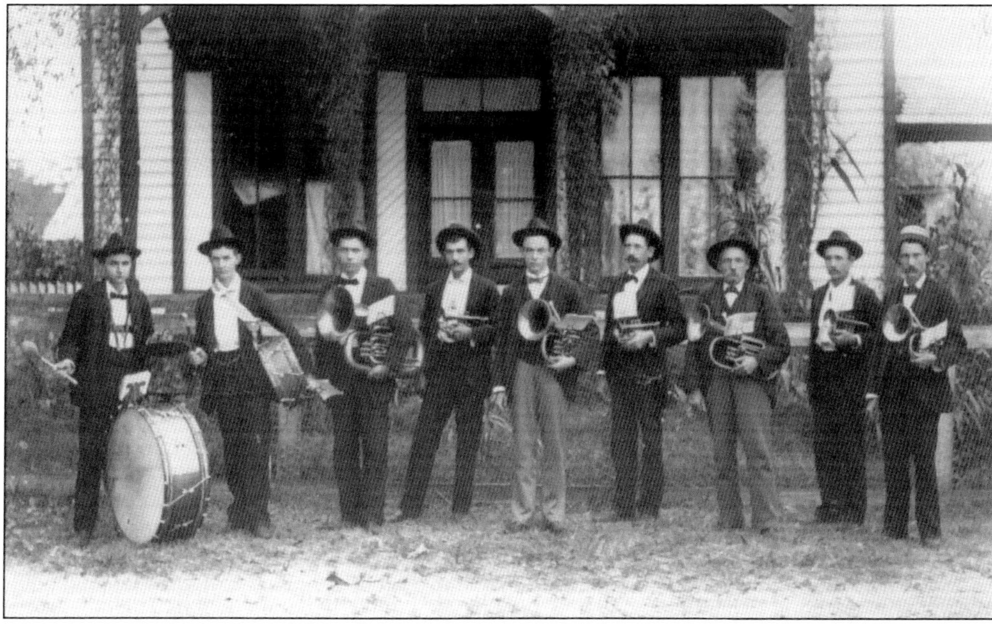

The Bartow Brass Band poses for a group photograph sometime in the 1890s. The band is composed of bass and snare drums, tuba, three baritone horns, and three cornets. The band had numerous performance opportunities; early newspaper accounts report on dances, parades, concerts, church functions, social events, and any number of dramas and other activities conducted at the opera houses. (Courtesy State Archives of Florida, Frisbie Collection.)

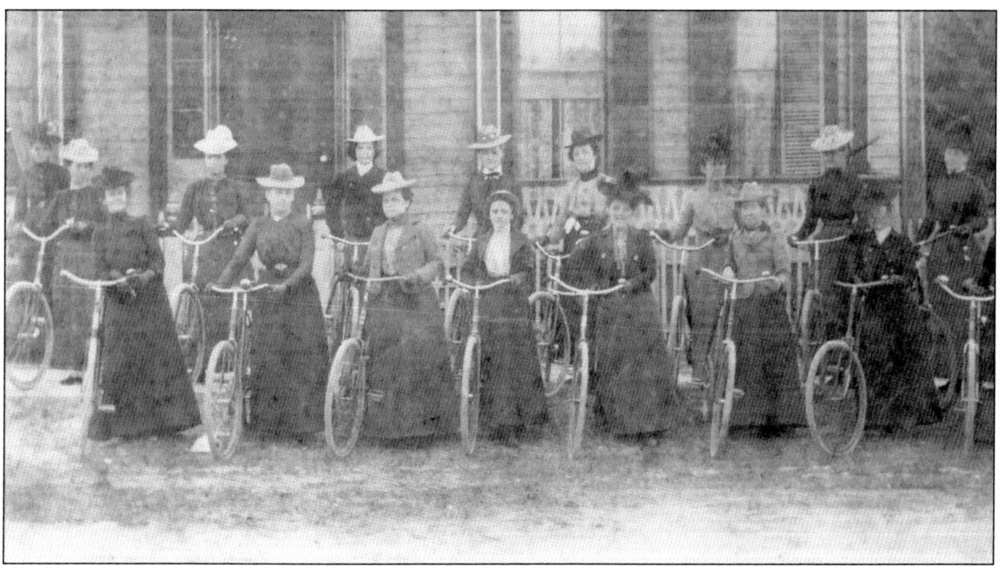

The late 1890s and early 1900s was the heyday for bicycles, as evidenced in this photograph of women cyclists outfitted with hats, coats, and gloves. Bartow's bicycle shop, started by John Wiggins, was turned over to John A. Gresham in 1903, who continued in the business for over 40 years. The shop maintained up to 50 bikes for rentals. (Courtesy State Archives of Florida, Frisbie Collection.)

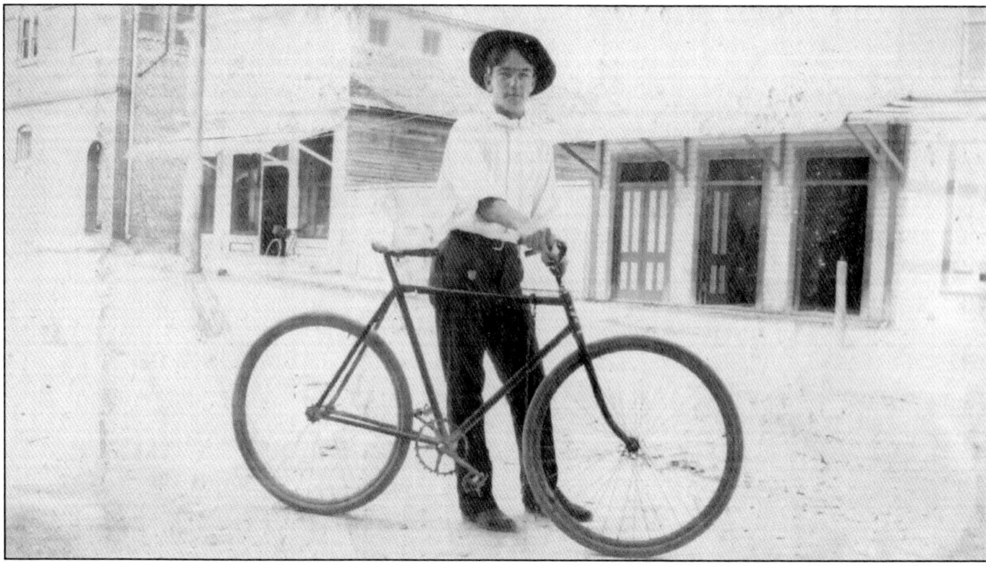

Bicyclist Benjamin Franklin Childs stands on Central Avenue with a broken chain draped over the crossbar. There is another bicycle with a basket in the background. Bicycles were an extremely popular and affordable means of transportation. The hard clay streets were perfect for racing, and a competition course was laid out from the courthouse, down Main Street to Oak Avenue, and to Pearl Street and Broadway Avenue. (Courtesy Bo Raulerson.)

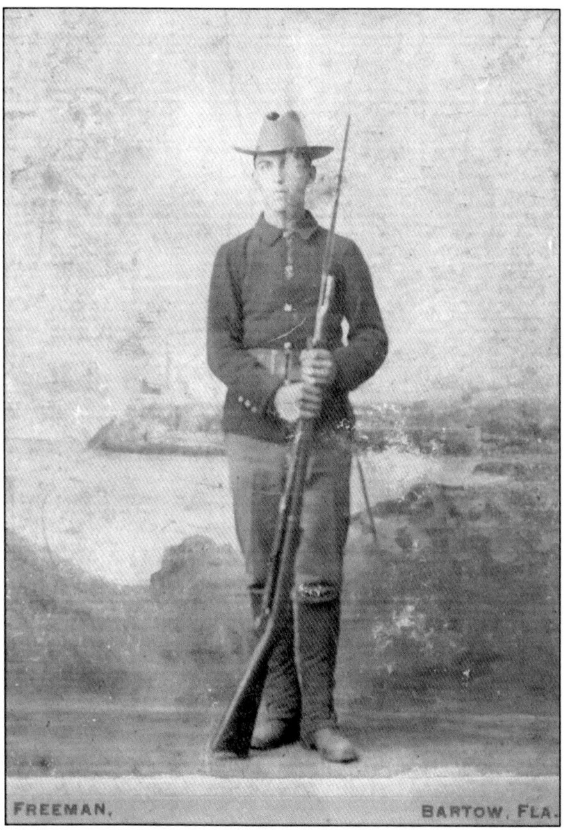

An unidentified soldier of the Spanish-American War, in uniform with rifle and field gear, poses for the camera of George P. Freeman. The soldier was very likely a member of Company C, 3rd United States Volunteers, and one of 13 Bartowans who enlisted and served in Cuba. Two Bartowans, Streaty Smith and Hugh Blount, fell in the war and are buried in Arlington National Cemetery. (Courtesy W.L. Harris collection.)

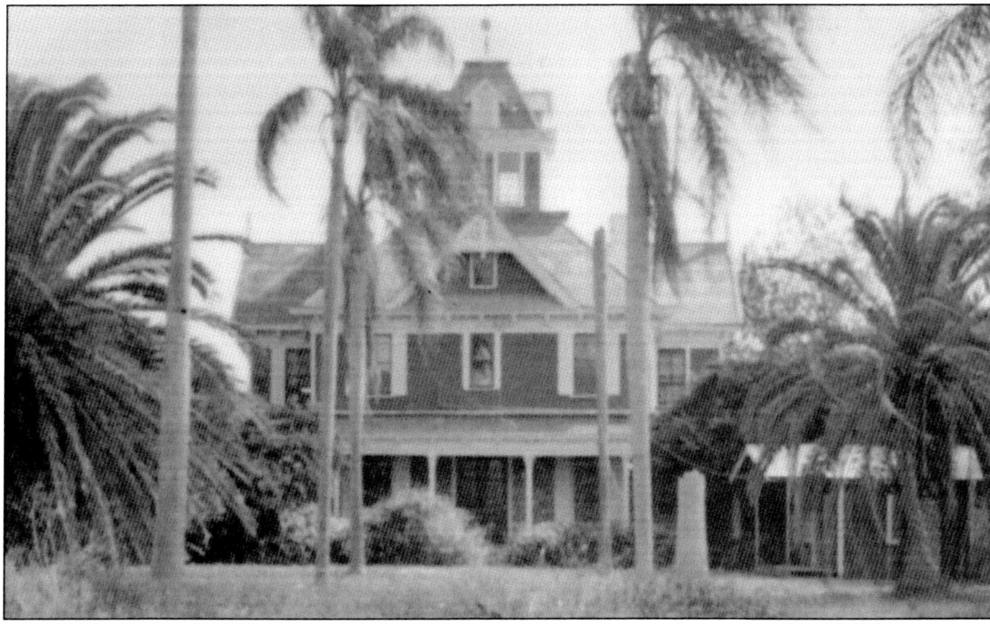

The William B. Varn Home, built in the late 1860s, was a four-story showplace southeast of Bartow. The tallest home in the area, it included crystal chandeliers and copper bathtubs. Varn, a noted citrus grower, produced the first crop of sweet oranges and the first budded grove. The home and properties were demolished to make way for phosphate mining in the 1960s. (Courtesy State Archives of Florida, Frisbie Collection.)

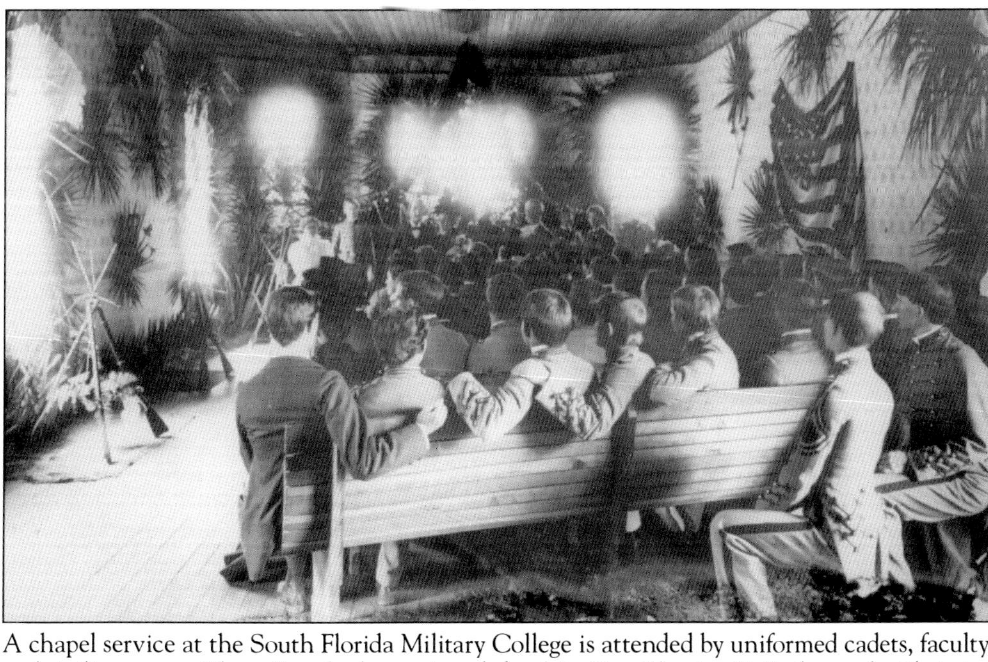

A chapel service at the South Florida Military College is attended by uniformed cadets, faculty, and civilian guests. The college had an assigned chaplain, Rev. Fleming G. Railey, and a Christian Cadet Corps. The room contains pews, stacked rifles, palmetto fronds, swords, and a flag. The window configuration and angled walls identify the chapel as being located in the south tower. (Courtesy State Archives of Florida, Frisbie Collection.)

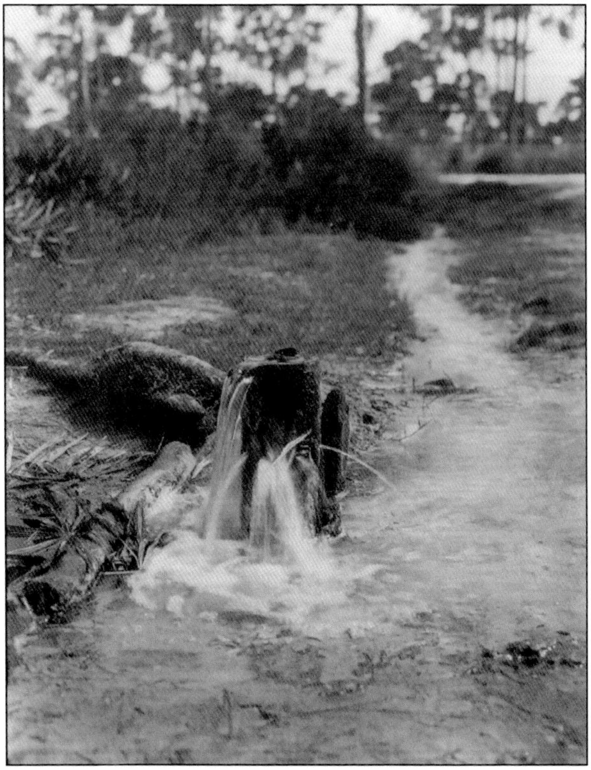

Artesian wells were common in the area. Following the 1903 hurricane, city water, drawn from a 200-foot-deep artesian well, and household sources were contaminated with *bacillus coli communis*. The downpour flooded three open cesspools on the outskirts of town, defiling the water. The ensuing 1904 epidemic resulted in 250 cases of fever and 11 deaths. A new well of unquestioned quality was installed in 1905. (Courtesy State Archives of Florida, Frisbie Collection.)

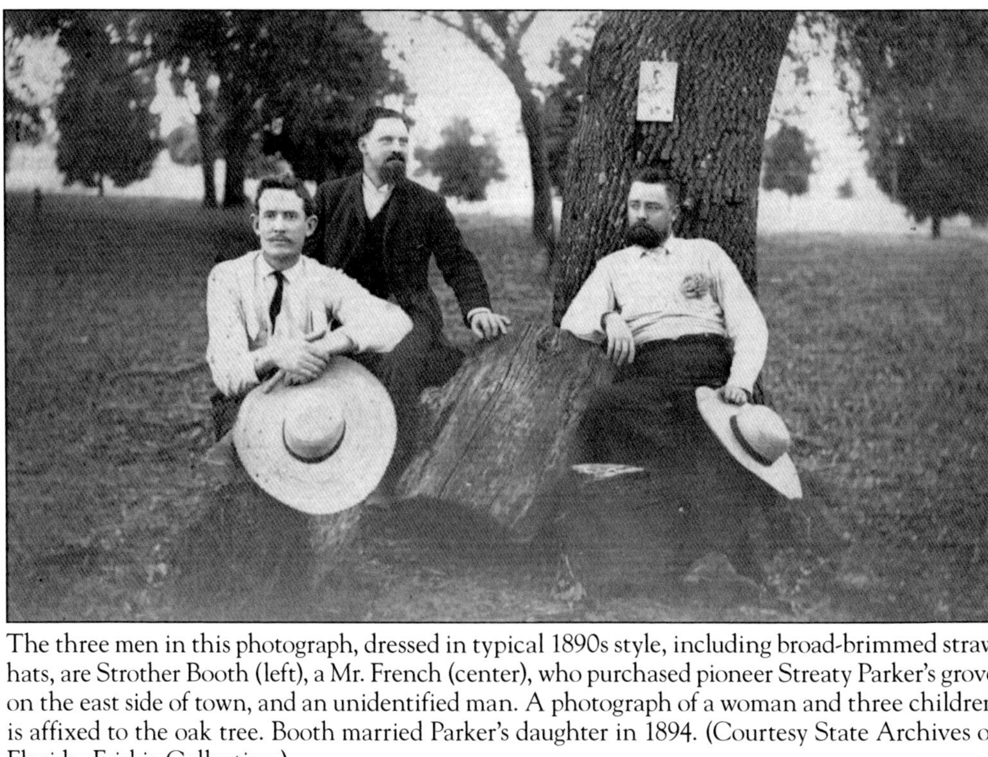

The three men in this photograph, dressed in typical 1890s style, including broad-brimmed straw hats, are Strother Booth (left), a Mr. French (center), who purchased pioneer Streaty Parker's grove on the east side of town, and an unidentified man. A photograph of a woman and three children is affixed to the oak tree. Booth married Parker's daughter in 1894. (Courtesy State Archives of Florida, Frisbie Collection.)

Daisy Dietrich Parker, shown here in her wedding dress, was the daughter of Streaty Parker and Mary Eve Blount. Her grandfather was Readding Blount, the founder of Bartow. She married bookkeeper and grove owner Strother Booth of Bartow on October 17, 1894. They resided in Alturas. (Courtesy State Archives of Florida, Frisbie Collection.)

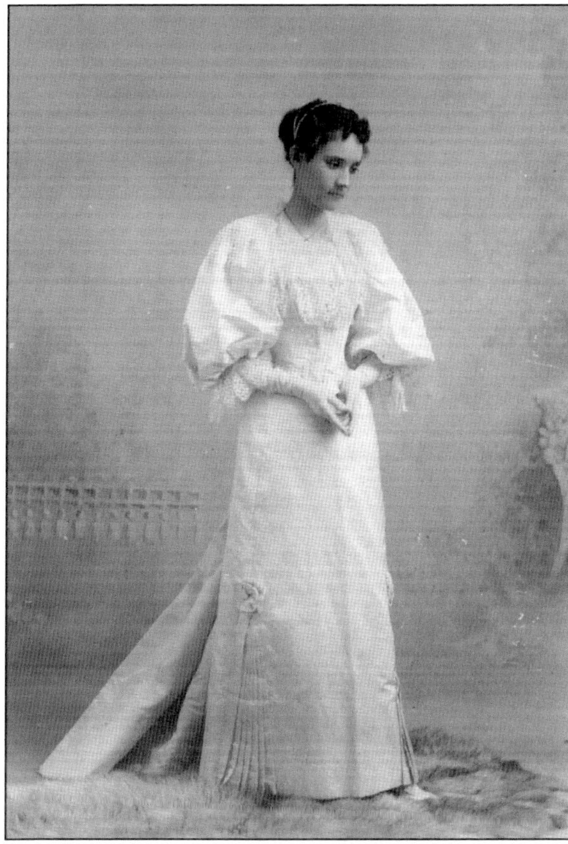

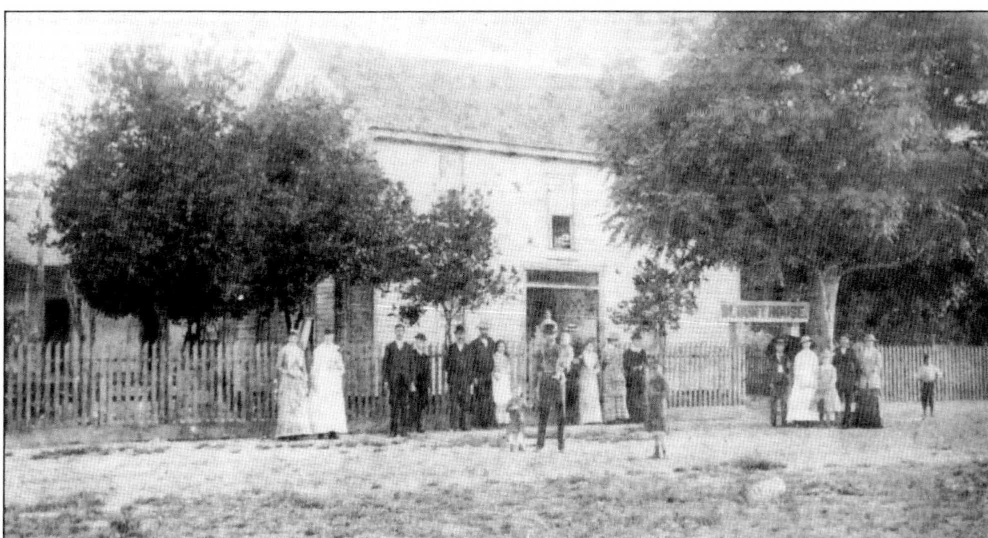

Guests pose in front of the Blount House, located on the southeast corner of Main Street and Carpenter Avenue. The hotel was built in the late 1860s as a residence and was acquired by the widow of Dr. A.V. Mann, who operated it as the Bartow House through the 1870s until 1882, when Riley Blount purchased it and renamed it for the first family of Bartow. (Courtesy State Archives of Florida.)

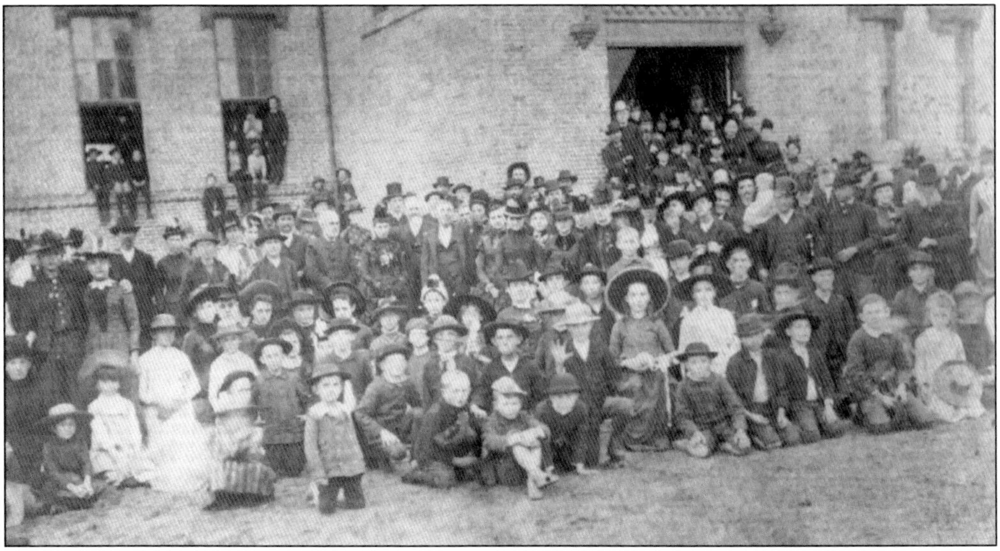

Jacob Summerlin returned to Bartow from Orlando to attend the grand opening and dedication of Summerlin Institute on January 2, 1889. He is just left of center, hatless, to the right of the bearded man. Summerlin died on November 4, 1893, and is buried in Bartow's Oak Hill Cemetery. He could claim many honors in his lifetime, yet chose a single epitaph: "Founder of Summerlin Institute." (Courtesy State Archives of Florida, Frisbie Collection.)

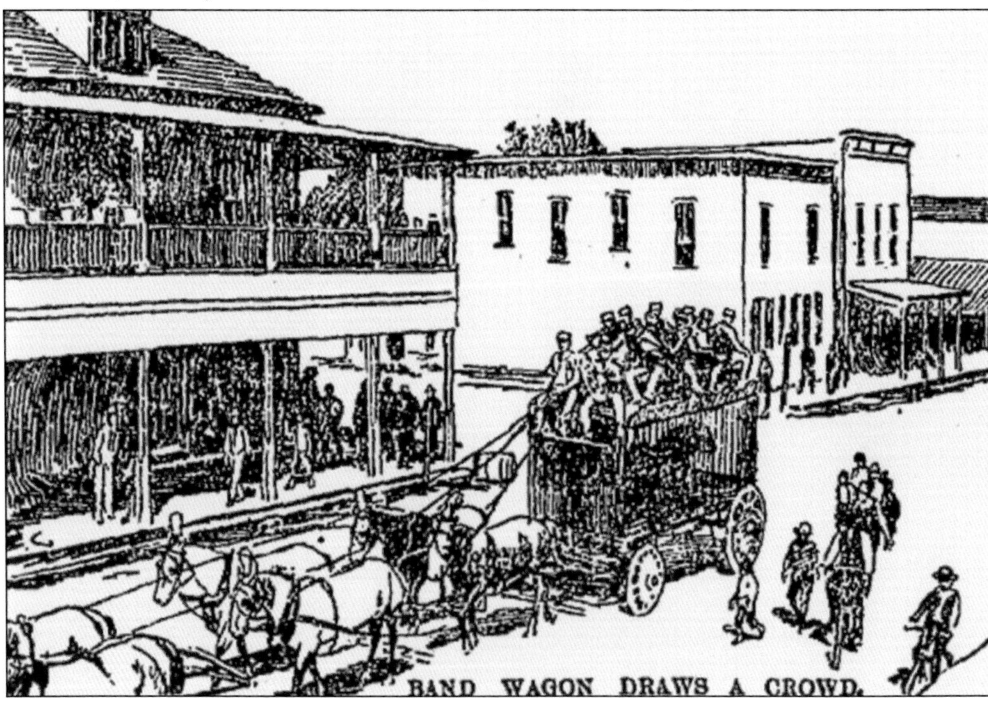

Before newspapers had the capability of printing photographs, they were redrawn and then published. This 1894 image of a circus parade in Bartow appears in a Chicago newspaper. The Harris Nickel Plate Show's six-horse menagerie and bandwagon, complete with "wild animal," plays to the crowd on Main Street just past Wilson Avenue. The building on the left is the Tremont House, situated on the northwest corner. (Courtesy W.L. Harris collection.)

Dressed to the nines are Oakley Lanier (left), Strother Booth (center), and Arthur Forsythe. Top hats, double-breasted coats, and high collars were typical of formal dress near the turn of the 20th century. It is likely that this photograph was taken in association with Strother's marriage in October 1894 to Daisy Parker. (Courtesy State Archives of Florida, Frisbie Collection.)

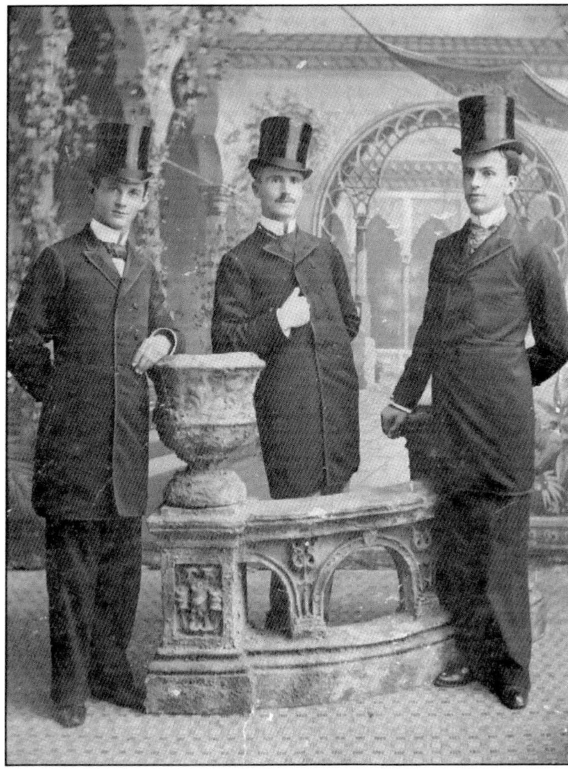

William B. Lyle's office was a hub for buying and shipping vegetables and fruit. The men in the photograph are C.F. Furnall (left), Harry Freeman (center), and Charles Walker. The small building was located at the northeast corner of Davidson Street and Broadway Avenue. In 1896, Lyle was supplying the Vanderbilts' Biltmore House near Asheville, North Carolina, with locally grown strawberries. (Courtesy State Archives of Florida, Frisbie Collection.)

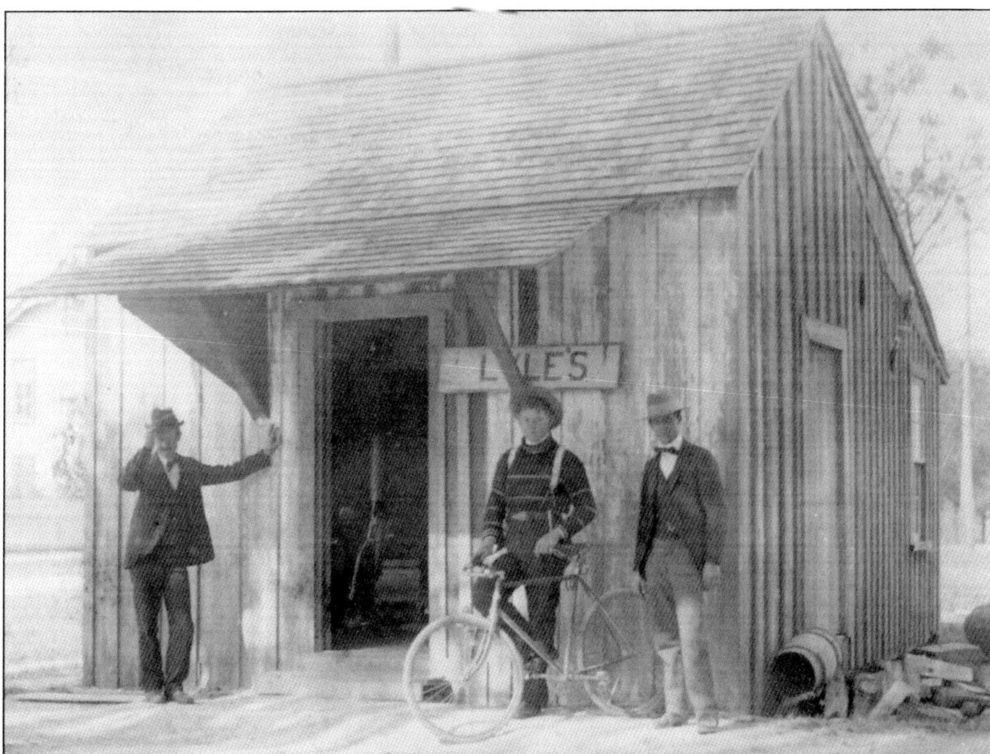

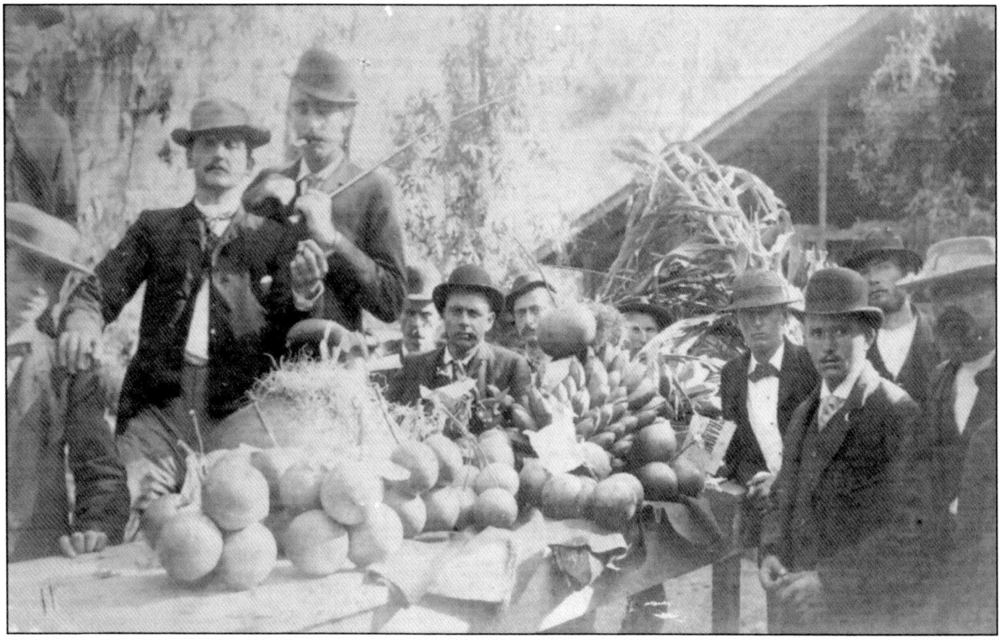

William B. Lyle, a prominent grower and shipper, is seen here wearing a derby and holding a buggy whip behind a display of fruit at the Polk County Fair. The fair opened in Lakeland on March 1, 1895, and allowed growers and merchants to display a wealth of crops and goods to the public. (Courtesy State Archives of Florida, Frisbie Collection.)

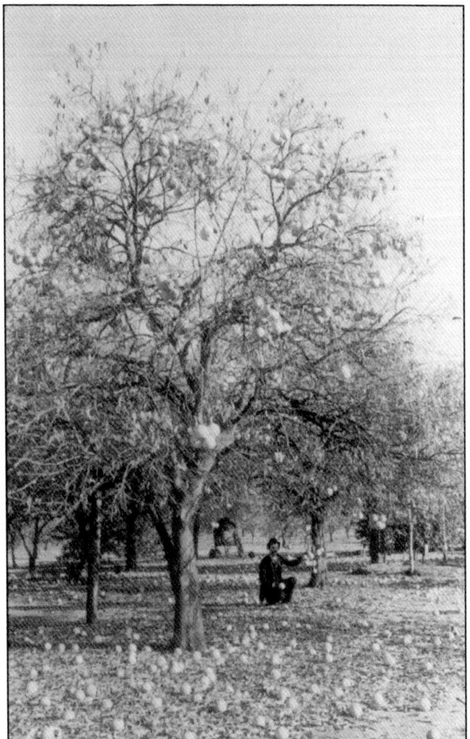

Grapefruit and leaves cover the ground in 1895 after plummeting temperatures took a toll on the citrus industry. The huge setback for citrus growers in the region prompted many Bartowans to move south to the new town of Miami. One notable, William M. Burdine, reemerged as a successful department store mogul destined for national fame. (Courtesy State Archives of Florida, Frisbie Collection.)

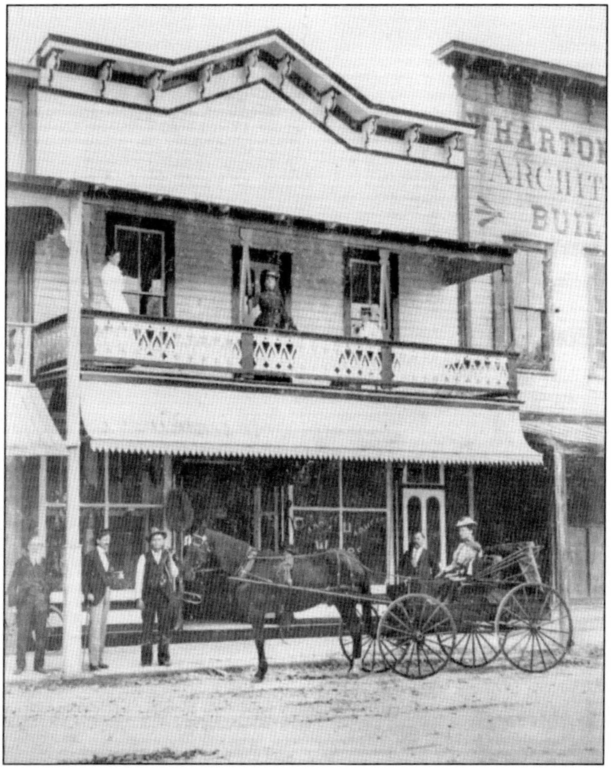

This harness shop is next to Edwin R. Wharton's office. The shop outfitted horses with leather goods and tack and supplied harnesses and gear for wagons. Wharton was an early architect, finding employment and ready work in the growing town of Bartow. He designed the Benjamin Holland house on East Stanford Street and other homes in the city. (Courtesy State Archives of Florida, Frisbie Collection.)

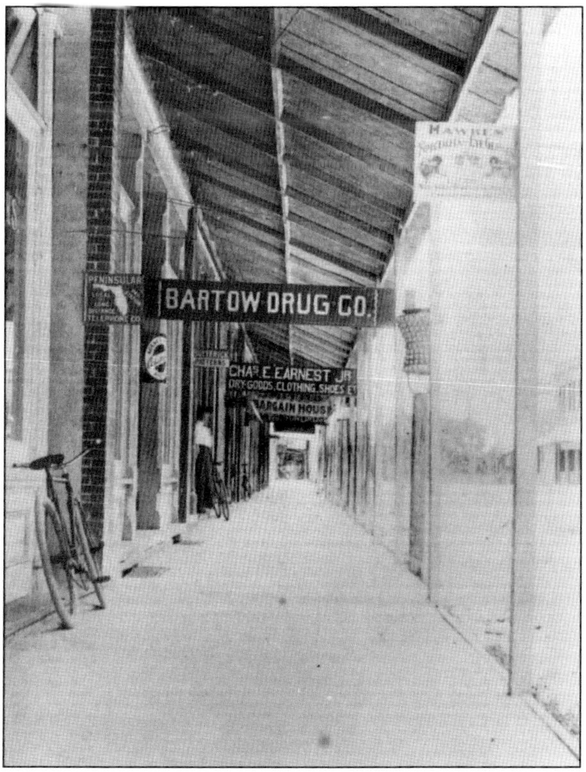

Bartow's first telephone was installed in 1899, and this pedestrian view of Main Street's 100 block, showing the Peninsular Telephone exchange, recalls the day when Mayor William Hampton Johnson phoned Mayor Francis L. Wing of Tampa. The call, on January 21, 1902, was Bartow's first long-distance phone call. Other establishments seen here are Earnest dry goods and clothing, Smith's Bargain House, Wilson Drugs, and Davis Cash dry goods. (Courtesy State Archives of Florida, Frisbie Collection.)

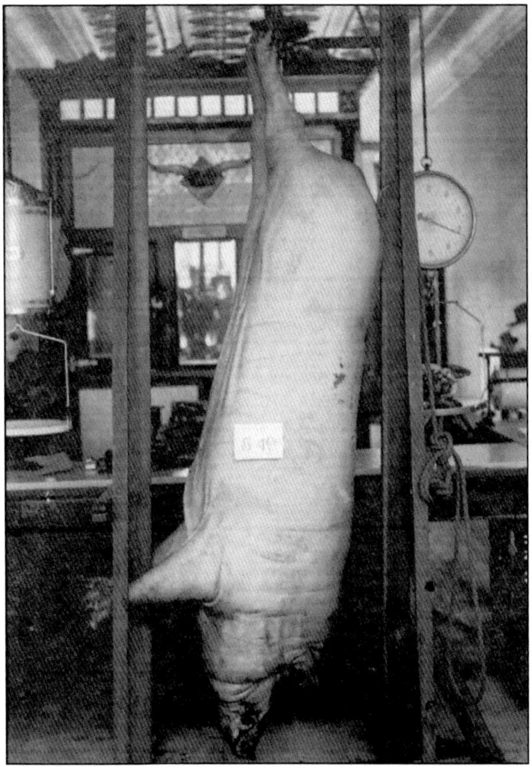

In the days before modern supermarkets, meat was purchased at the meat market or butcher shop. Silas Lee Caldwell's "Jimmy the hog" registered 549 pounds at the butcher shop. Note the roll of packing paper on the counter at right and the suspended scales for weighing meats in full view of the customer. (Courtesy Barbara and Wallace Orr, Lynda Belle and David Black family.)

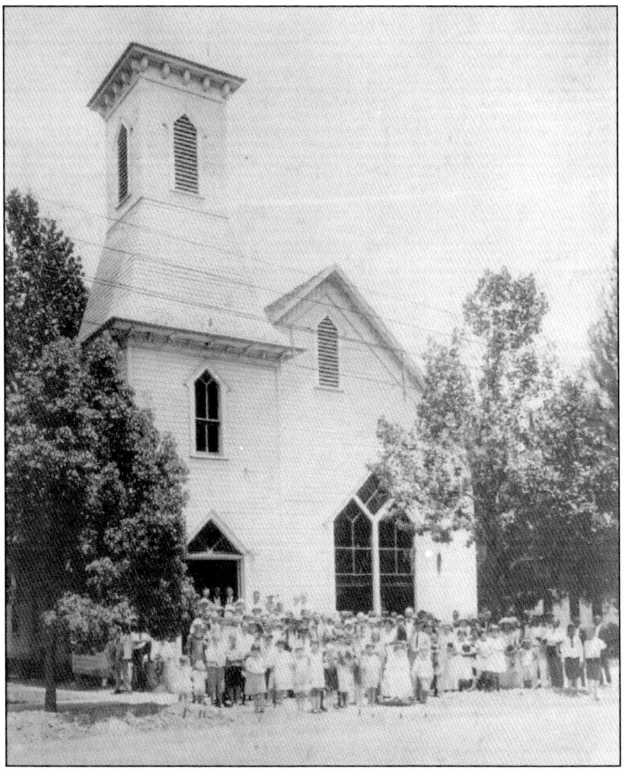

The First Baptist Church, built in 1899 and dedicated on July 11, 1900, is pictured with the Sunday school and congregation about 1924. The church traces its origins to 1873 and the ministry of Rev. Jeremiah Hayman, who is credited with inaugurating many congregations in the state. The church was formerly called Concord Church and Bartow Baptist, and took its present name in 1889. (Courtesy State Archives of Florida, Frisbie Collection.)

Four

City of Oaks
1900–1919

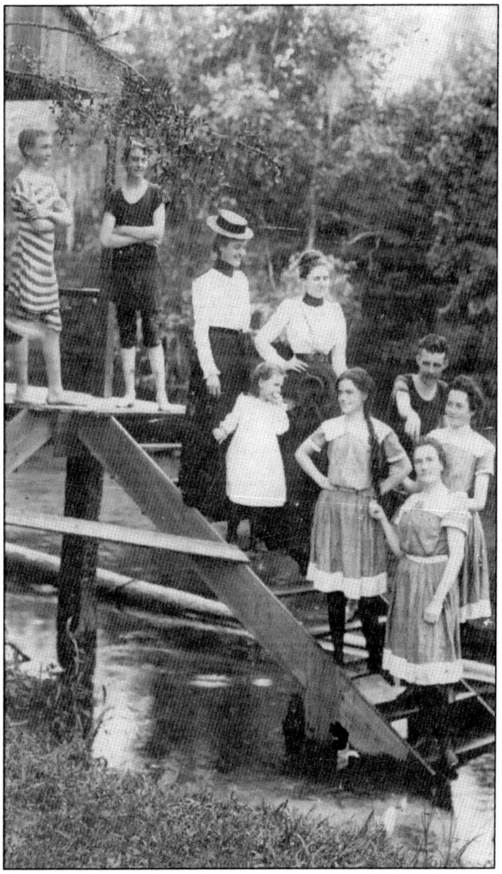

This is a photograph of a Kissengen Springs outing for the Caldwell family of Bartow. The family members are appropriately dressed for swimming in the latest styles, presenting a catalog of appearances. The boys wear two-piece, round-neck, short-sleeved striped tops and knee-length trunks. The girls' wool swimwear sports sailor collars, waistbands, and long black stockings for modesty. (Courtesy Barbara and Wallace Orr, Lynda Belle and David Black family.)

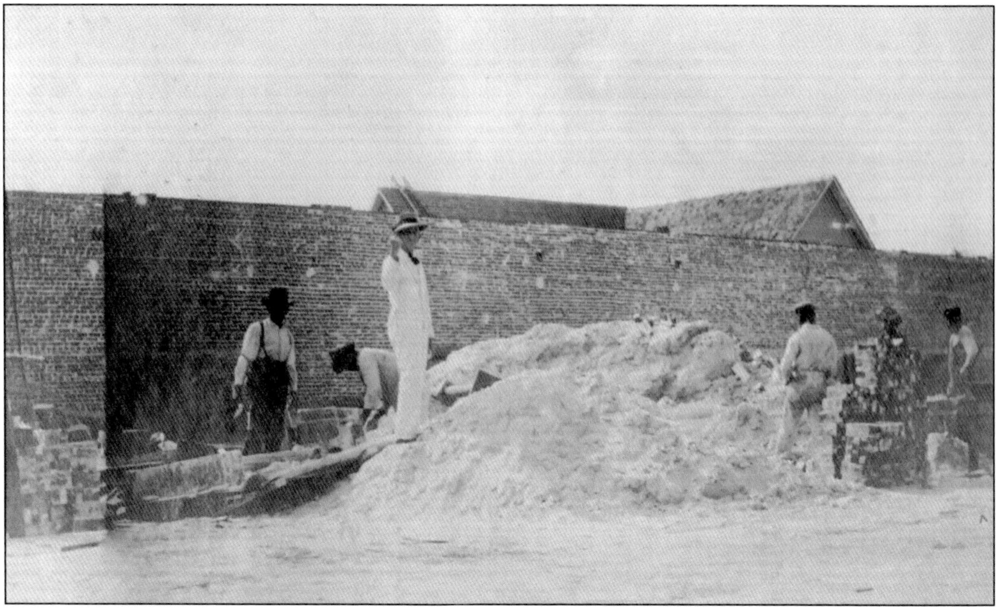

This 1890s photograph shows C.H. Irwin's brickyard in full production. Irwin leased the city's clay pit to produce smooth, red, lemon, and black bricks. His initial run ranged in the thousands, to the satisfaction of local builders. Pebble flaws were soon eradicated, producing superior blocks, and clay used for streets was now employed in building walls. Irwin's bricks can still be seen in many present-day buildings. (Courtesy Bo Raulerson.)

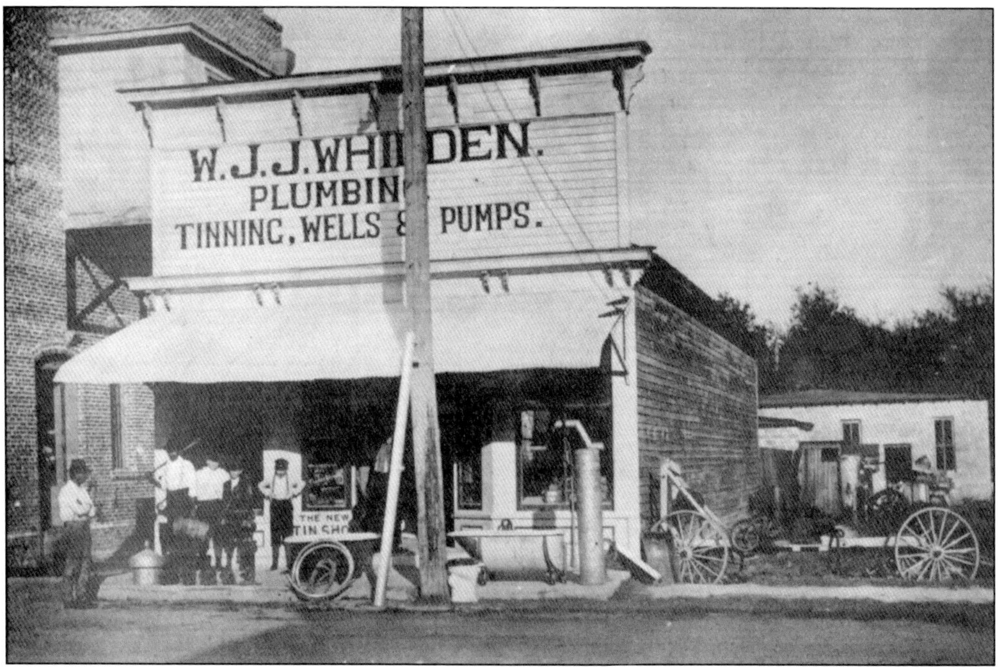

This photograph, taken in the early 1900s, shows W.J.J. Whidden's plumbing store, located on Central Avenue facing west. Whidden advertised itself as the "new" tin shop and provided well-digging services, tinning, and hardware sales. Bathtubs line the sidewalk. At right is the back of the Courier Informant Building. (Courtesy State Archives of Florida, Frisbie Collection.)

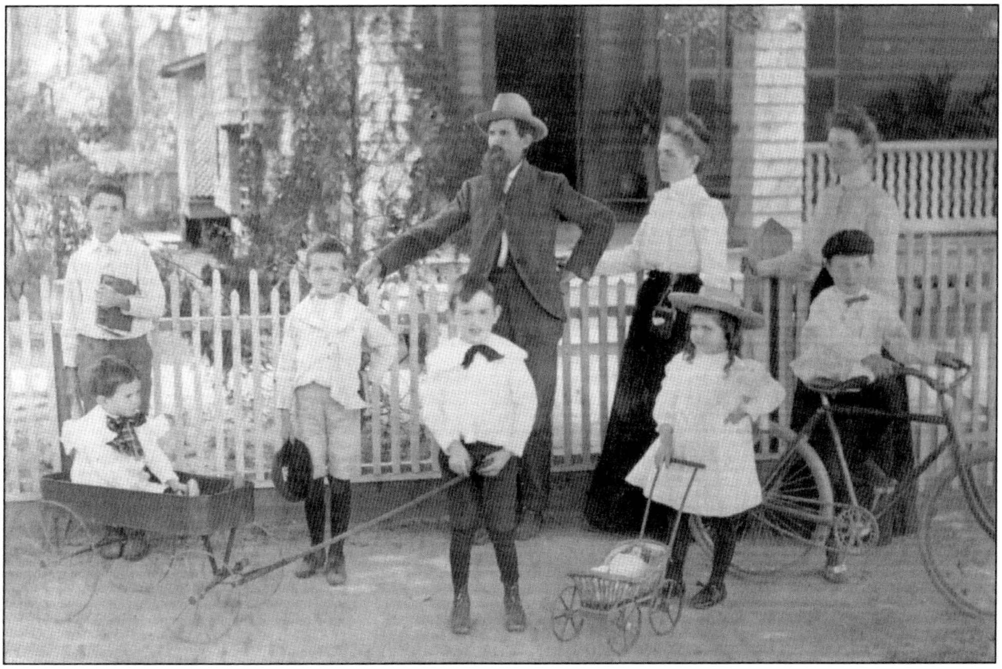

The Holland family poses at their home on Stanford Street in 1902. Spessard Holland, standing at left holding a book, became a World War I hero, county judge, governor, and US senator from Florida. Benjamin F. Holland stands by the fence. Next to him are his wife, Fannie Virginia, and her sister Nora Spessard McNeer (far right). The other children are, from left to right, Francis McNeer, Frank Holland, James McNeer, Virginia Holland, and Selden McNeer. (Courtesy State Archives of Florida.)

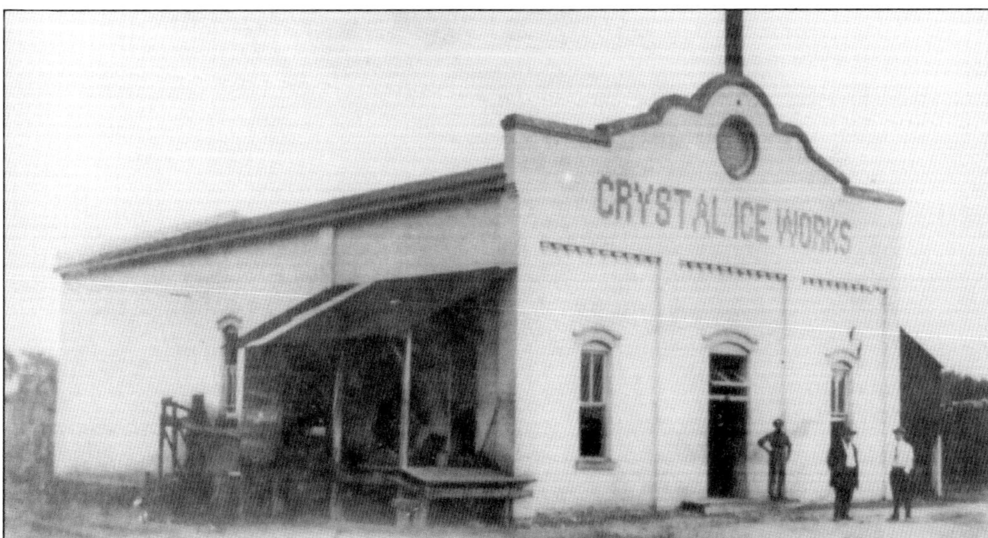

The white brick building trimmed in blue was Crystal Ice Works, reputed to be the third absorption process ice plant in America. Since 1886, the plant was located on West Pearl Street and serviced the city and surrounding communities. In 1894, the plant offered public baths for 15¢ and a tank for swimming. The plant was expanded and continued ice delivery through 1978. It is shown here in 1906. (Courtesy State Archives of Florida, Frisbie Collection.)

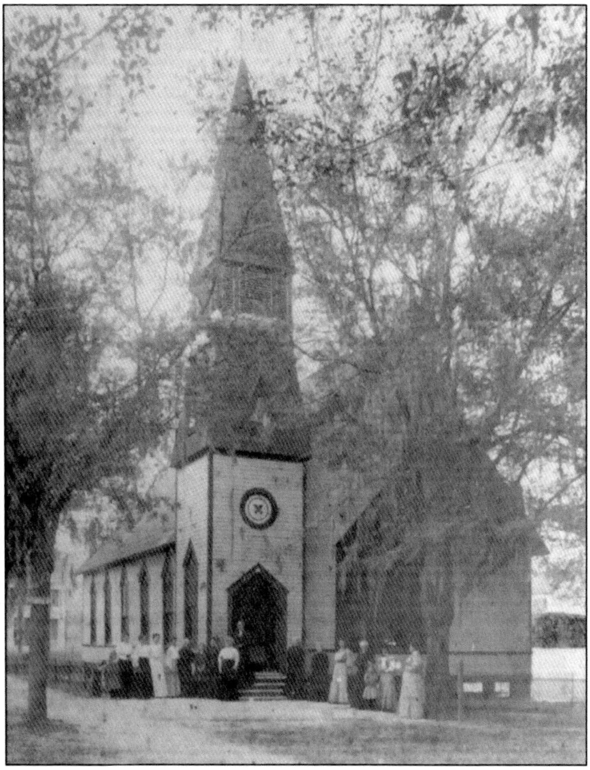

The First Presbyterian Church Women's Auxiliary assembles in front of the church on Florida Avenue in 1906. Sixth from the right is Charlotte Ann Torrey, widow of the former ambassador to the King of Siam. The steeple was removed in 1932 and the sanctuary oriented north to south. The original structure survives as the interior of the present church fellowship hall. (Courtesy First Presbyterian Church of Bartow.)

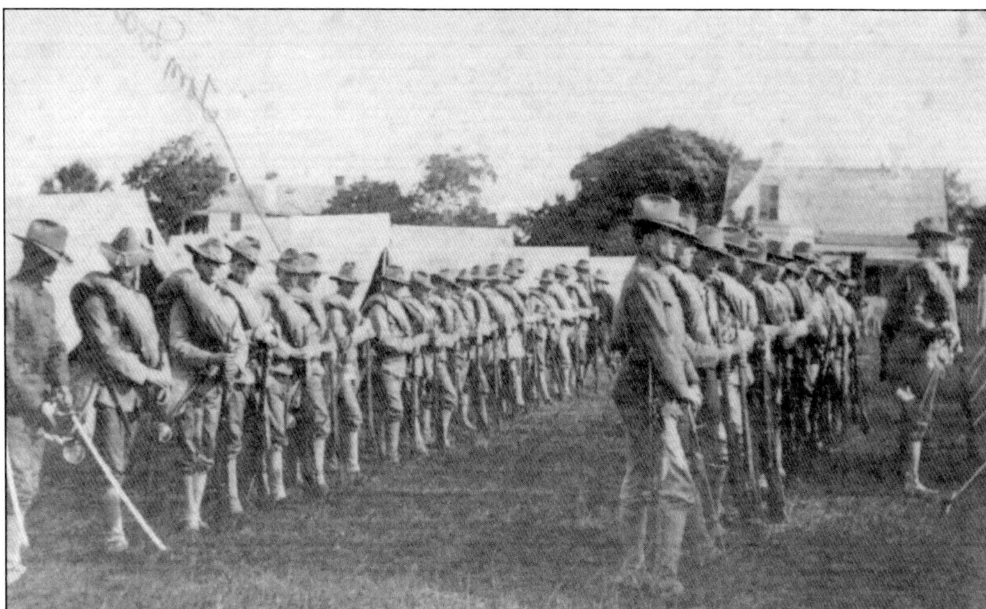

The "Oak City Guards," officially Company G, 2nd Regiment, Florida State Troops, was constituted in 1899 and served through 1905. It drilled at the armory on the northeast corner of Summerlin Street and Broadway Avenue. An element of the unit was honored to march behind the hearse in the Buffalo, New York, funeral cortege of Pres. William McKinley after his 1901 assassination. (Courtesy W.L. Harris collection.)

The 1904 South Florida Military College football team gathers on the back steps of the school. The campus consisted of 13 acres south of present-day Stuart Street and east of South Broadway Avenue. This group of young men holds the distinction of having played the first football game in the county, on Thanksgiving Day 1903. Company A squared off against Company B on the parade field. (Courtesy State Archives of Florida, Frisbie Collection.)

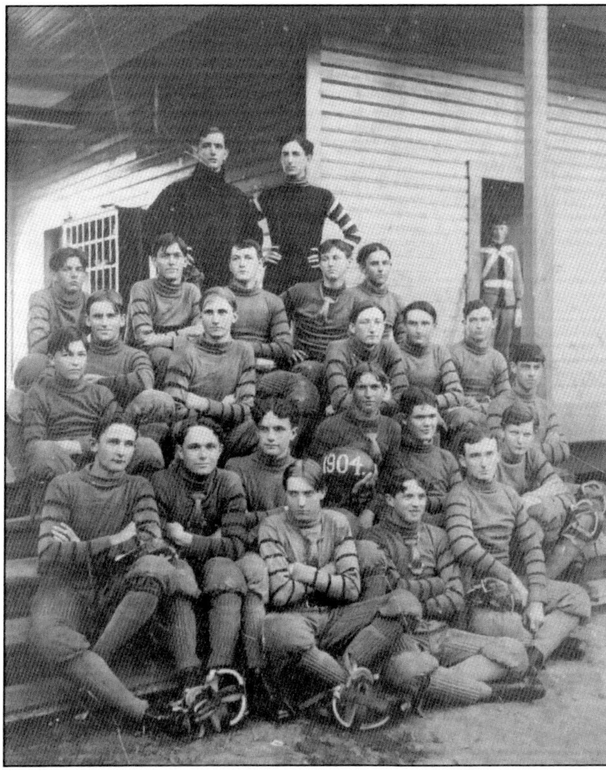

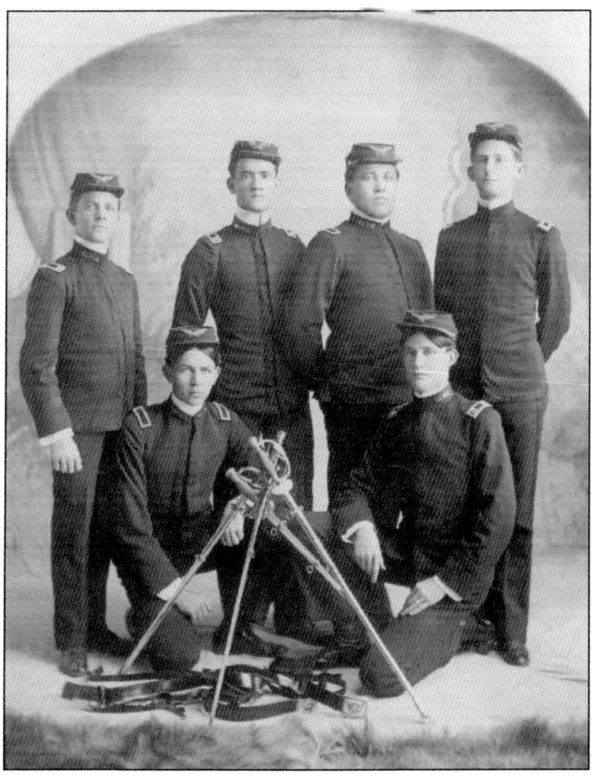

The South Florida Military College class of 1904 cadet staff poses behind stacked swords. One year later, the school merged with other Florida colleges, establishing the University of Florida in Gainesville. The military college was founded by Maj. Gen. Evander M. Law in 1895 and was in existence for a decade. A monument marks the grounds on the west end of Tharp Street. (Courtesy State Archives of Florida.)

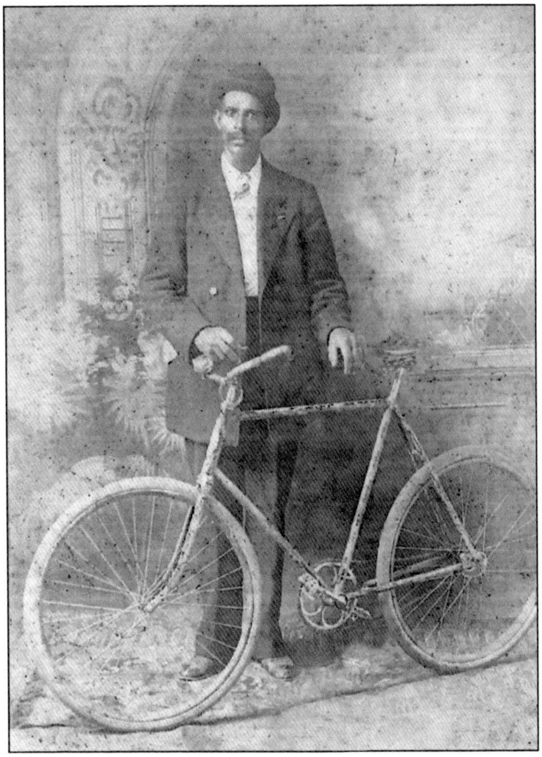

Thomas Waldon of Brittsville stands next to his bicycle in this 1890s photograph. Waldon was a fruit packer and successful farmer residing in the African American community originally called Over the Branch, which merged into West Bartow. Thomas's second wife, Artie, was the daughter of Prince Johnson, a former slave, whose vote was a factor in the incorporation of Bartow on July 1, 1882. (Courtesy Historic L.B. Brown House.)

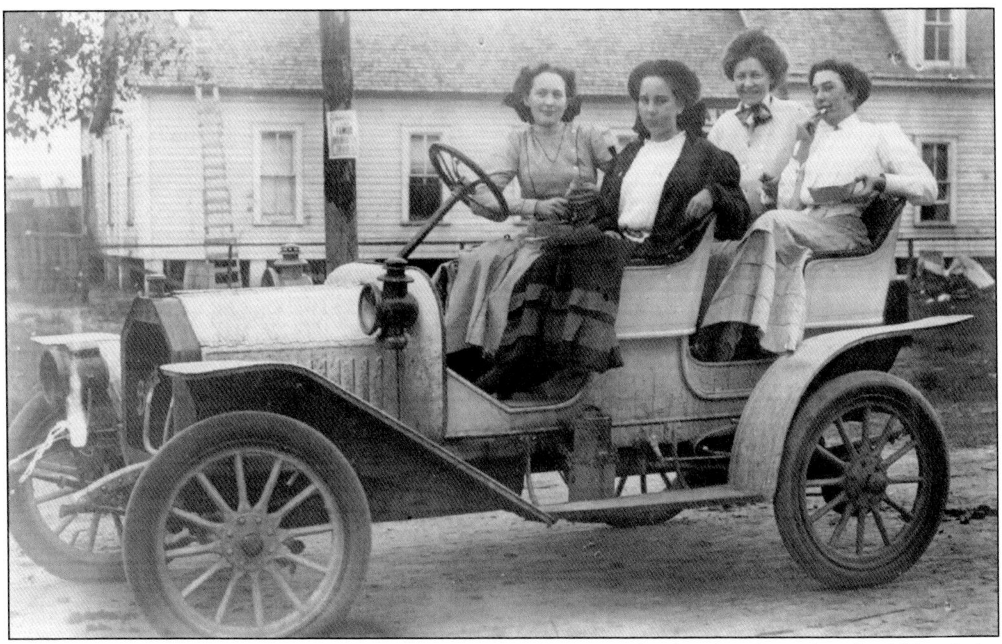

Taking a ride in J.B. Samples's 1905 Buick are, from left to right, his daughter Sarah, Abbie Lyle, Marie Willard, and Bernice Lyle. Among the automobile firsts in Bartow are the following: first car owner, W.P. Newkirk in 1903; first collision, Dr. Edwin Law, who hit a tree; first gasoline station, Standard Oil on Second Avenue; and first dealership, Erle L. Wirt REO sales. A 1905 round-trip to Winter Haven took 54 minutes. (Courtesy State Archives of Florida, Frisbie Collection.)

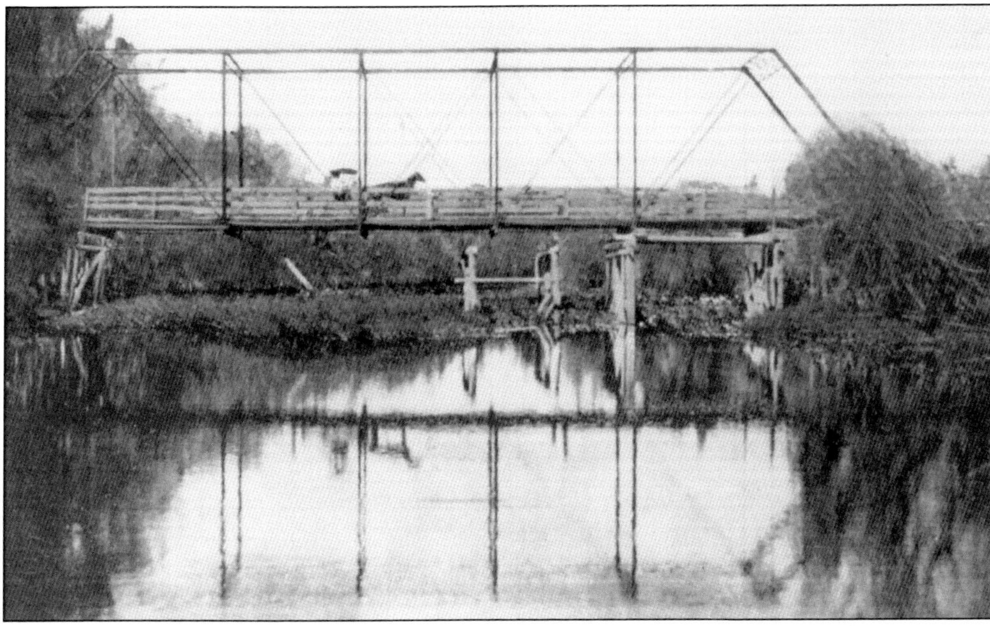

This photograph of the iron bridge over the Peace River was taken after its completion in 1901. It was a vast improvement over the single-lane wooden bridge, allowing traffic to travel east to Eagle Lake and Winter Haven. In earlier days, a skiff was used to ferry wagons across the river. The remnants of the wooden bridge can be seen in the background. (Courtesy State Archives of Florida, Frisbie Collection.)

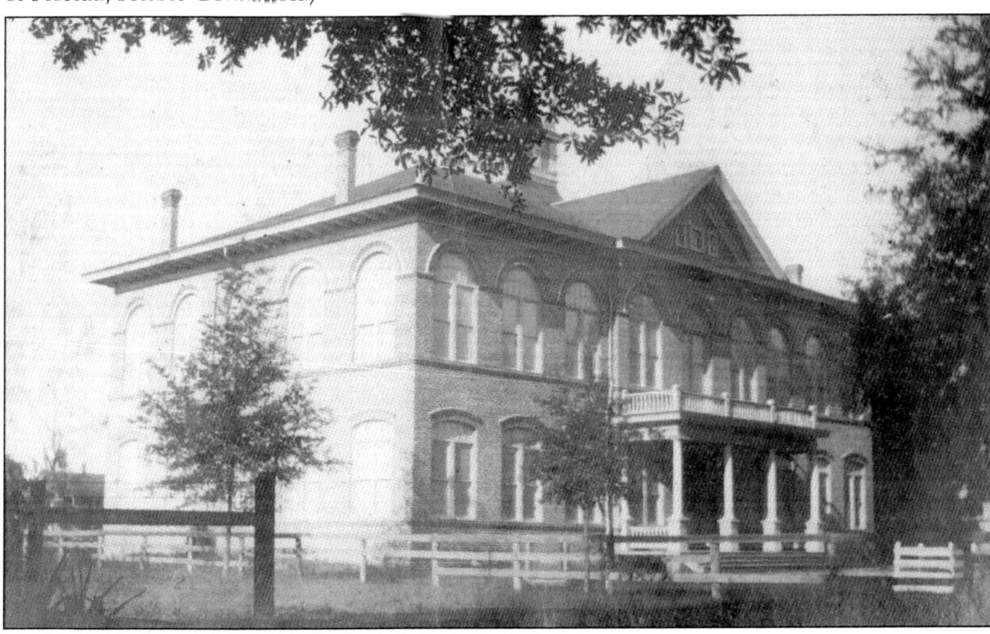

As the city's population grew, the need for more classrooms was met with the construction of a new high school building, housing grades 7 through 12. The building, seen here in 1905, was located east of the original 1887 Summerlin Institute on Stanford Street, which became the grammar school. The new high school's second-floor auditorium was used by the community and school. (Courtesy State Archives of Florida, Frisbie Collection.)

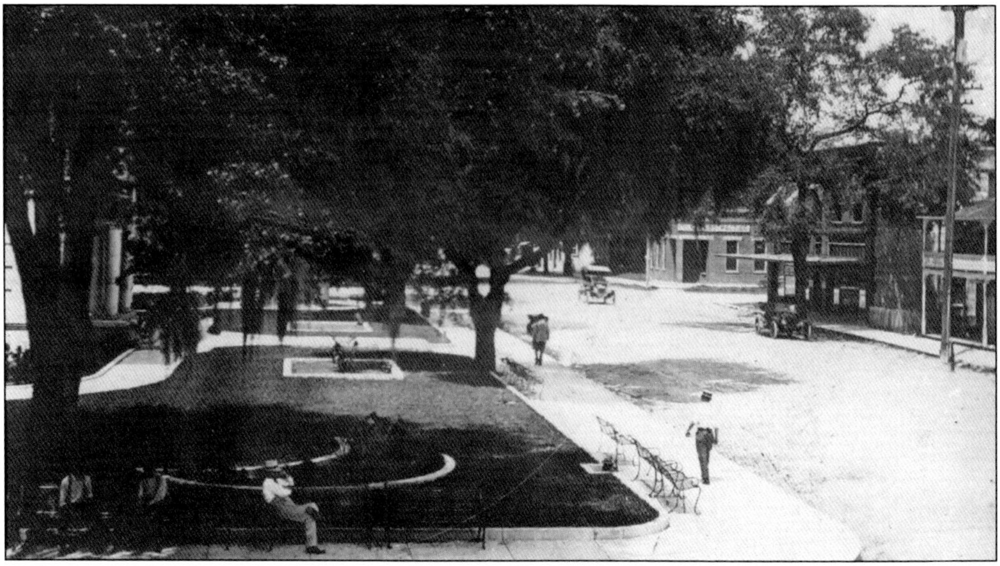

Early cars and moss-laden oaks are evident in this photograph of the courthouse square facing Central Avenue in the early 1920s. The Polk County Abstract Company can be seen to the right of the Ford Model T in the street. The 1926 courtroom additions have not been built onto the courthouse, which still presents a landscaped square adorned with the iron benches that lasted into the 1960s. (Courtesy State Archives of Florida, Frisbie Collection.)

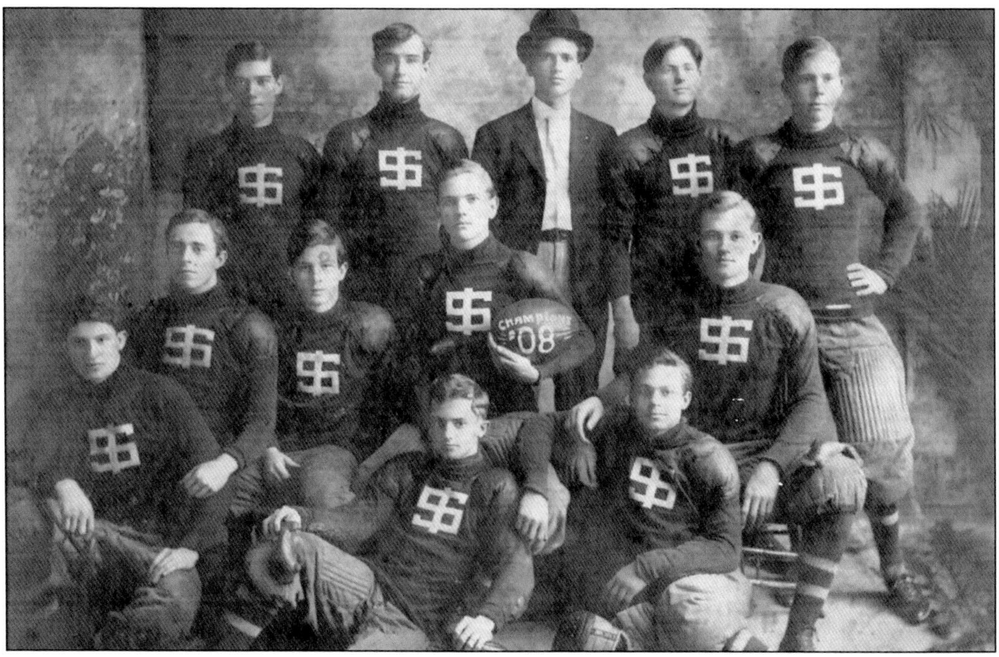

The Summerlin Institute 1908 football players were the undisputed Florida champions, having played several other schools and one college team to secure the right to the title. Shown here are, from left to right, (first row) Noel Stanley, Lee Overbay, and T.L. Marquis; (second row) Emerson Harless, Rader Merritt, Borden Wilson, and Cecil Wilson; (third row) James Van Fleet, Joe Woodard, coach Glen Skipper, Louis Snedigar, and Frank Wilson. (Courtesy State Archives of Florida, Frisbie Collection.)

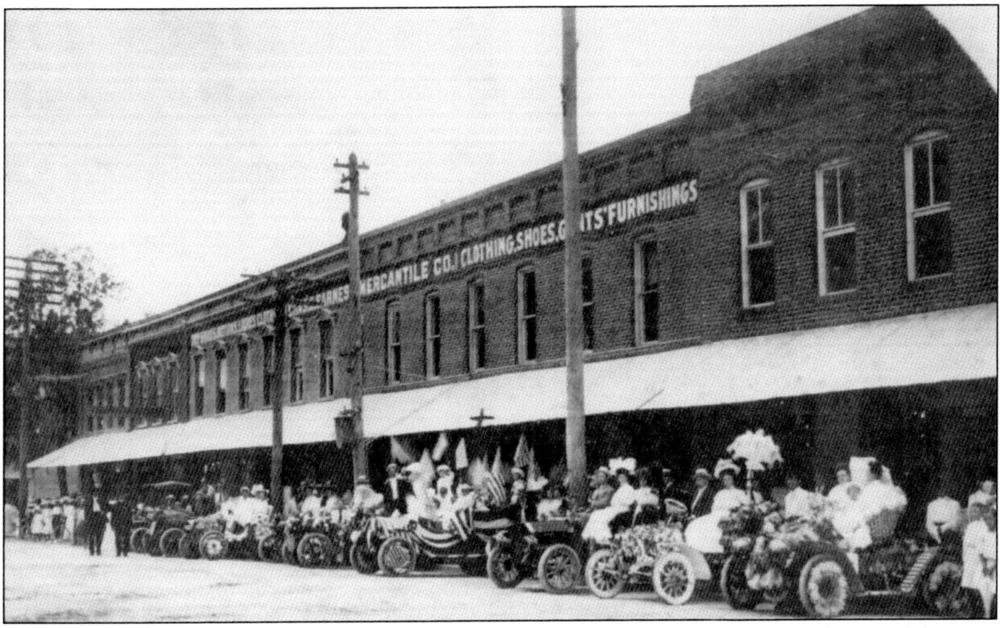

In the 100 block of Main Street, automobiles line up for the dedication parade in celebration of the new county courthouse in 1909. The vehicles display a wide range of decorative themes. Two years earlier, there were 14 registered automobiles in the city. The vehicles were joined by horses and bicycles to commemorate the new hall of justice. (Courtesy State Archives of Florida, Frisbie Collection.)

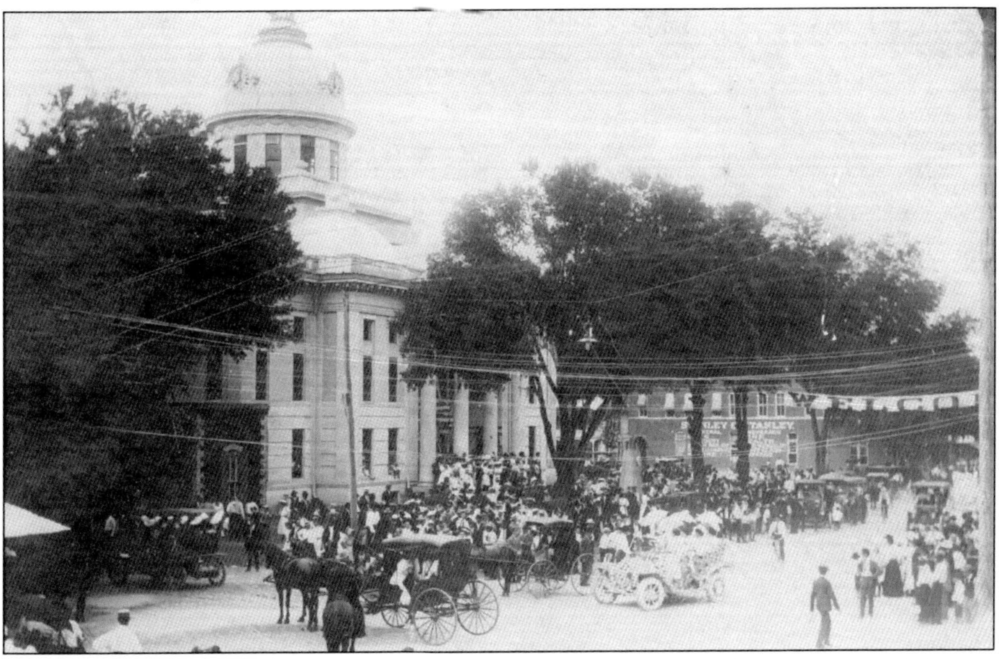

June 25, 1909, was a gala day in Bartow, as seen in this photograph of the celebration of the new courthouse. The event drew over 6,000 citizens, who heard speeches and witnessed a parade of horses, buggies, and decorated automobiles. The celebration concluded with barbecue meals served to the public at the city's grounds two blocks north. (Courtesy State Archives of Florida.)

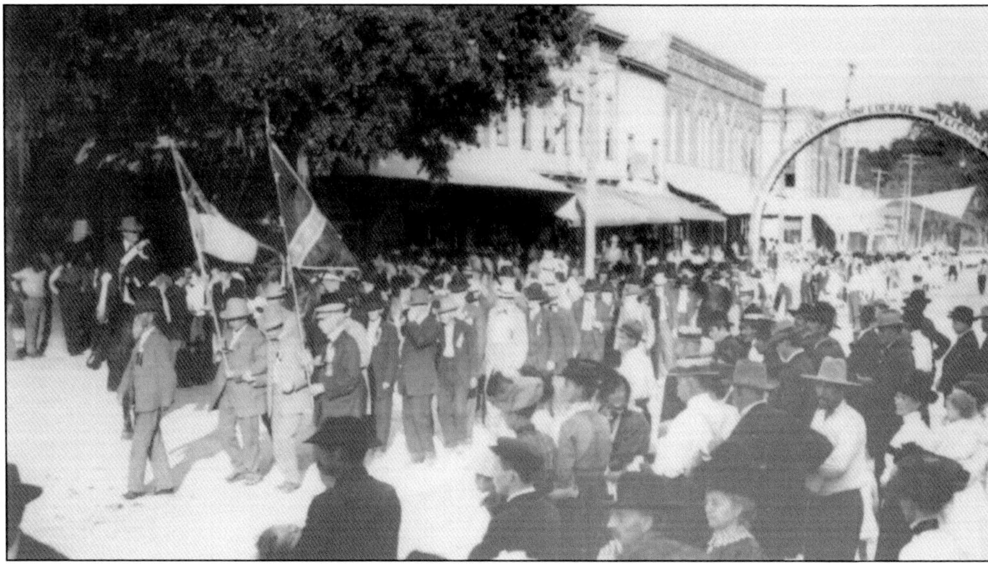

The October 1910 reunion of the United Confederate Veterans allowed old soldiers to once again march to the strains of music and cheering crowds on Bartow's Main Street. Gen. Evander M. Law leads the parade. A veteran plays a harmonica behind the color guard carrying the Confederate national and army battle flags. The event goes unnoticed by the sleeping toddler in the left foreground. (Courtesy State Archives of Florida, Frisbie Collection.)

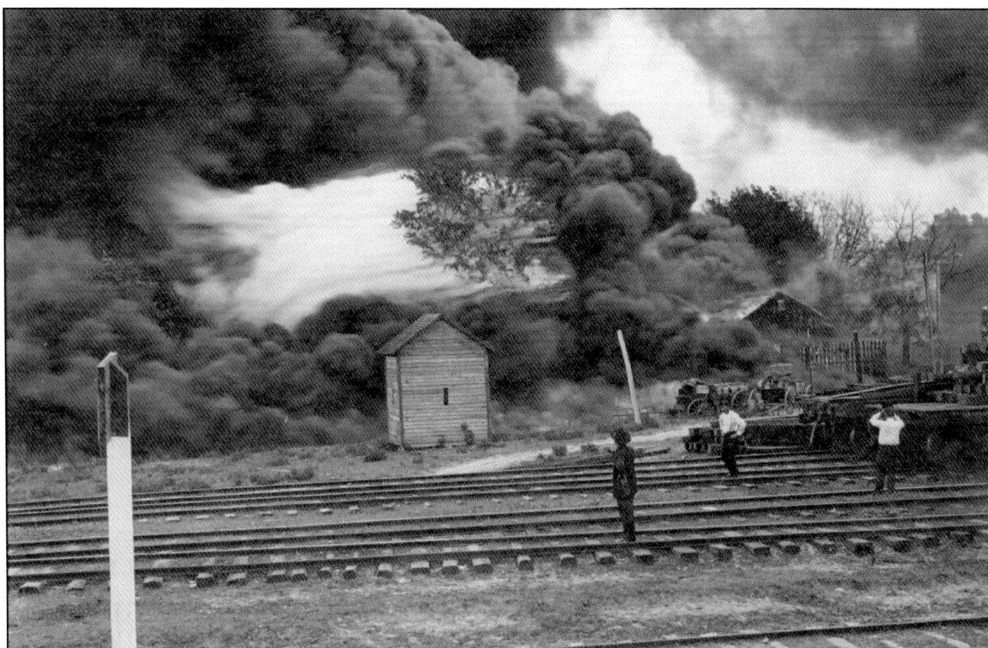

The great fire of 1910 engulfed an entire block on Second Avenue (present-day L.B. Brown Avenue), destroying 15 homes and businesses. A restaurant fire spread to Standard Oil's facility, exploding tanks containing thousands of gallons of fuel. Flames like giant curtains rose 200 feet and burned for two days without abate. It was a miracle that only property, and no life, was lost. (Courtesy State Archives of Florida, Frisbie Collection.)

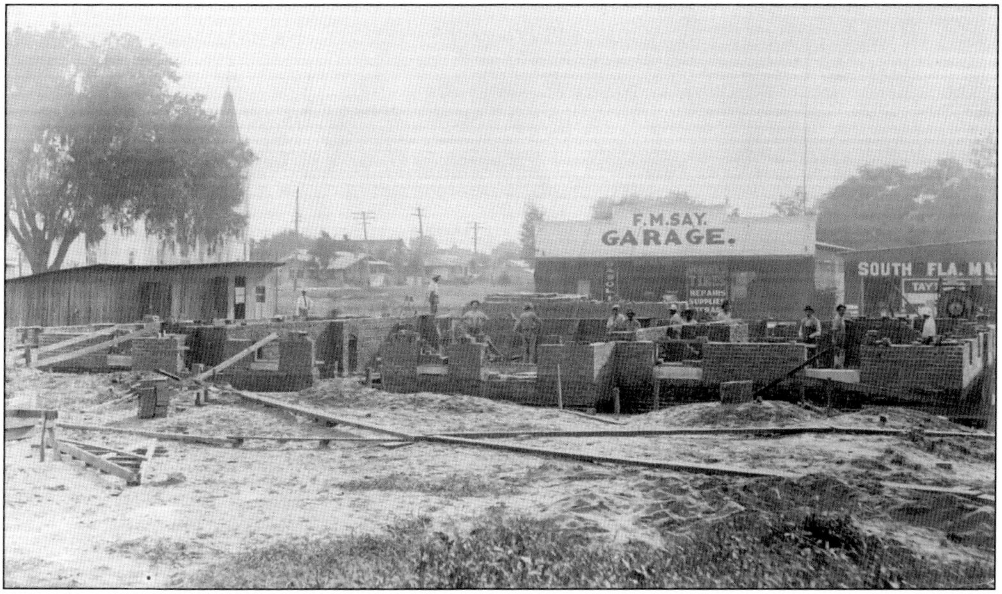

Construction of the new post office, at the southeast corner of Central Avenue and Summerlin Street, commenced in 1917 and covered over half a block. The steeple of the First Methodist Church, Say's Garage, and the South Florida marble works can be seen in the background. In 1972, the adjacent city hall was razed and a new addition to the post office building and a parking area filled the block. (Courtesy State Archives of Florida, Frisbie Collection.)

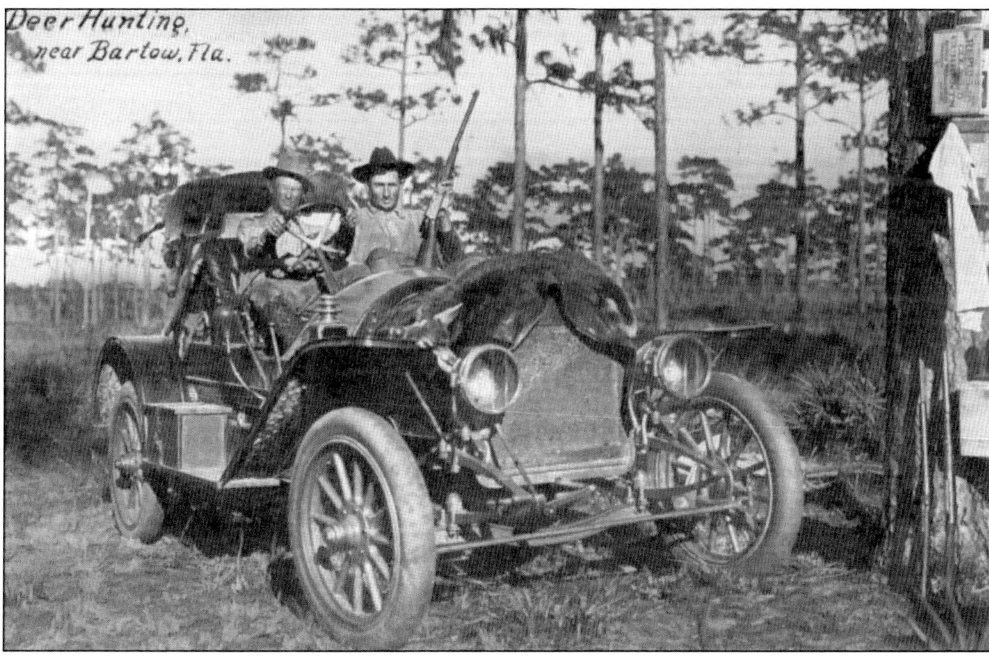

Automobiles provided outdoorsmen with a new means of travel through nearby woods. These hunters have bagged two deer, evidenced by one stretched across the front of the car and one draped across the back. The unimproved lands around the city were rich in wild game; a few years earlier, one mighty nimrod named Pap Hankins tallied 117 bears. (Courtesy State Archives of Florida, Frisbie Collection.)

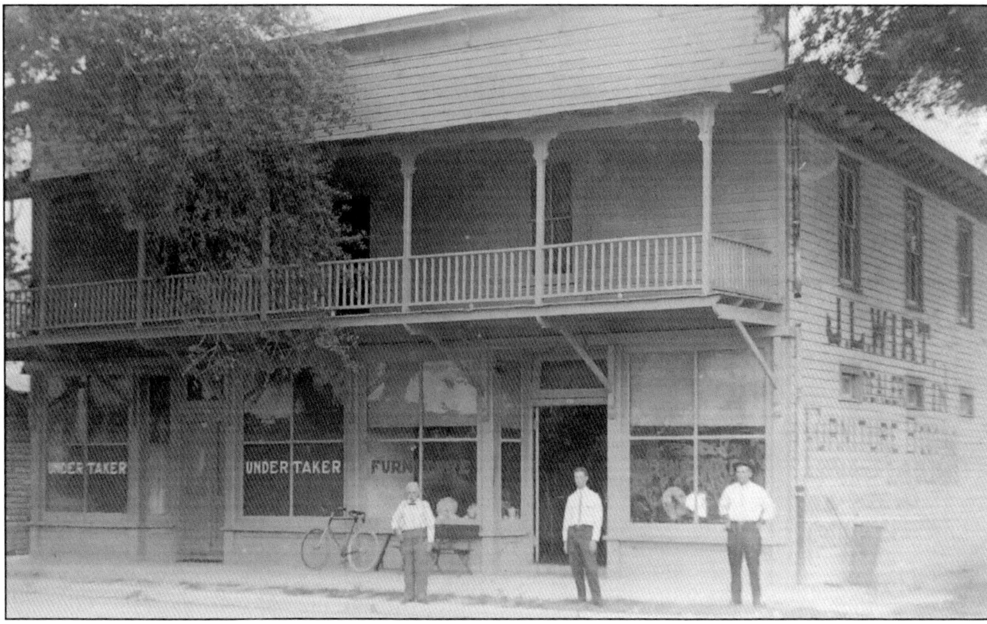

Funeral arrangements and embalming were provided by J.L. Wirt and Theron E. Wirt, undertakers, who pose for this c. 1910 photograph on Wilson Avenue. Funerals were a sideline of cabinet shops and furniture stores until Henry P. Whidden Sr., former Wirt employee and graduate of embalming college, founded Whidden Funeral Home in 1925 on Oak Avenue. In 1937, he moved to East Main Street and Clark Avenue. (Courtesy State Archives of Florida, Frisbie Collection.)

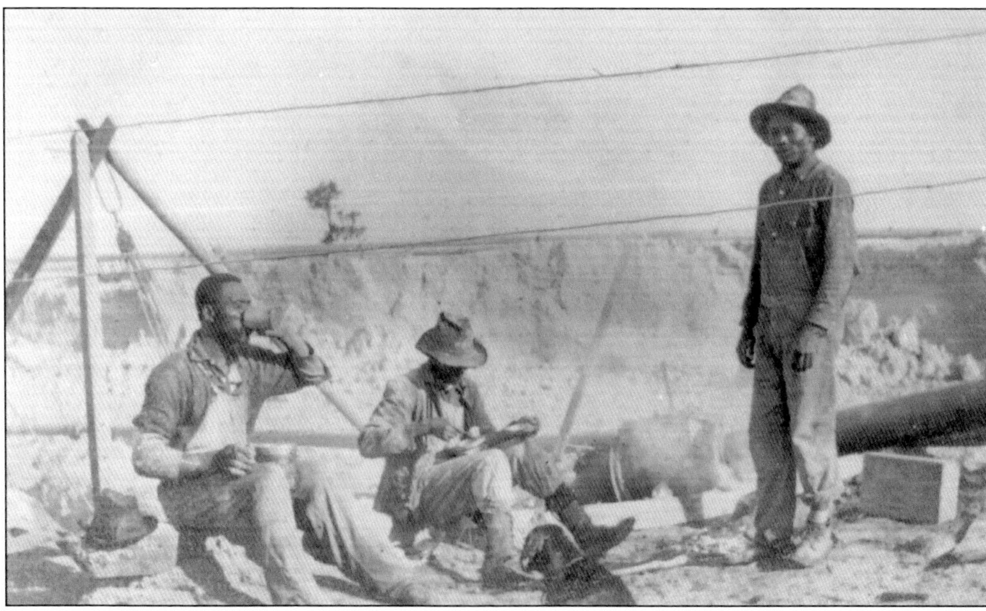

This phosphate pit crew takes a break in the 1910s. Laborers worked shifts averaging 10 to 12 hours and were paid up to $2.60 per day in the local mines. Overburden (earth) was removed by draglines to reach phosphate deposits, where the phosphate, sand, and clay were blasted with water. The mixture was pumped to a plant for further processing. (Courtesy State Archives of Florida, Frisbie Collection.)

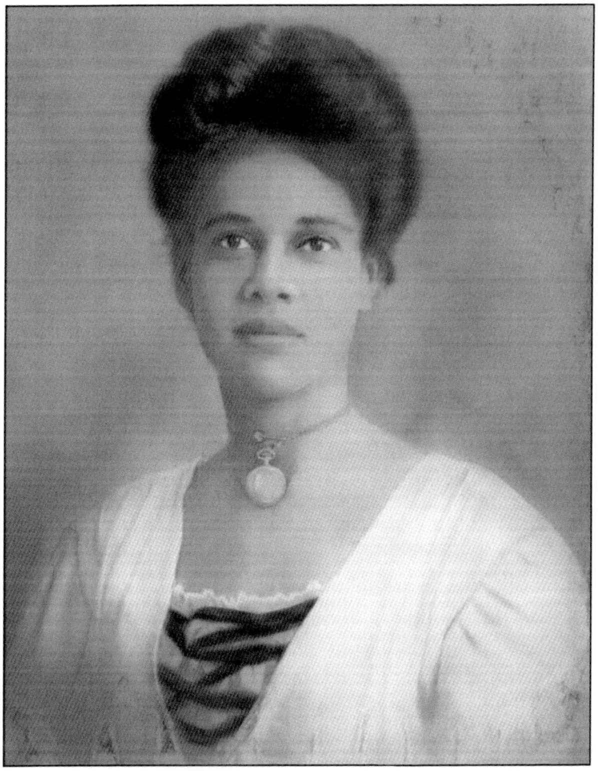

Rosa Ganns McNeill was a graduate of Spelman College in Atlanta, Georgia, and the wife of Bartow's first black physician, Dr. Ledge W. McNeill. She was employed at Union Academy High School. A teacher of extraordinary talent, she tutored Lela Burkett, who became, on June 4, 1928, the first African American high school graduate in Polk County. (Courtesy Historic L.B. Brown House.)

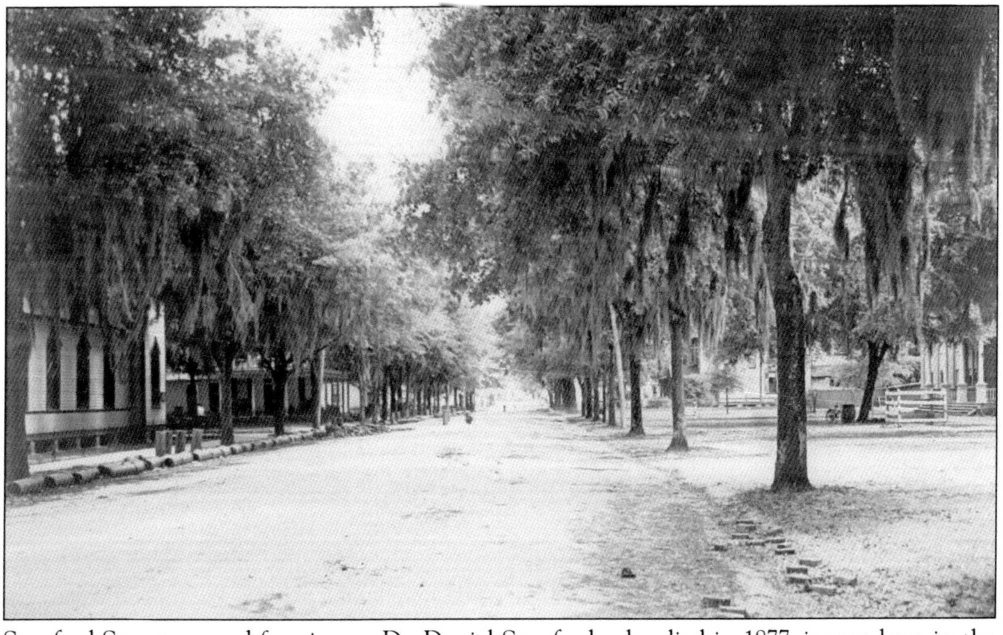

Stanford Street, named for pioneer Dr. Daniel Stanford, who died in 1877, is seen here in the early 1900s. The left side of the street, alongside First Presbyterian Church, is lined with sewer pipes. The oaks lining the clay street were the product of an 1894 city beautification project that resulted in the planting of 1,000 water oaks. In just a few years, Bartow would be known as the "City of Oaks." (Courtesy W.L. Harris collection.)

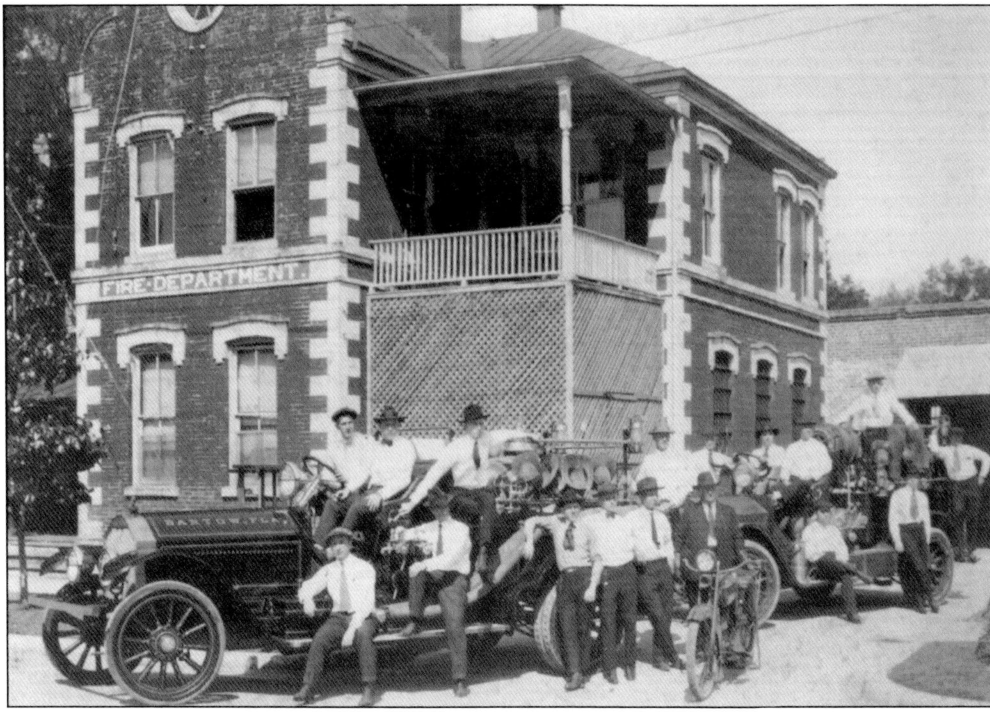

The volunteer fire department poses with engines No. 1 and No. 2, a motorcycle, and equipment in front of its new fire station in 1914. The station was previously the county jail, built in 1887 and located on the northeast corner of Broadway Avenue and Church Street. The iron bars of the old jail still guard the windows on the right. (Courtesy State Archives of Florida, Frisbie Collection.)

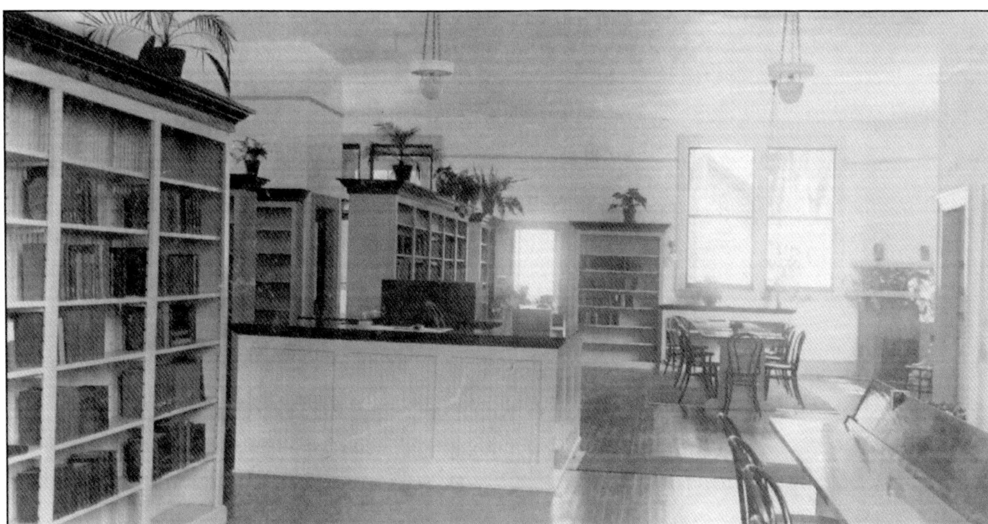

The interior of the Carnegie library is flooded with natural light to assist in reading. It was built in 1915, on the corner of Stanford Street and Wilson Avenue. The project to receive Andrew Carnegie's grant to build and fully stock a library was spearheaded by librarian Samuel Sharpless Green. A library association had established a public library as early as 1897. (Courtesy State Archives of Florida, Frisbie Collection.)

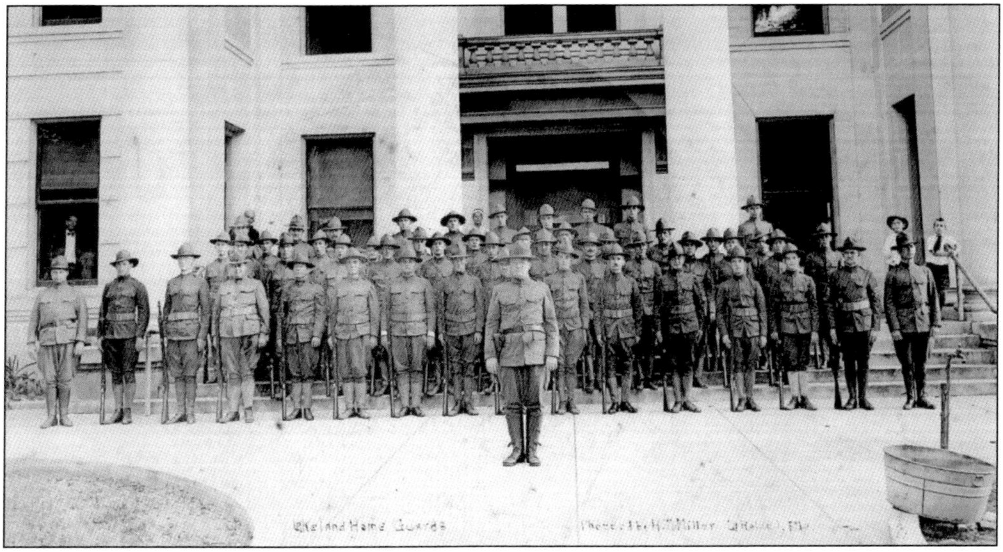

A company of the Polk County Home Guard stands at attention on the steps of the courthouse in 1918. A World War I defense measure allowed the formation of Home Guards to replace mobilized National Guard units. Home Guard companies were organized in Mulberry, Lakeland, Fort Meade, and Bartow. Polk's Home Guard battalion was commanded by Maj. T.W. Gary of Bartow. (Courtesy State Archives of Florida, Frisbie Collection.)

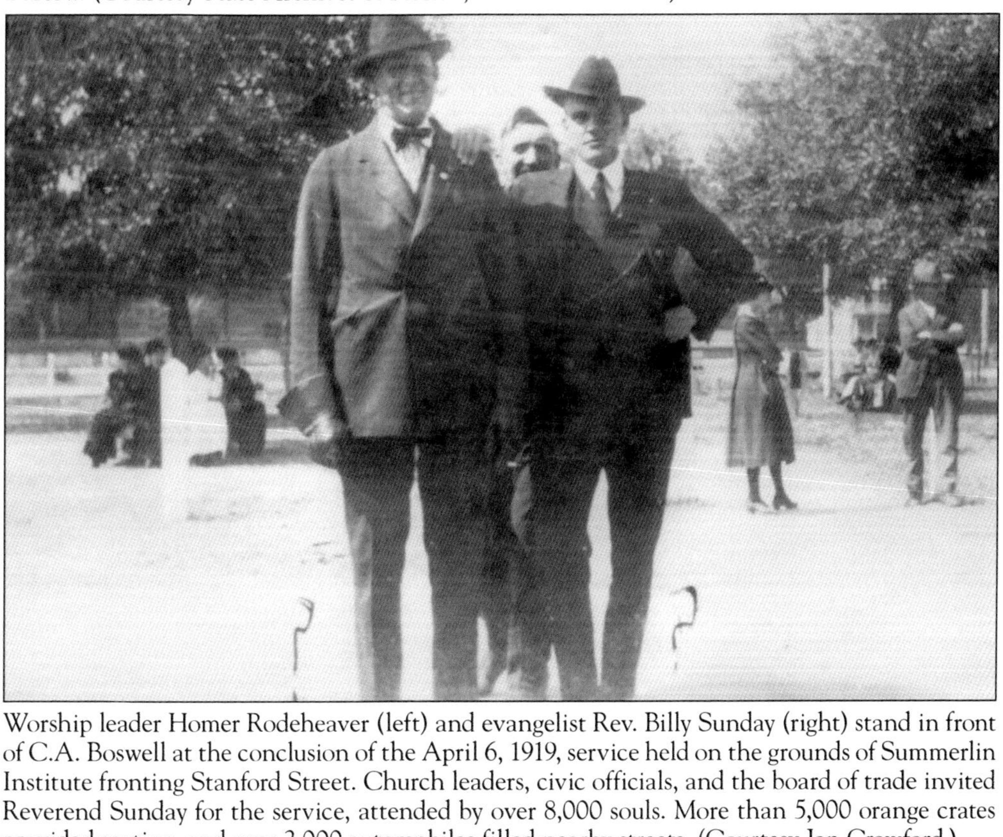

Worship leader Homer Rodeheaver (left) and evangelist Rev. Billy Sunday (right) stand in front of C.A. Boswell at the conclusion of the April 6, 1919, service held on the grounds of Summerlin Institute fronting Stanford Street. Church leaders, civic officials, and the board of trade invited Reverend Sunday for the service, attended by over 8,000 souls. More than 5,000 orange crates provided seating, and over 2,000 automobiles filled nearby streets. (Courtesy Jan Crawford.)

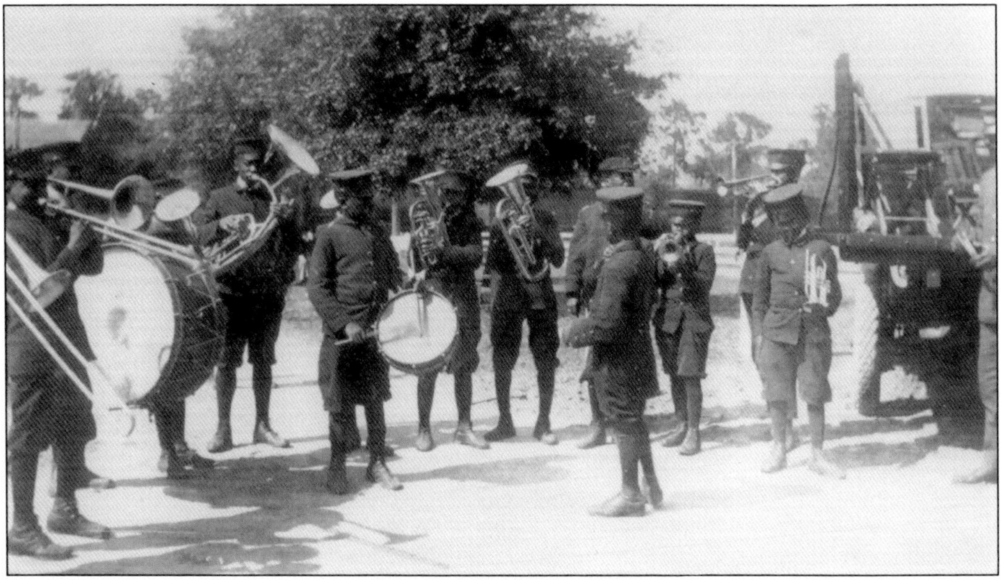

The African American young people's band, composed of percussionists and brass players attired in knickers, hats, and uniforms, presented a professional image for the one-day evangelical service by Rev. Billy Sunday. The April 6, 1919, service was no small event, as the band accompanied Rev. Sunday's worship leader, Homer Rodeheaver, and a massed choir in a musical prelude, choruses, and hymns, joined by thousands. (Courtesy Jan Crawford.)

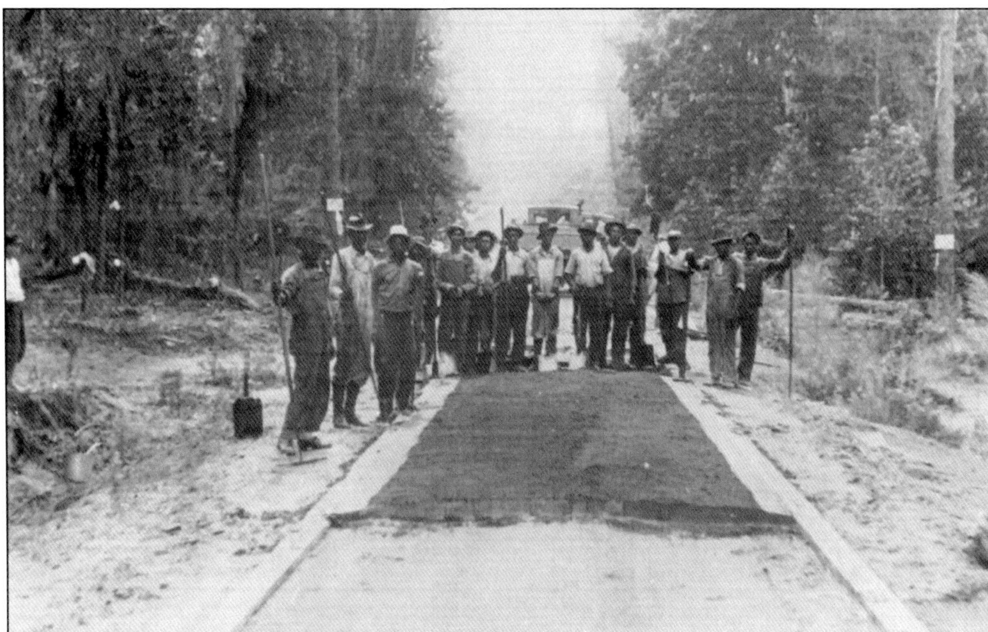

A road crew lays asphalt over a clay and phosphate base near Bartow. In 1916, "Imperial" Polk County contracted for 217 miles of asphalt road to connect all of the cities with the county seat. The sobriquet "Imperial" was coined upon completion of the roads in 1919—as all roads once led to Imperial Rome, so all roads in "Imperial Polk" led to Bartow. (Courtesy State Archives of Florida, Frisbie Collection.)

Five

Boom to Bust
1920–1929

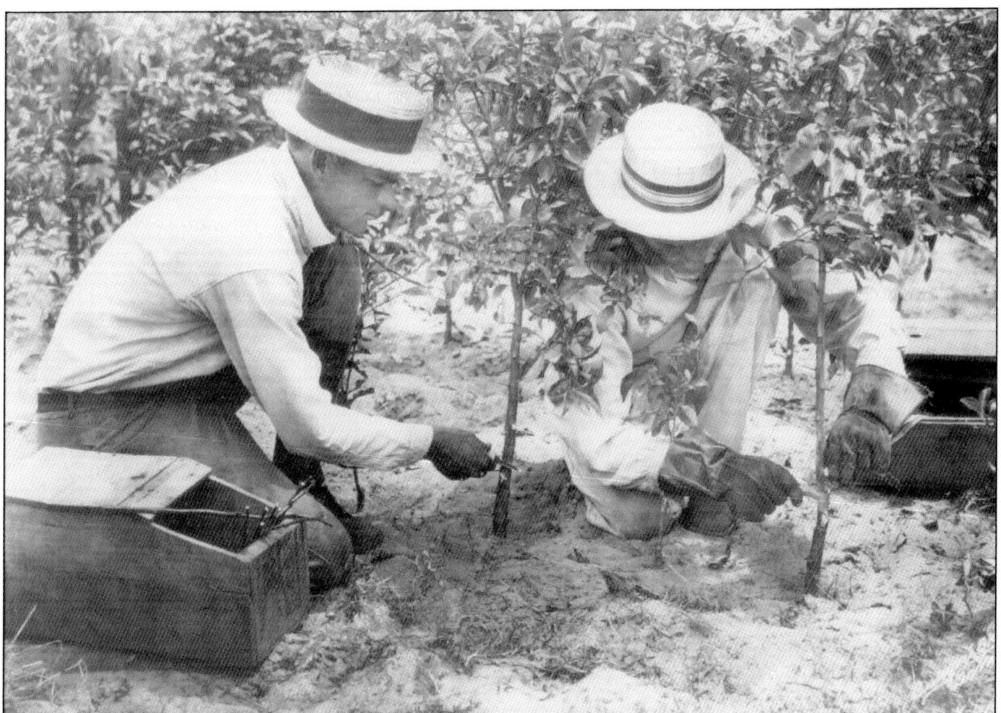

Sporting straw skimmer hats typical of the Roaring Twenties, these men are budding citrus trees for Lake Garfield Nurseries. One man makes the small slice on the seedling rootstock while the other inserts the desired budwood and carefully wraps the bud in place. Lake Garfield Nurseries was a leader in supplying oranges, grapefruit, tangerines, lemons, limes, kumquats, and tangelos to citrus growers throughout the county. (Courtesy State Archives of Florida, Frisbie Collection.)

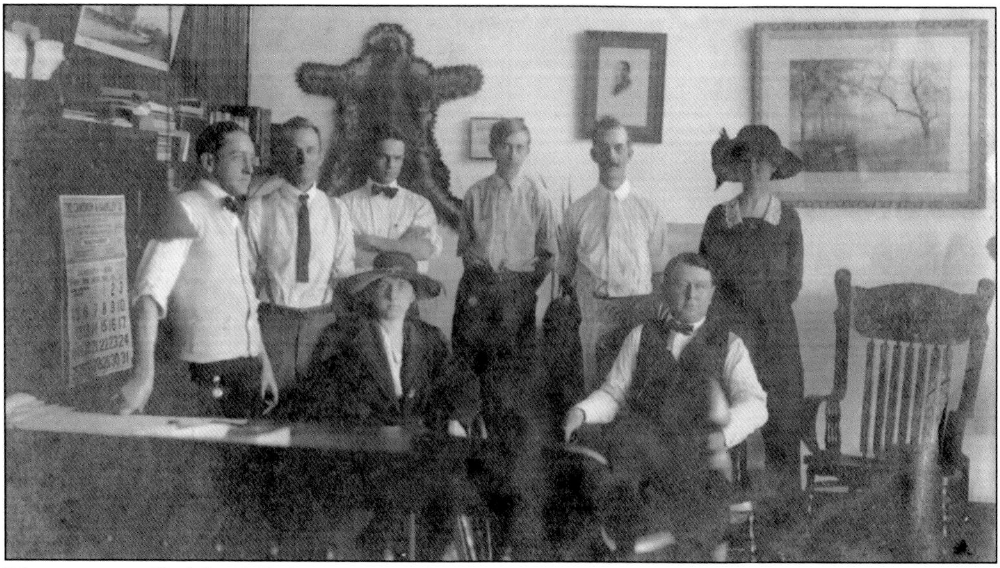

The entire staff of the *Polk County Record* newspaper is assembled for this 1920 photograph. The office at that time was located at 156 East Summerlin Street, on the north side near Central Avenue. Shown here are, from left to right, (seated) society editor Charlotte Varn and editor and publisher James G. Gallemore; (standing) Willie Witherspoon, two unidentified employees, Marion Burkholder, unidentified, and Mrs. J. (Frankie) Gallemore. (Courtesy State Archives of Florida, Frisbie Collection.)

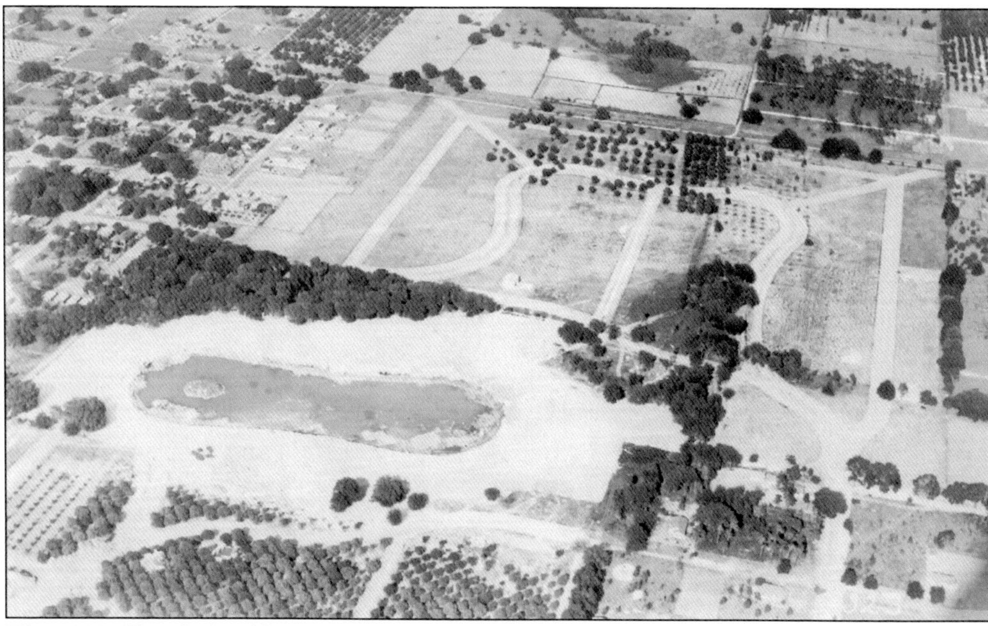

The 1920s Florida land boom was in full swing at the time of this aerial photograph of the Hacklake subdivision being laid out. Albert Theodore Hackl was the developer who inspired the subdivision, with its man-made lake and island. The loaf-like Lakeshore Boulevard, renamed Conant Street and Hackl Boulevard, winds among orange groves awaiting homes. For many years, the island displayed a Christmas tree during the holiday season. (Courtesy State Archives of Florida, Frisbie Collection.)

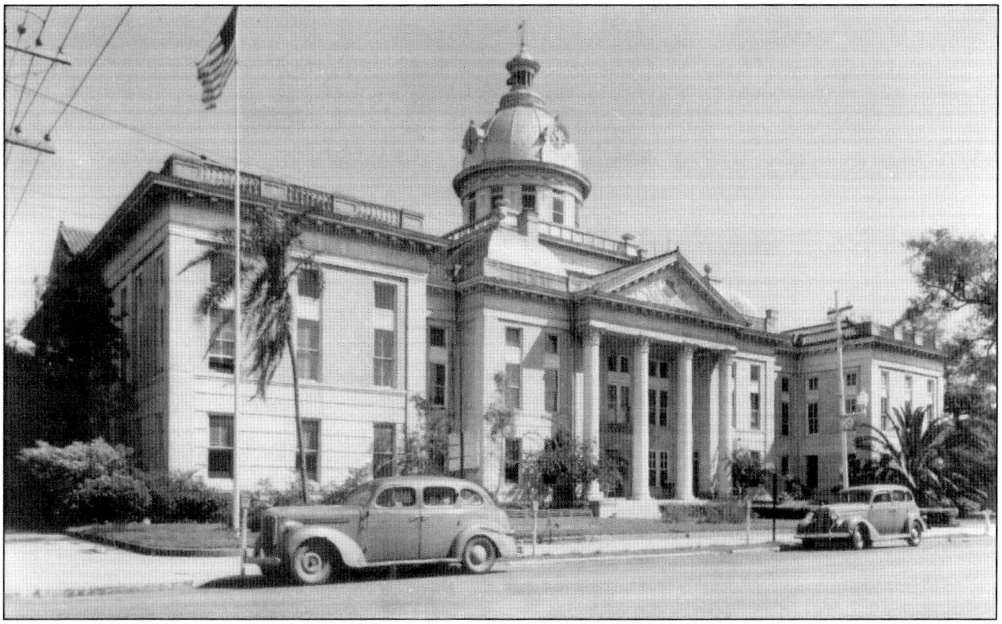

The 1909 Polk County Courthouse appears in full architectural splendor in 1940. The east and west wings were added in 1926. Corinthian capitals and Romanesque balustrades crown the roofline. The bell in the cupola tolled the hours from a central weight-driven clockwork in the dome. For years, green benches lined the square, offering repose for pedestrians. (Seiler News photograph, courtesy W.L. Harris collection.)

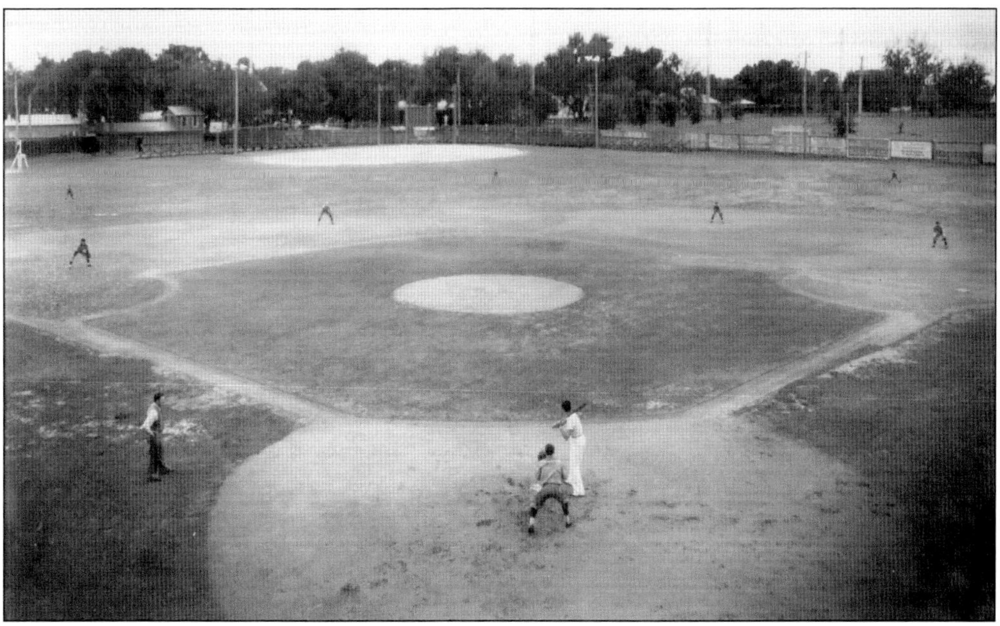

The Bartow Baseball Grounds is seen in this 1920s photograph looking southwest toward the railroad crossing at Broadway Avenue. Baseball was played here starting in 1883. The fence was erected in 1897 and advertises Head & Edwards haberdashers and Warren Hosmer Dodge. In 1919, Bartow fielded the Bartow Polkers as a charter team of the Florida State League. The grounds were later renamed Bartow Athletic Field. (Courtesy Greater Bartow Chamber of Commerce.)

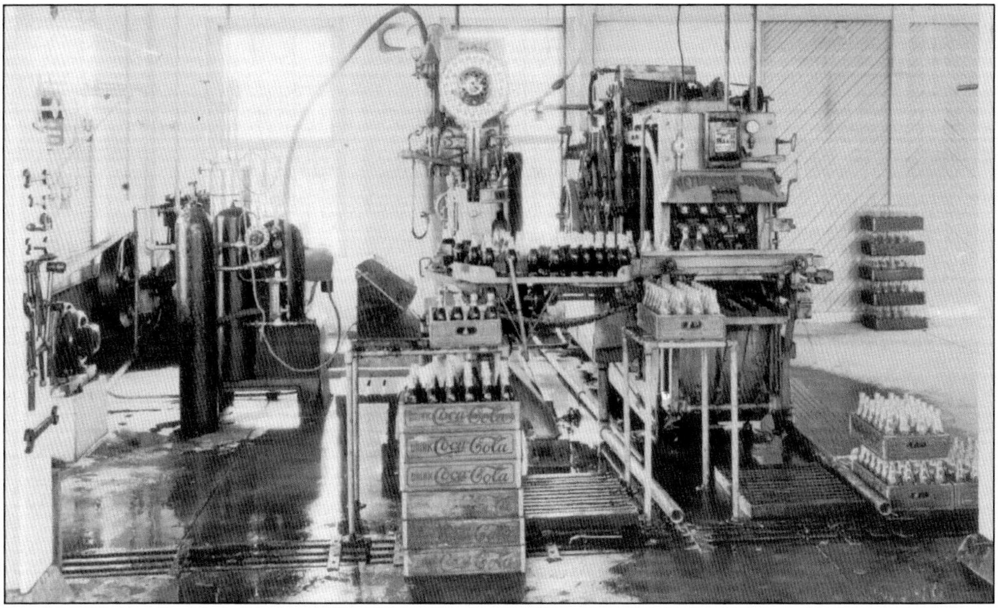

The bottling of Coca-Cola is seen in full operation in this 1910s photograph. The wooden 24-bottle crates bear the iconic Spencerian-script trademark. The Coca-Cola bottling plant, located on Summerlin Street, was owned by Lynn Grady Bruce, a prominent businessman in Bartow and Winter Haven. Bartow's Coke plant was established in 1914, eventually moving to Winter Haven as the Ridge Coca-Cola Bottling Company. (Courtesy State Archives of Florida, Frisbie Collection.)

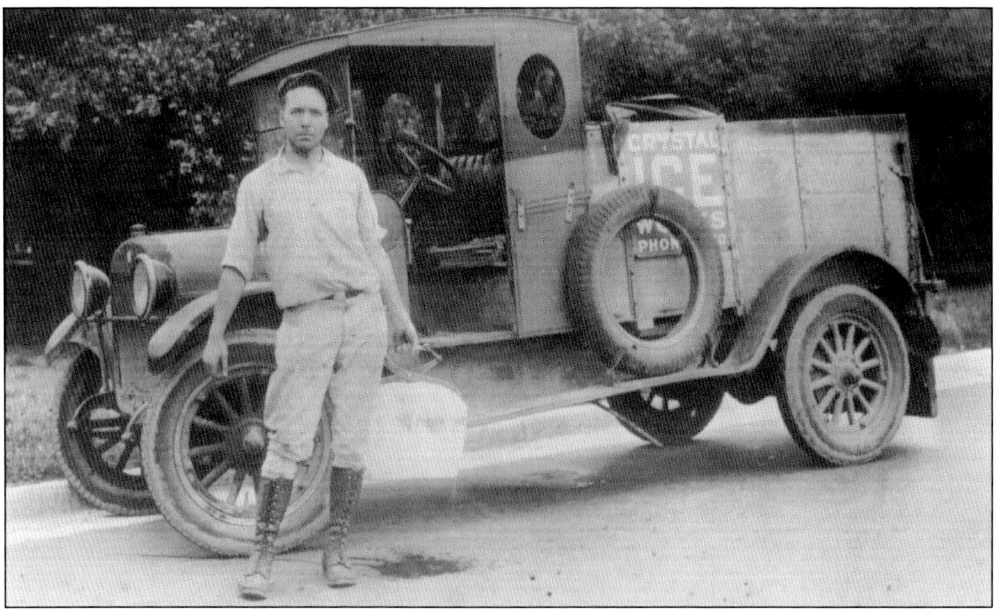

Iceman Willie G. Harris stands beside a blue-and-gray Crystal Ice Works truck. Ice was delivered daily on six city routes and to neighboring towns. Manufactured in 300-pound blocks, the frozen commodity was distributed crushed or in small blocks. A huge freezer at the ice plant was available for cold-storage needs. The business closed in 1978 after 91 years of service. (Courtesy W.L. Harris collection.)

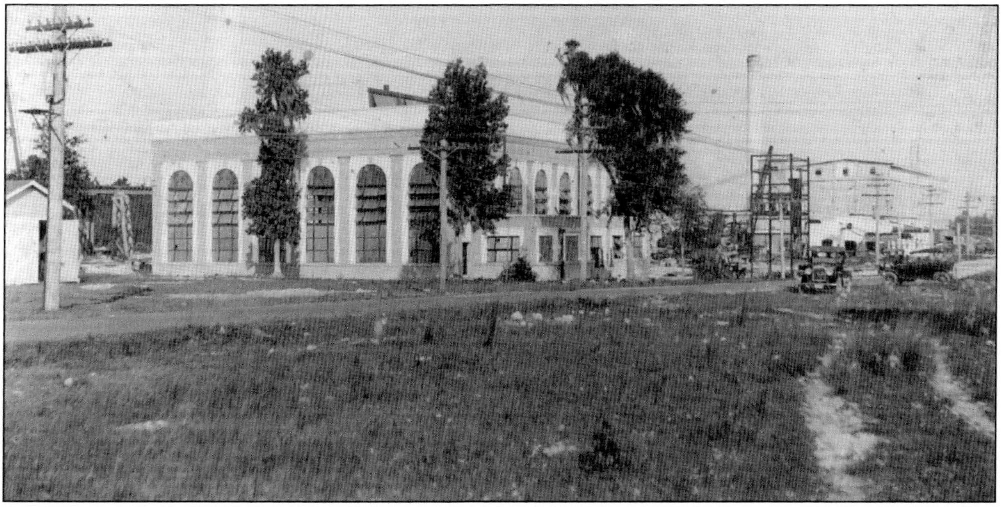

Morris Fertilizer Company and the small town of Morris were established in 1919, a couple of miles west of Bartow on the north side of present-day US Highway 60. This photograph shows the electrical power plant and other buildings on the right. The town's residences were further west. Armour Fertilizer purchased the operation in 1923 and closed the plant two years later, resuming operations in 1949. (Courtesy State Archives of Florida, Frisbie Collection.)

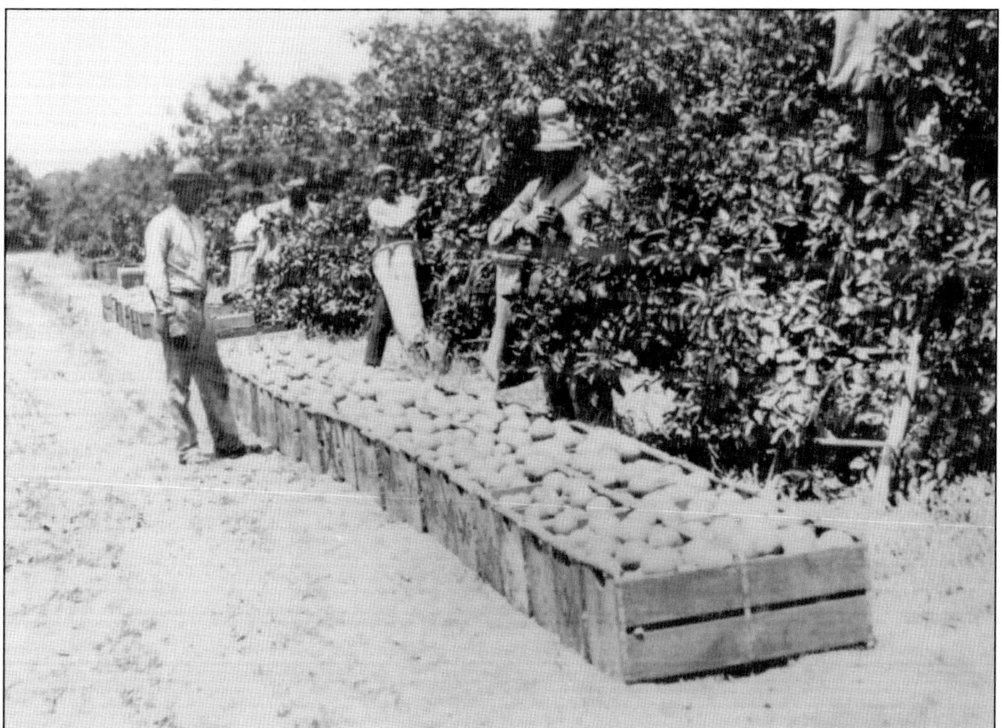

Crews of workers bearing canvas pick sacks load grapefruit into crates for Lake Garfield Nurseries. The Roux Crate and Lumber Company's mill at Lake Garfield manufactured the boxes and crates, and the company provided crates to the citrus and truck farm industry throughout the state. Roux was in operation from the early 1920s to 1942. Crates turned upside down provided quick and handy seating for public events. (Courtesy State Archives of Florida, Frisbie Collection.)

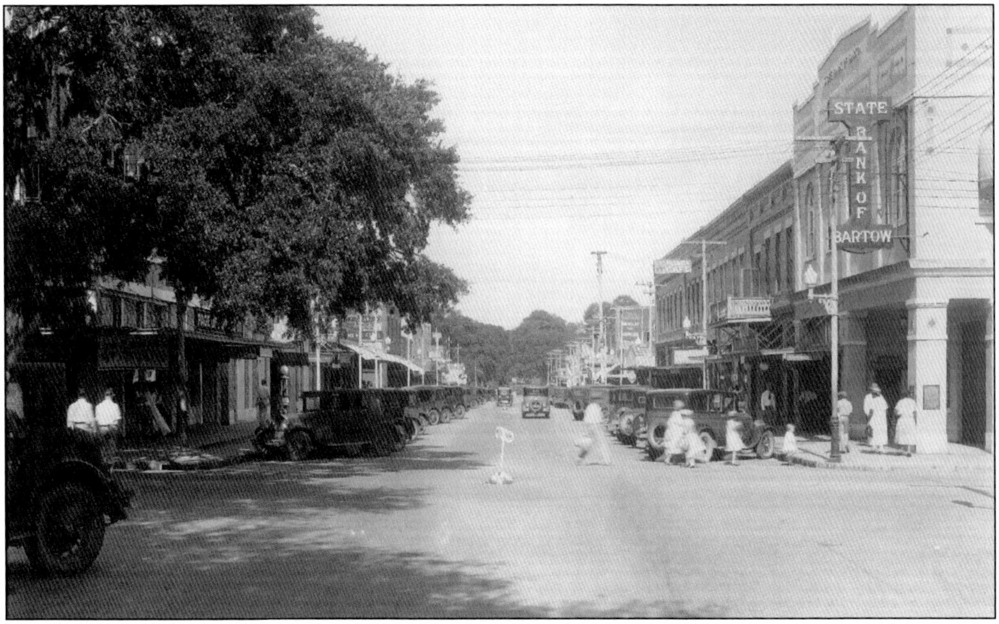

This view looking west from Central Avenue on Main Street reveals the 1920s land boom prosperity. The State Bank of Bartow (far right) occupies the site of the former opera house on the corner. Next to it are Wilson Drugs, Whidden Arcade, and Plaza Cafe. Further down the street, John Gresham advertises bicycles and supplies. Bartow's policeman is in the lower left. (Courtesy State Archives of Florida, Frisbie Collection.)

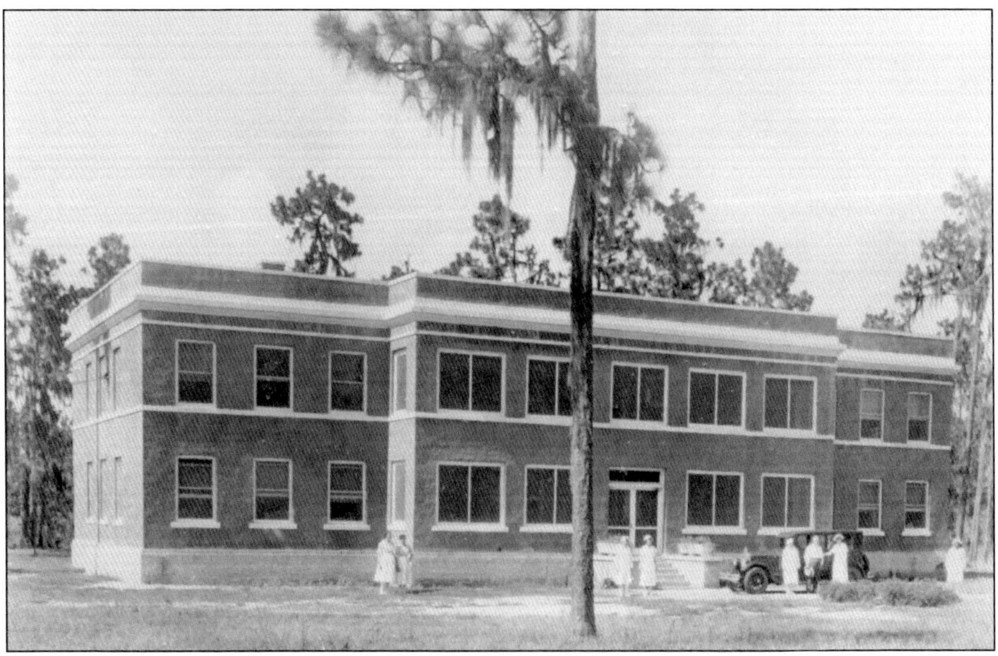

Dr. Robert L. Hughes and nursing staff stand in front of the newly built Polk General Hospital, located at the east end of Georgia Street. The 26-bed county hospital, completed in 1926, was designed to care for the indigent and less fortunate. The hospital closed in 1995. (Courtesy State Archives of Florida, Frisbie Collection.)

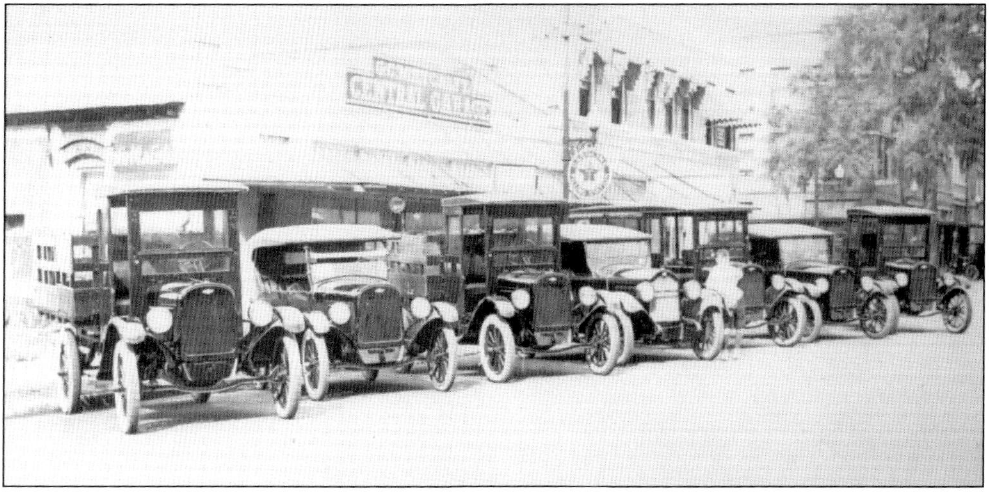

Metcalfe's Central Garage and Texaco filling station was located across from the post office on Central Avenue, just south of Summerlin Street. The 1922 Record Building is to the immediate right of the garage. The four trucks and three of the automobiles are Chevrolets. The top of the gravity-fed gas pump can be seen above and behind the second truck. (Courtesy State Archives of Florida, Frisbie Collection.)

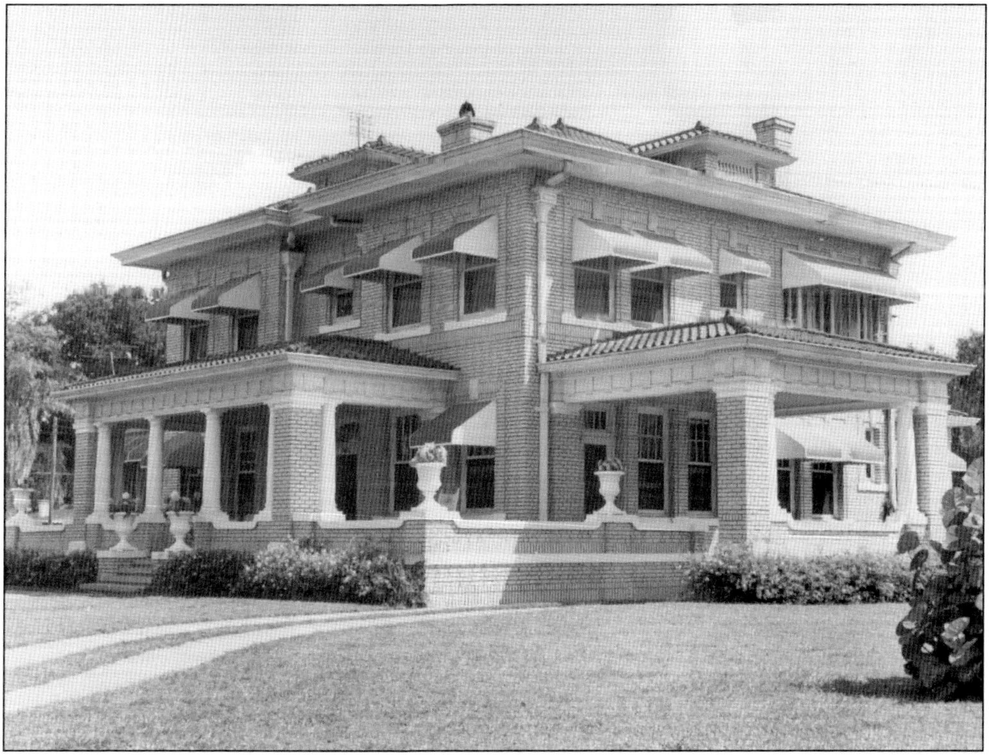

The home of Hugh Wear, a prominent businessman and developer, is seen in the 1920s. The home, covering the entire southwest block of East Main Street and Oak Avenue, had white facings and was built of his signature Shawnee light yellow brick. There was an additional apartment in the rear. Wear's home burned to the ground in the 1990s. (Courtesy State Archives of Florida, Frisbie Collection.)

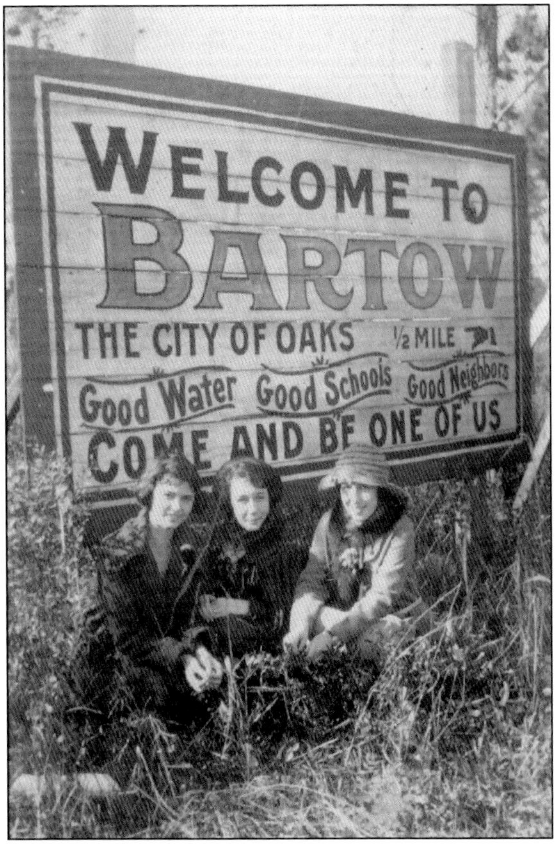

Rosa Caldwell (left), Sara Caldwell (center), and Ruth Gillon smile beneath a "Welcome to Bartow" sign in the early 1920s. The town promoted its "good water, good schools, good neighbors." (Courtesy Barbara and Wallace Orr, Lynda Belle and David Black family.)

The Union Railroad station pictured here was Bartow's third passenger station since 1885. It was located at the north end of Depot Street and First Avenue, where Atlantic Coast Line's tracks were crossed by those of the Seaboard Air Line Railroad in 1913. The point of intersection was the site of the new station, completed in 1915, providing convenience for passengers of both railroads through the 1950s. (Courtesy State Archives of Florida, Frisbie Collection.)

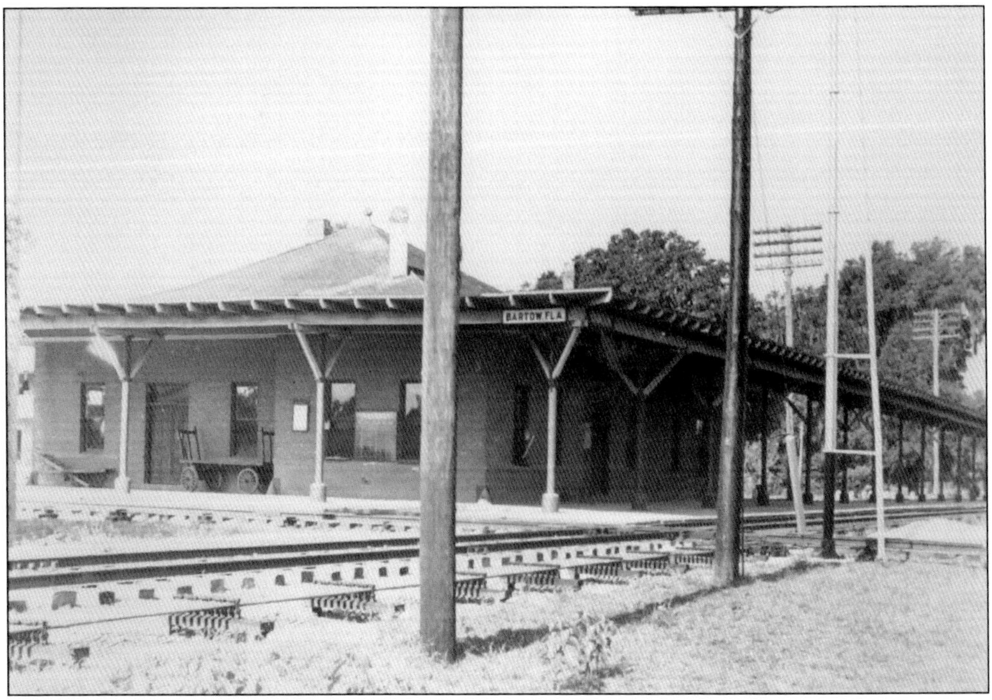

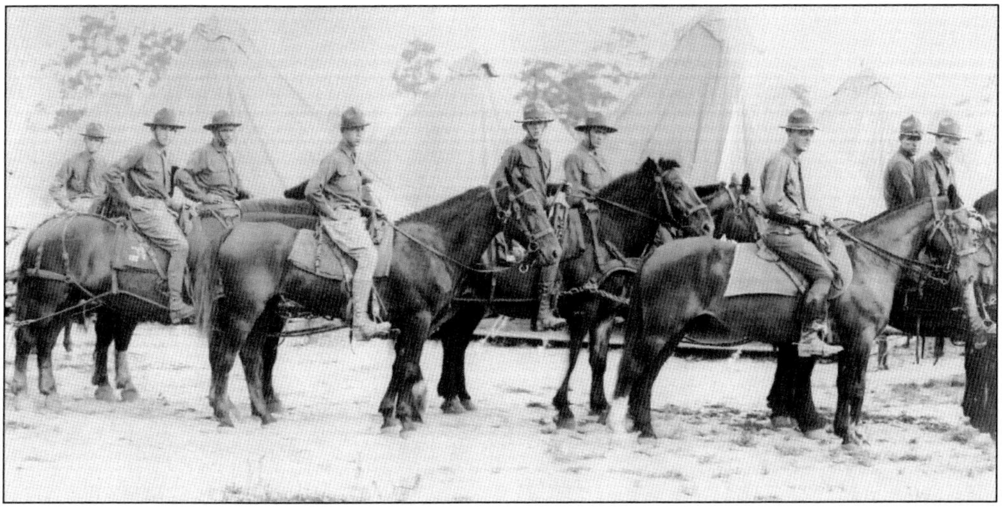

The National Guard was reorganized after World War I by Capt. Roger Lyle and designated Headquarters Detachment, 2nd Battalion, 116th Field Artillery in 1923. This photograph shows Bartow's horse artillerymen training at Fort Bragg, North Carolina, the following year. Weekly drills were held on the lawn of Bartow City Hall until the "old armory" on Blount Street was refurbished with an assembly hall, supply building, and stables. (Courtesy W.L. Harris collection.)

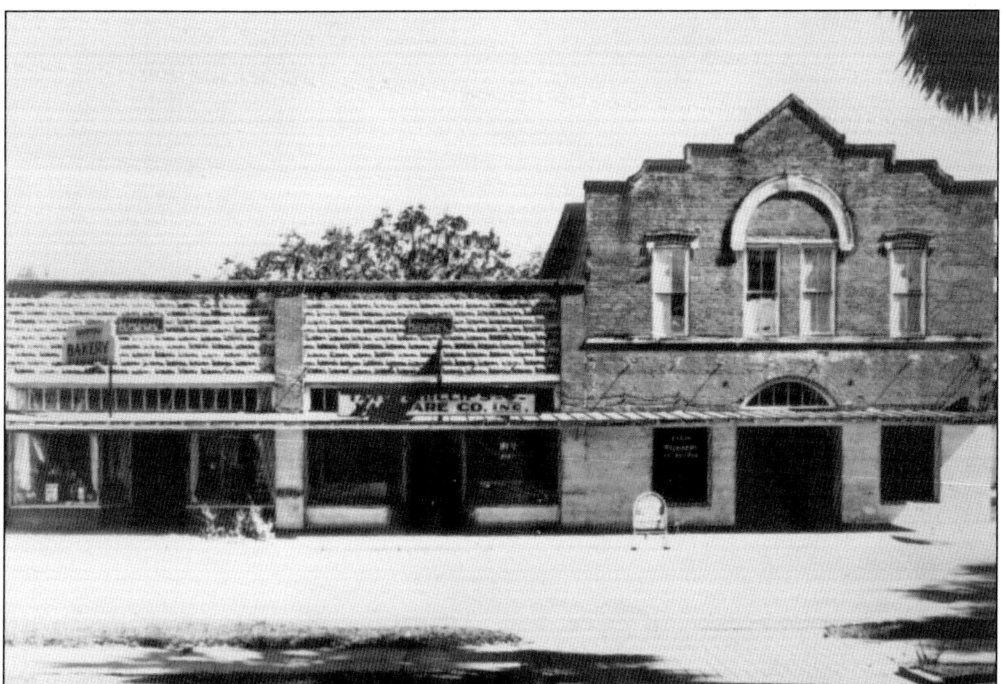

The structure on the right is the second Masonic Lodge, built in 1884. Meetings were held on the upper floor. The adjacent building is occupied by the Bartow Bakery and Tate Phillips Hardware. The arch and keystone on the lodge provide an added architectural highlight and figure in the symbolism of Royal Arch Masonry. The buildings still stand on Wilson Street behind the present-day post office. (Courtesy State Archives of Florida, Frisbie Collection.)

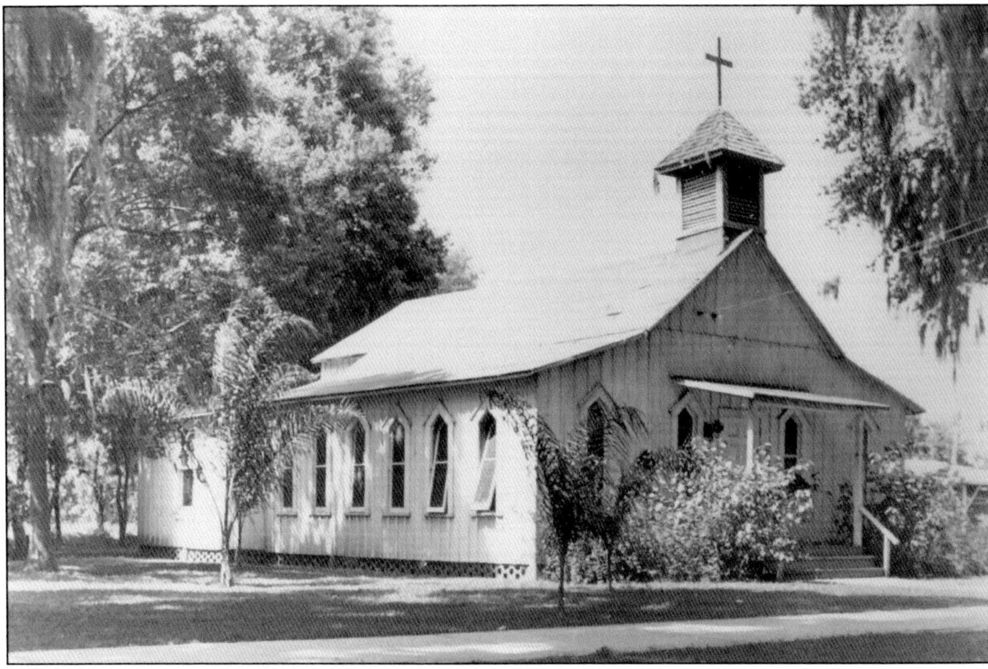

St. Thomas Roman Catholic Church, seen here in the 1940s, was originally a small home on West Church Street. Remodeled and expanded in 1913, it served the parish until 1956. Catholics organized a congregation in Bartow in 1884, but the death of the local priest delayed efforts for a sanctuary. Meetings were held at the Lemon Street home of John Woodard during the interim. (Courtesy State Archives of Florida, Frisbie Collection.)

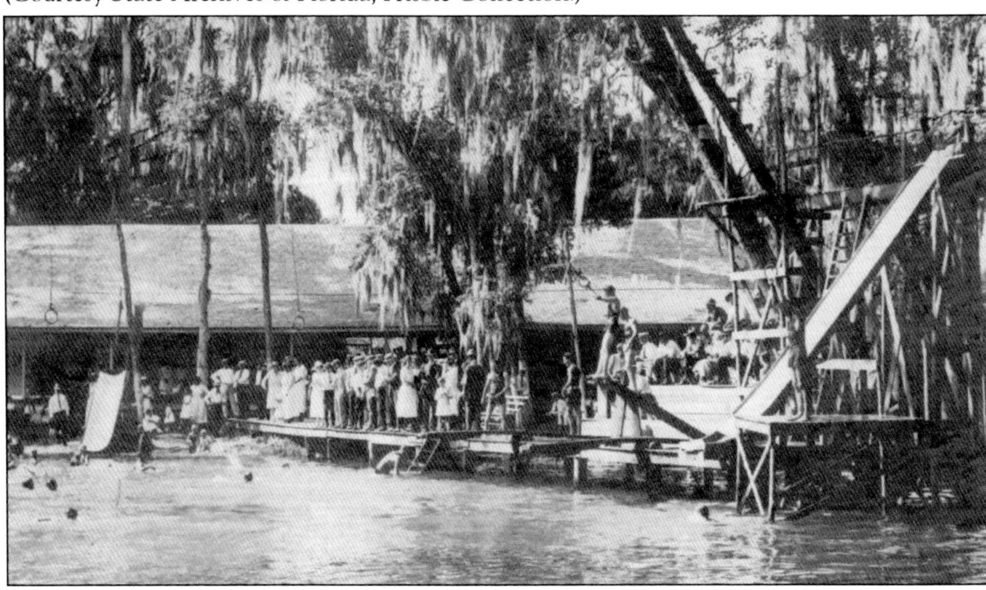

A dance pavilion, restaurant, slides, and swings illustrate the tremendous development of Kissengen Springs as a recreational site. Horse rides, picnic areas, and electric lights were added. The spring's popularity was secure even during the Depression; management advertised the cost-saving logic for families to "spend their vacation at the springs!" (Courtesy State Archives of Florida, Frisbie Collection.)

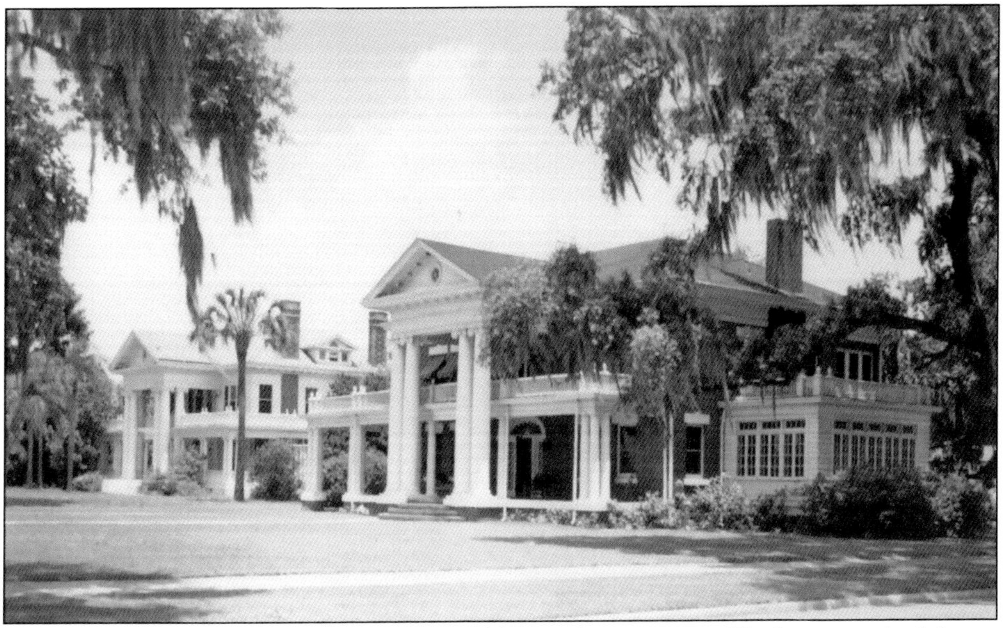

The Swearingen homes adorn Church Street like jewels in a crown. The home on the left was built by William B. Swearingen in 1912. The brick residence on the right was built in 1925 by William's brother John J. Swearingen. John was a lawyer, grove owner, and vice president of the State Bank of Bartow. Both homes were built in the Greek Revival style. (Courtesy State Archives of Florida, Frisbie Collection.)

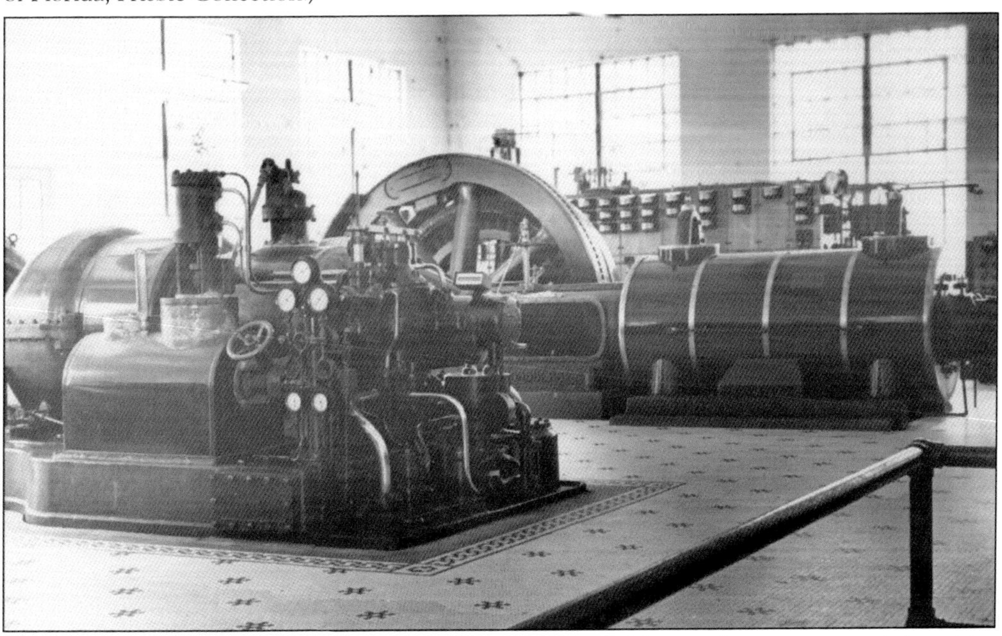

This image of the interior of the power plant, built in 1903, reveals generators of electricity resplendent in their palace of light. The Bartow Municipal Light & Water plant was located at the north end of Central Avenue at Church Street and dated to 1897. Until 1953, the power plant also provided energy to run the city's water pump, lifting 15,000 gallons per hour. (Courtesy State Archives of Florida, Frisbie Collection.)

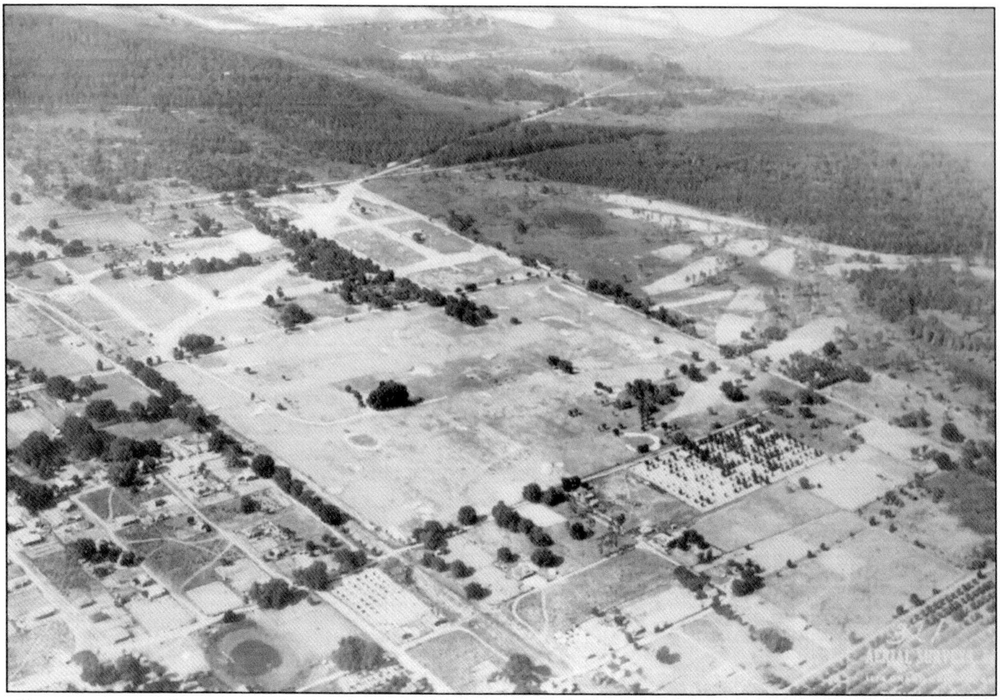

This is an aerial view of the Bartow Golf Course shortly after its completion and opening in 1921. The 18-hole course was designed by Scottish-born Donald James Ross, one of the most influential golf course designers in the history of the sport. The expanse of trees across the upper half marks Peace River, and beyond are the mined areas of Excelsior Phosphate Company. (Courtesy State Archives of Florida, Frisbie Collection.)

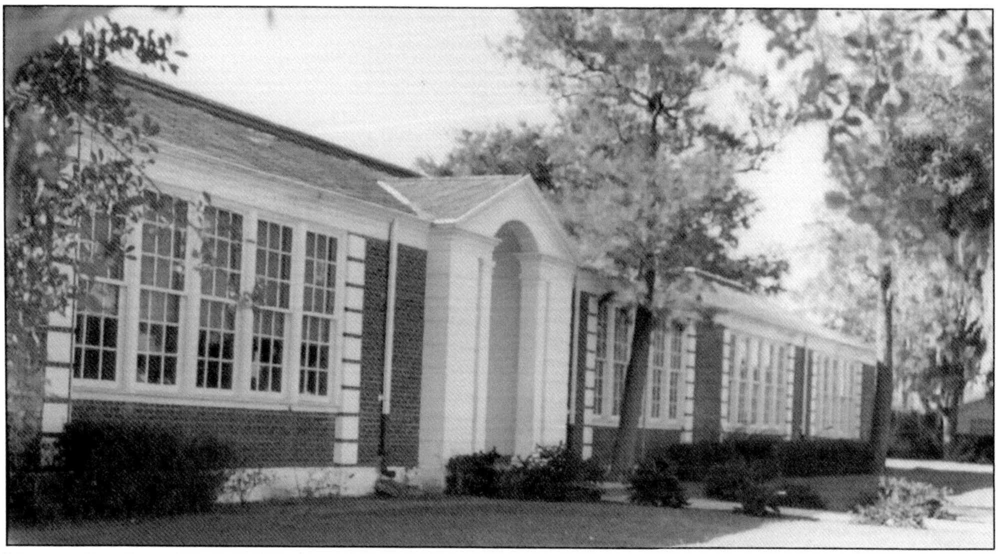

Union Academy High School, with its redbrick exterior, white facings, and central arch, was built in 1929 on East Wabash Street as an African American school during segregation. Founded in 1897, it was the outgrowth of two earlier schools dating to 1887. The 1897 school was a two-story frame building on Fourth Avenue and was named for the Freedmen's Bureau school in Gainesville. (Courtesy State Archives of Florida, Frisbie Collection.)

Six

PERSEVERANCE 1930–1939

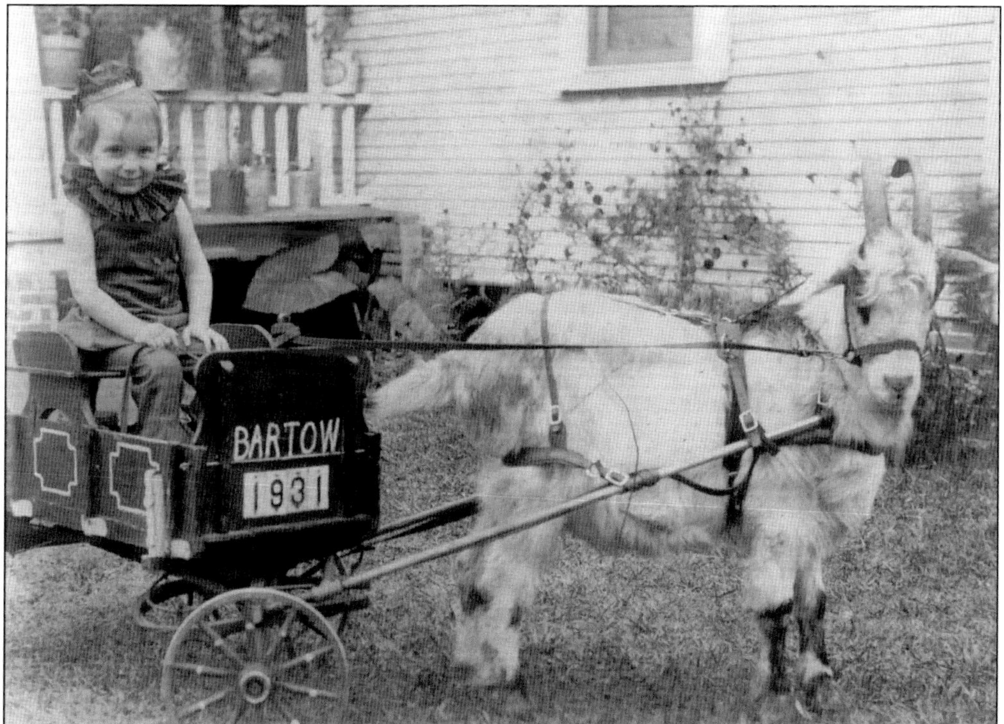

The Depression prompted an enterprising photographer to make house calls with a set of unusual props, capturing memories and lasting images for families. The goat, cart, and an assortment of costumes were available for the photographic moment. Edna Bernice Harris poses in front of her home on Sunset Avenue in 1931. Similar photographs are found among Bartow's older families. (Courtesy W.L. Harris collection.)

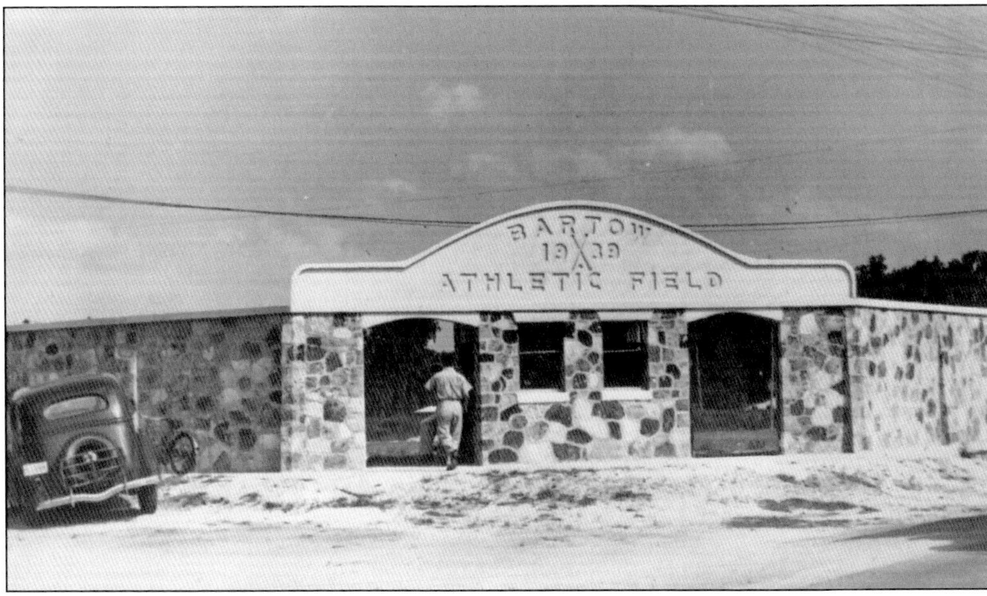

The 1939 Bartow Athletic Field's gatehouses and walls were built of local stone as a federal works project. East of Broadway and south of Blount Street, the facility contained baseball and softball diamonds, locker rooms, bleachers, and concession stands. From 1883, the field hosted city, minor, and Negro leagues baseball teams as well as softball leagues, the Crickette Club Halloween carnival, and American Legion turkey shoots. The site was cleared and by 1976 was the home of the Citrus and Chemical Bank. (Courtesy State Archives of Florida.)

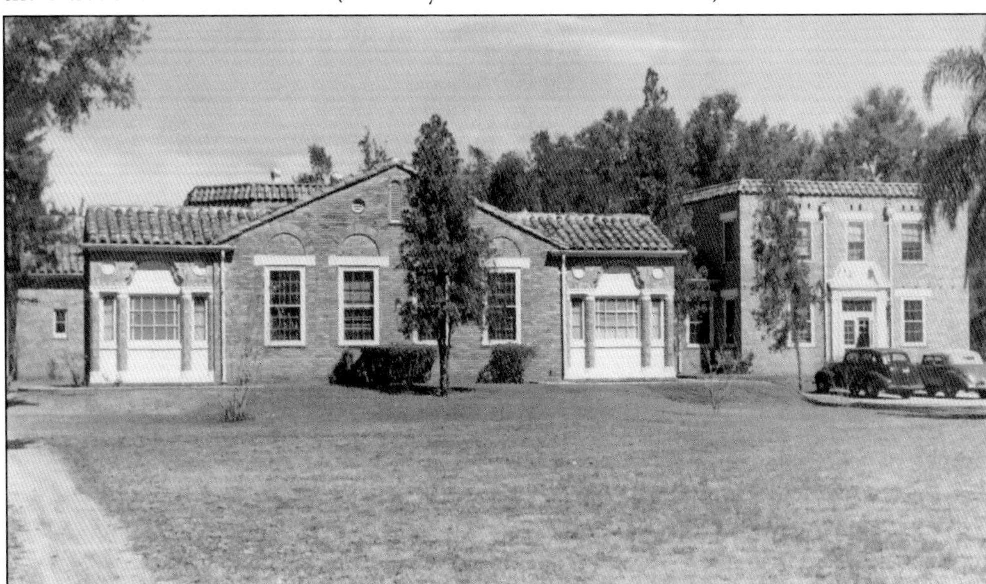

The Bartow City Hospital, on East Main Street, was founded in 1924, This photograph shows the completed 1926 wing. The hospital officially opened on March 1, 1928. By the 1950s, more additions were built, including an obstetrics building, "the Stork Club." In 1980, the hospital was enlarged to include 56 beds and three operating rooms. Bartow Memorial Hospital relocated in 1999, becoming Bartow Regional Medical Center. (Courtesy State Archives of Florida, Frisbie Collection.)

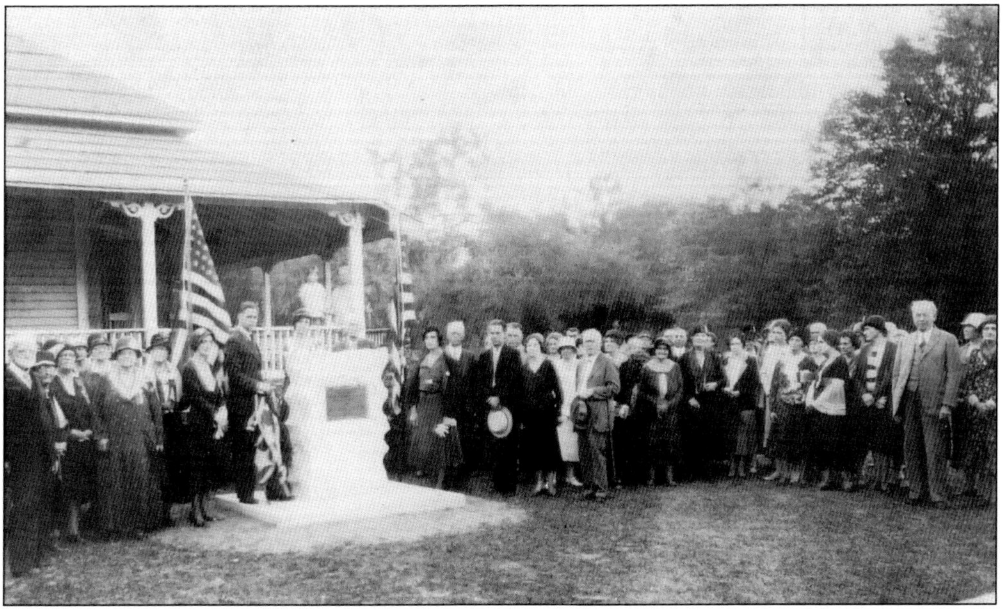

The 1932 dedication of the monument marking the final home of Bartow's beloved Maj. Gen. Evander McIvor Law, at the southwest corner of Summerlin Street and Broadway Avenue, was the culmination of years of planning by the Father Ryan Chapter No. 439, United Daughters of the Confederacy. Bank failures in 1929 halted the original plan to erect a statue in a park encompassing the entire block. (Courtesy State Archives of Florida, Frisbie Collection.)

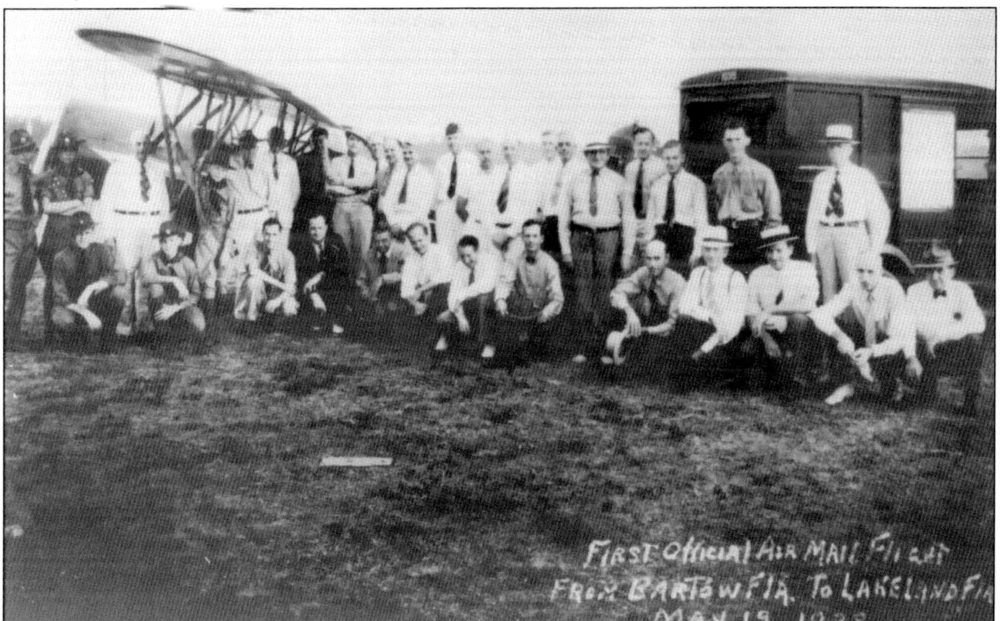

Boy Scouts, city officials, and postal employees pose for the inauguration of airmail service from Bartow to Lakeland on May 19, 1938. The mail was flown from Armour Field municipal airport, located south of present-day Highway 60 between County Road 555 and Woodlawn Avenue. It served the city until 1946. The land was donated by Armour Fertilizer and officially opened on January 15, 1931. (Courtesy State Archives of Florida.)

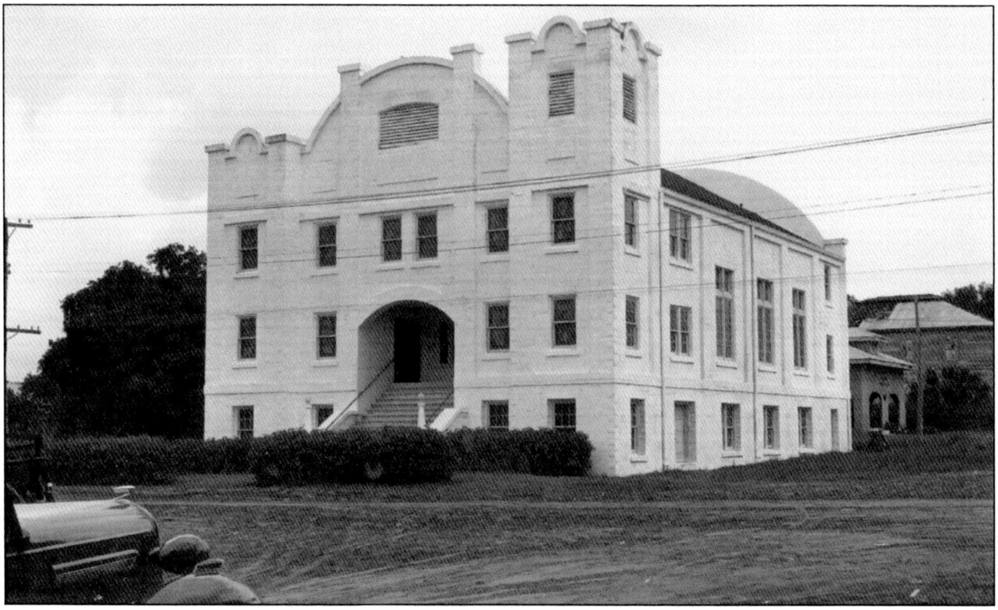

This 1930s photograph of Mount Gilboa Missionary Baptist Church also shows undertaker Lucius T. Hewing's funeral home and the Odd Fellows Hall. Hewing's Funeral Home was originally Oldham & Hewing Undertaking Parlor, and Union Academy held its first classes in 1897 in the two-story hall located at far right. Mount Gilboa's first services were held at a two-story building three blocks west. (Courtesy State Archives of Florida, Frisbie Collection.)

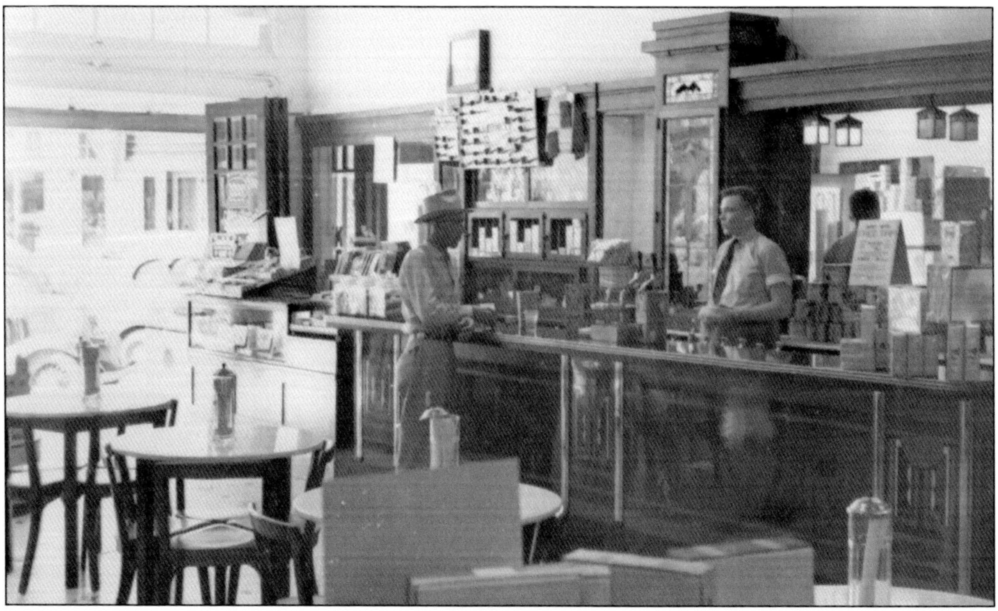

Wilson Drug Company was founded in 1894. This photograph was taken in 1933 at 215 Main Street. "Bud" Skipper is working the soda fountain. Straw containers, tables, pipes, mirrors, sundries, and a sign offering a chance to win a trip to the 1893 Chicago World's Fair were typical of such establishments. Wilson's first soda fountain was installed in 1901. The store advertised drugs, toiletries, stationery, cigars, fine candies, and quick delivery. (Courtesy State Archives of Florida, Frisbie Collection.)

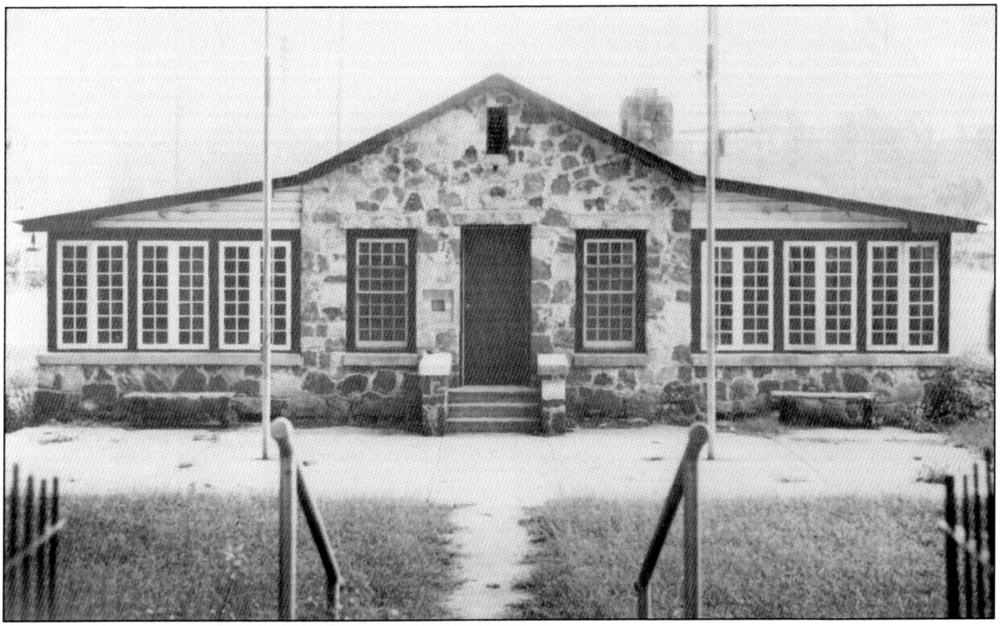

The Boy Scout House was built in 1938 as a Works Progress Administration project using local orange, brown, and buff-colored fieldstone. The meeting place served an active Scouting program, which was composed of two basic groups, Boy Scouts for younger boys, and, for older boys, a Sea Scout program sponsored in part by the Kiwanis Club. The building was razed in 1966. (Courtesy State Archives of Florida, Frisbie Collection.)

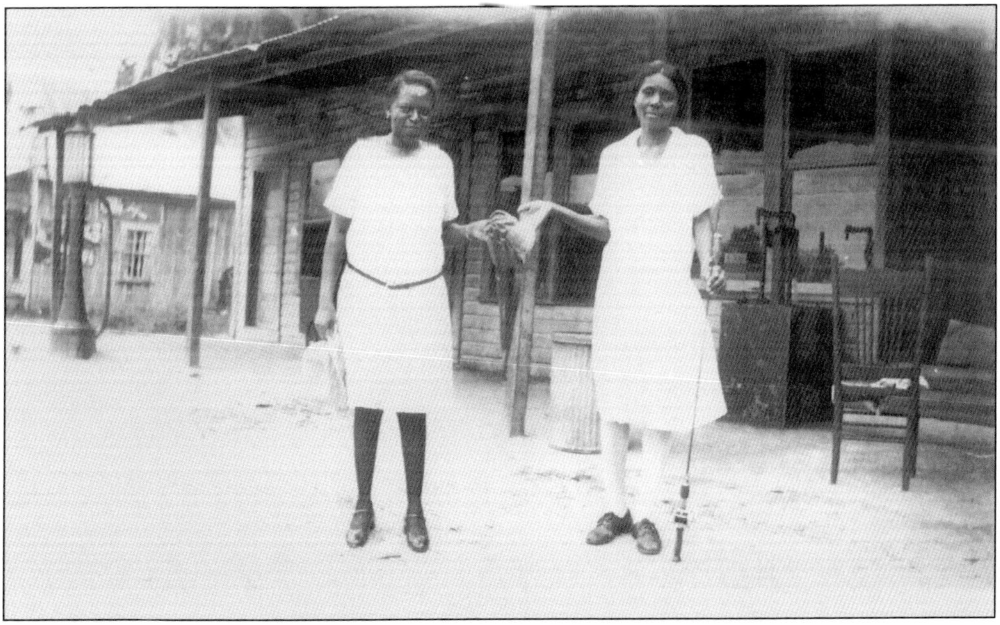

In this photograph, two unidentified women hold a largemouth bass caught with a top-water lure, reel, and rod. It was not uncommon for families to supplement the table with fish and wildlife during the Depression years. They are standing on Polk Street in front of Ben Williams's store. Note the large kerosene pump on the right and the gravity gas pump on the left. (Courtesy Historic L.B. Brown House.)

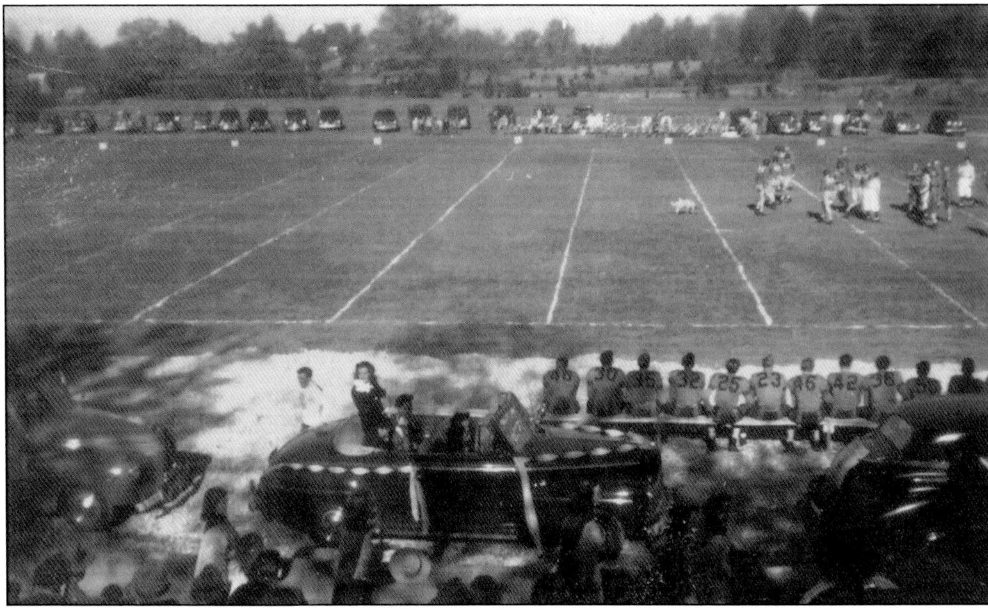

This photograph was taken at a high school homecoming parade during the 1940s at Bartow Municipal Field. The event was concurrent with the football game, and the dog on the field added to the memories. The field was located directly behind the high school building on Tharp Street and parallel to present-day Broadway Avenue. (Courtesy Barbara and Wallace Orr.)

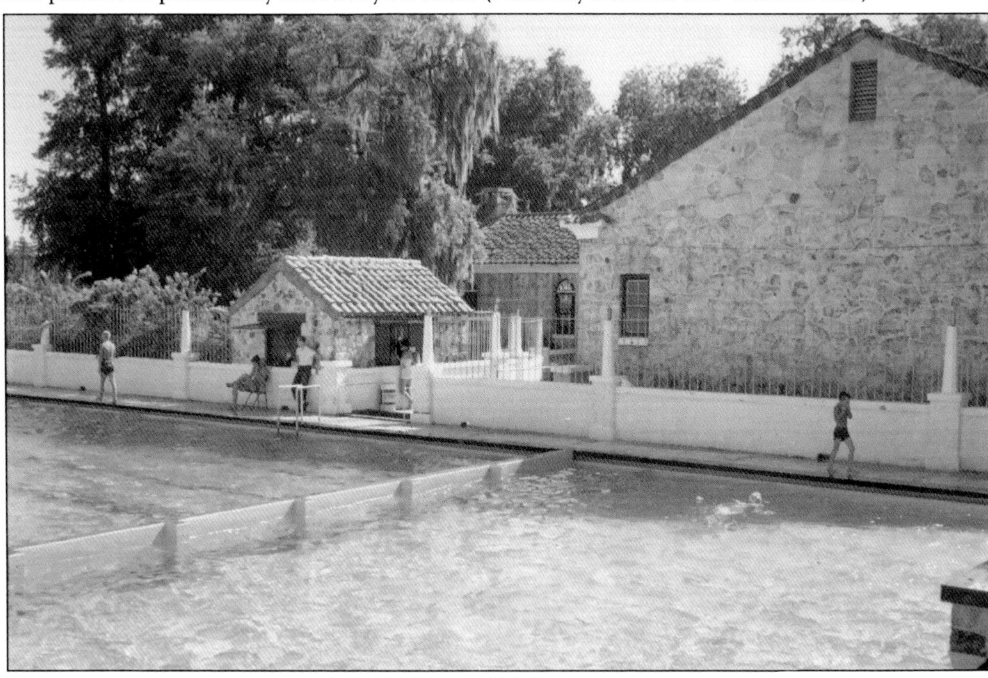

The community swimming pool, located directly behind the civic center, was completed in 1934 as a Civilian Works Administration project under President Roosevelt's Federal Emergency Relief program. It served the city for many years until being replaced by a new civic center in 1967. The pool, ranging in depth from 3 feet to 12 feet, had diving boards and a separate toddler's pool. (Courtesy State Archives of Florida, Frisbie Collection.)

Seven

On to Victory 1940–1945

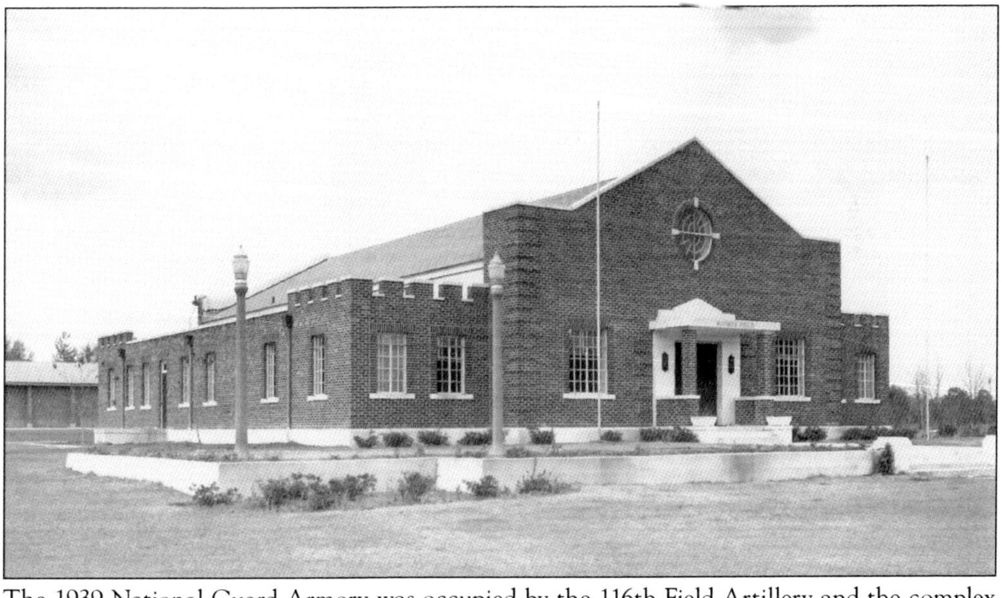

The 1939 National Guard Armory was occupied by the 116th Field Artillery and the complex was named Hughes Field, for deceased commander Capt. Robert L. Hughes. It contained a drill hall, offices, classrooms, supply room, weapons vault, and gun sheds. The Guard vacated the building when a new armory was constructed at the airport in 1974, after which the old armory was used for community events and as a polling place. (Courtesy State Archives of Florida, Frisbie Collection.)

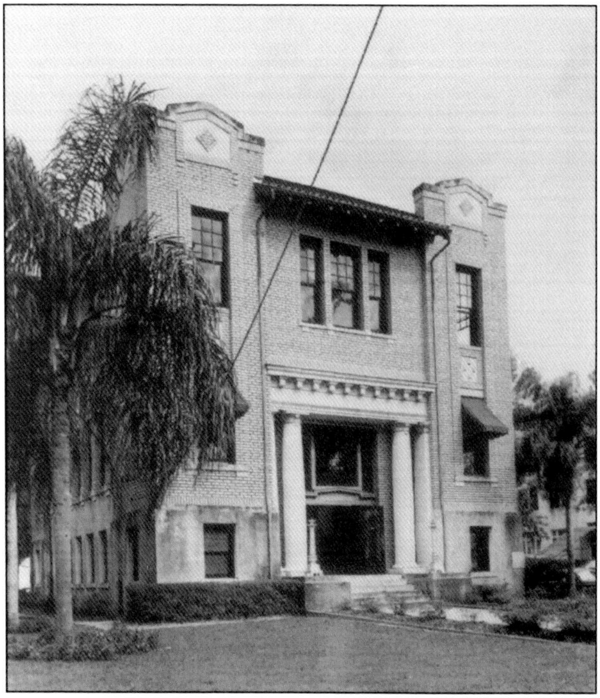

Bartow City Hall occupied the northeast corner of the intersection of Parker Street and Central Avenue. The building's white exterior was offset with yellow brick and a dark green tile roof. Completed on September 7, 1915, it was the heart of city government through 1971, when it was razed for the post office expansion. City hall moved in 1972 and again in 1982. (Seiler News photograph, courtesy W.L. Harris collection.)

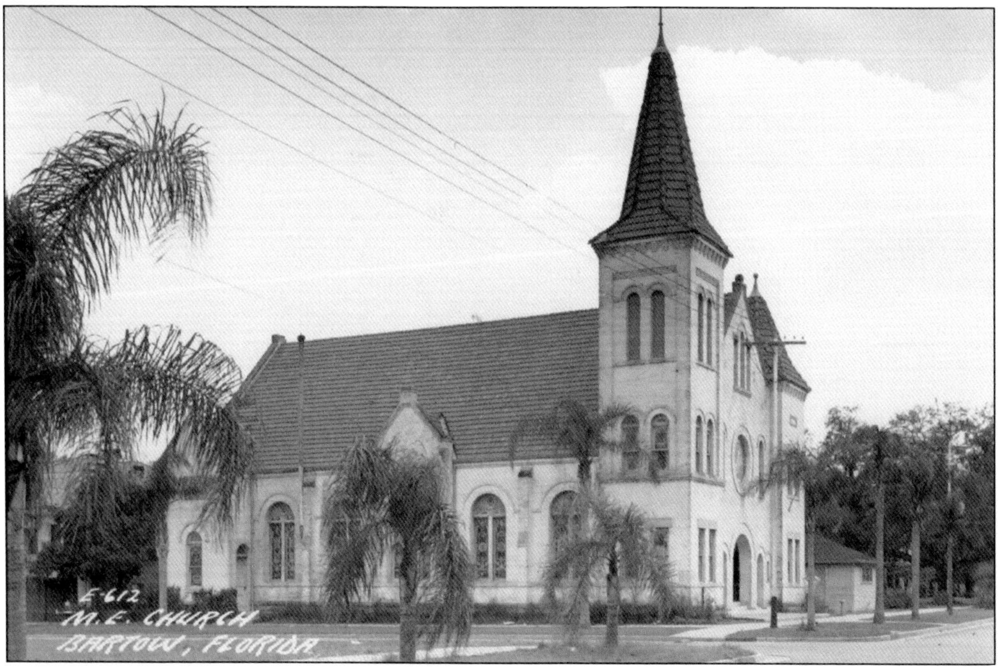

The First Methodist Church is shown in the 1940s. The church was constructed in 1906 and the next year held its first service in a new sanctuary fronting Broadway Avenue. The former church building on West Church Street was sold, dismantled, and its materials used to build two homes. Stained-glass windows were subscribed by the following early congregant families: Crum, Wilson, Earnest, Stanley, Jordan, Carpenter, Mann, and Bishop. (Seiler News photograph, courtesy W.L. Harris collection.)

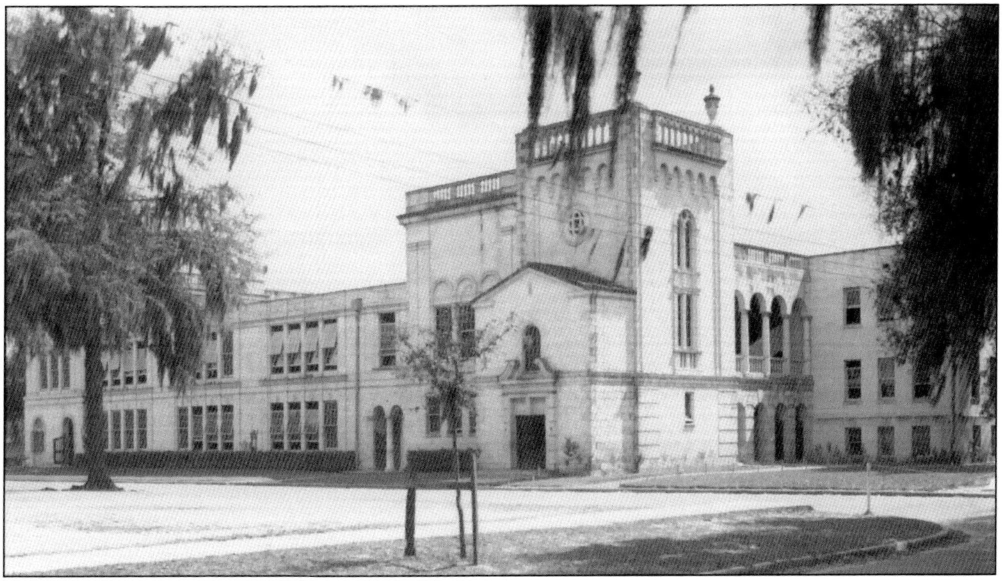

Bartow Elementary, seen here in 1940, was an imposing structure that served as the high school from 1917 to 1929. The original 1917 high school is on the right; the colonnade and classrooms to the left were built to connect the school to the City Auditorium. (Seiler News photograph, courtesy W.L. Harris collection.)

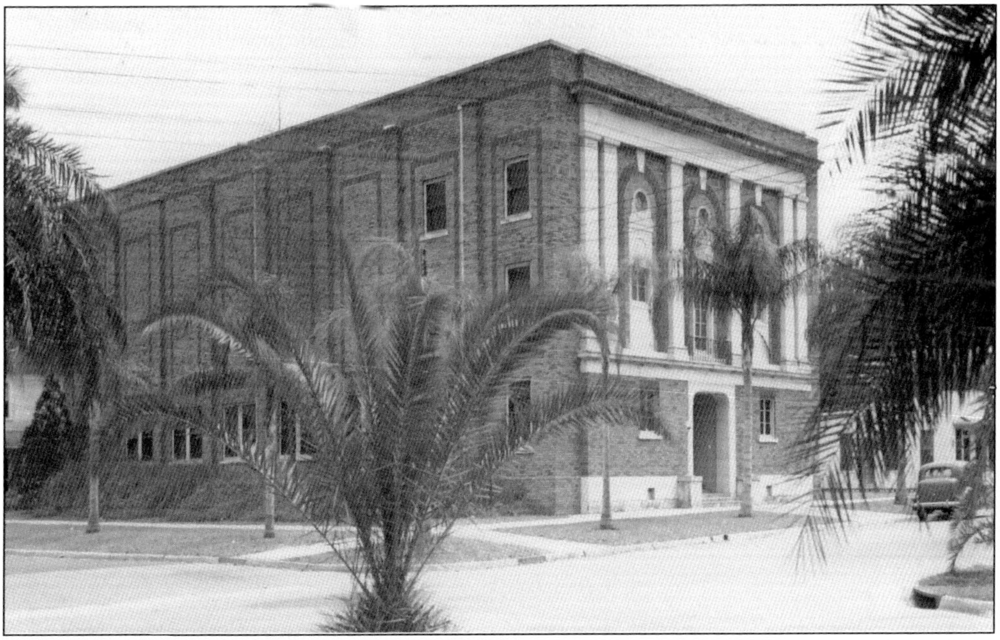

Palms abound on Florida Avenue in this 1940 view of the Masonic Temple and office of Dr. James Gilchrist. The building was completed in 1927 and was the third home of Tuscan Lodge No. 6, Free and Accepted Masons. Other Masonic groups and civic clubs called it home until the new civic center was constructed in the 1960s. (Seiler News photograph, courtesy W.L. Harris collection.)

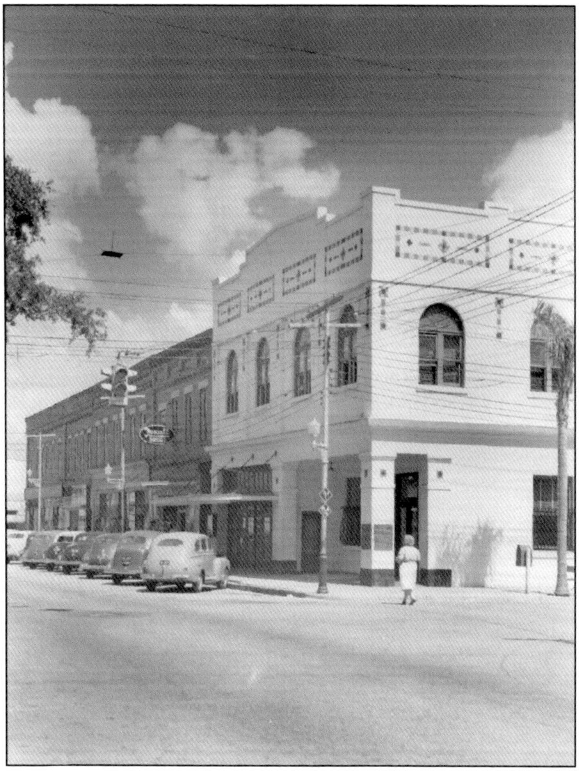

This 1940s photograph shows the Florida National Bank at Bartow, on the corner of Main Street and Central Avenue. The new bank was born out of the failure of the Polk County National Bank in 1929 at the height of the Depression, and was chartered on October 17, 1929. Doctors Robert L. Hughes and Heber P. Newman maintained offices upstairs. (Courtesy State Archives of Florida, Frisbie Collection.)

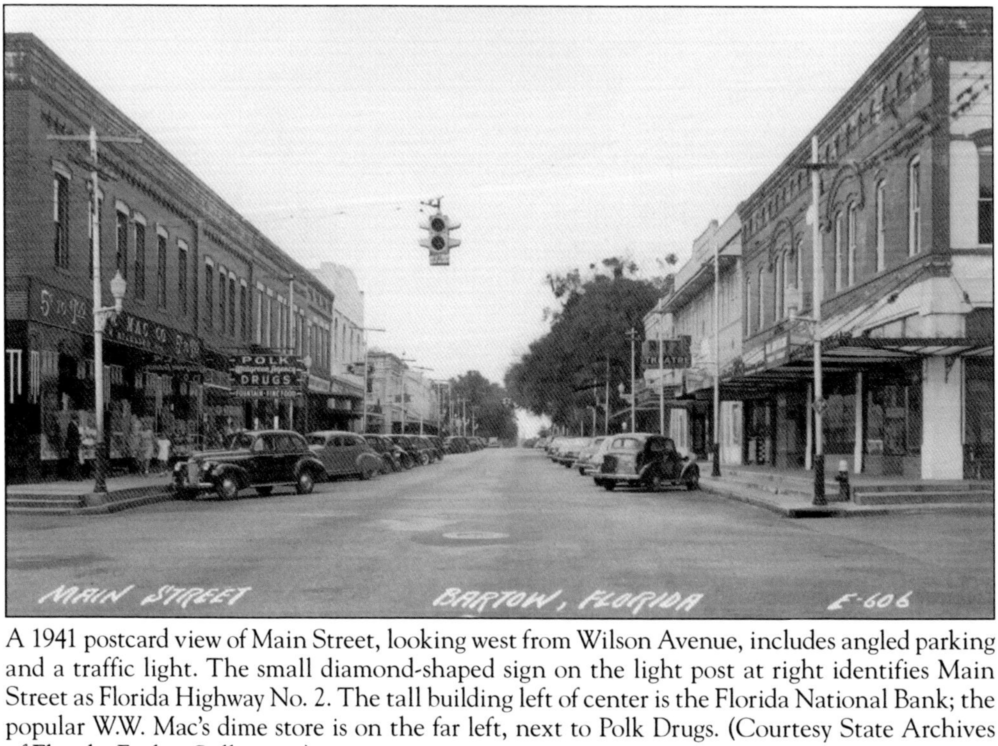

A 1941 postcard view of Main Street, looking west from Wilson Avenue, includes angled parking and a traffic light. The small diamond-shaped sign on the light post at right identifies Main Street as Florida Highway No. 2. The tall building left of center is the Florida National Bank; the popular W.W. Mac's dime store is on the far left, next to Polk Drugs. (Courtesy State Archives of Florida, Frisbie Collection.)

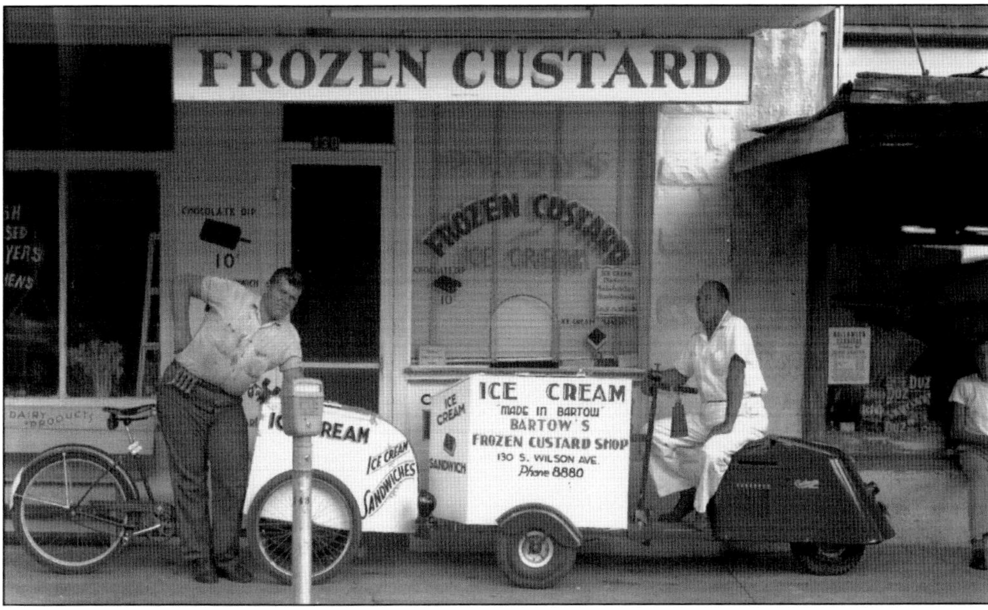

Two of Bartow's Frozen Custard ice cream carts and vendors are shown in this 1940s photograph. Five flavors—chocolate, vanilla, peach, strawberry, and cherry—were available by delivery or at a sidewalk window. Located at 130 South Wilson Avenue, the shop was sandwiched between Roberts Fish Market and Denham's grocery. A poster advertising the Crickette Club Halloween Carnival, which began in 1941, is displayed in the window to the right. (Courtesy State Archives of Florida, Frisbie Collection.)

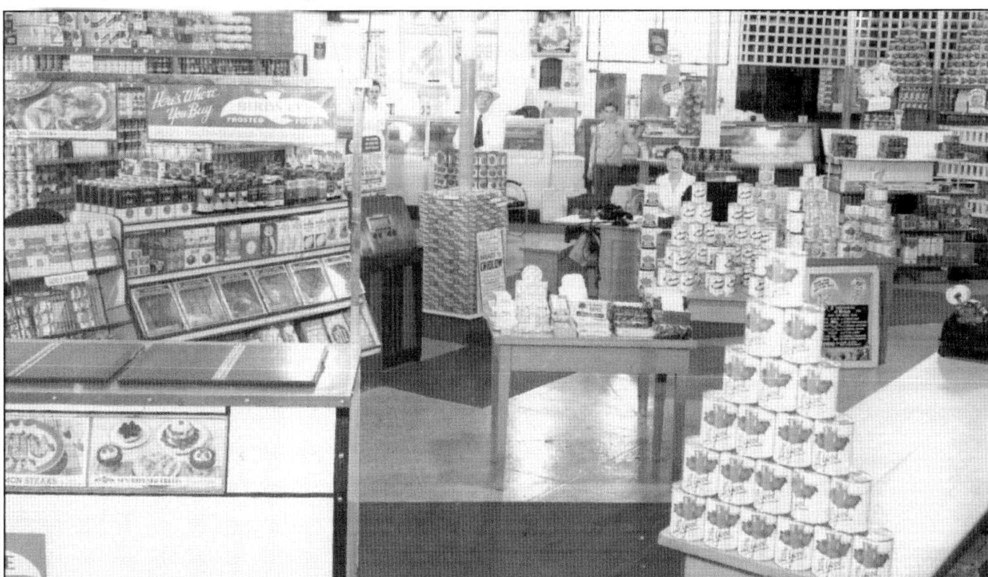

Hall's All American Grocery Store, seen here in the 1940s, presented a well-stocked, organized, clean, and modern shopping environment. One of 19 stores purchased by George Jenkins in 1945 to expand Publix Super Markets, it was located on the northeast corner of South Wilson Avenue and Summerlin Street. In 1945, Hall's was one of 26 grocery stores serving the community. (Courtesy State Archives of Florida, Frisbie Collection.)

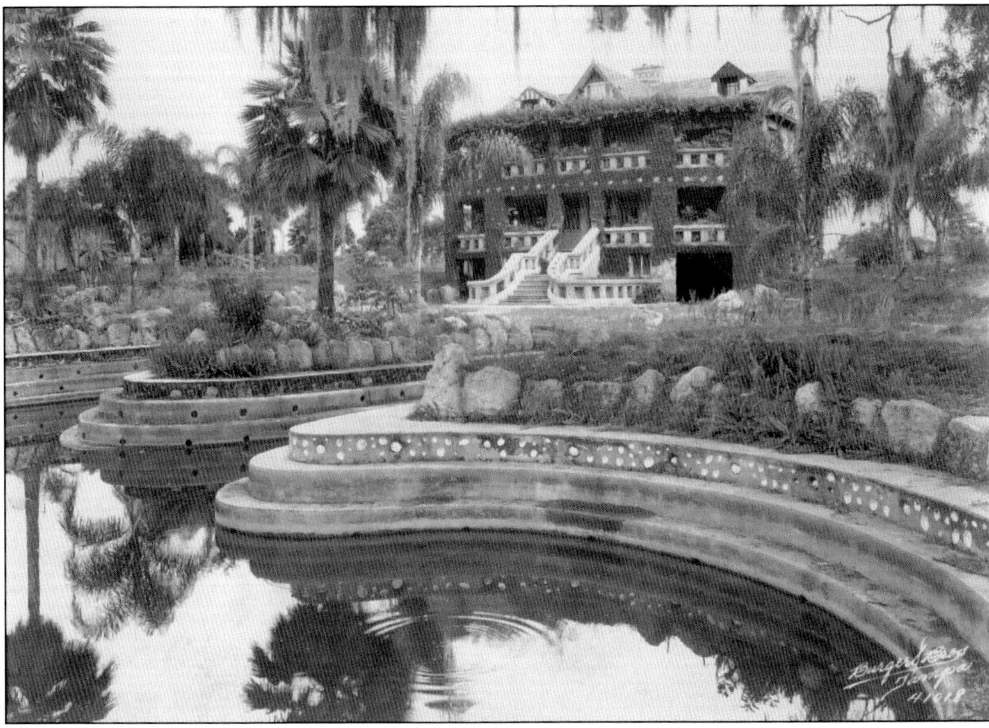

Conrad Schuck's Wonder House was built in 1926 and gained widespread attention in a *Ripley's Believe It or Not!* article. This 1940s view shows the three-story concrete mansion studded with tile work and surrounded by pools, bridges, and ornate gardens. Wondrous innovations included a rainwater cooling system, mirrored lights, and rotating closets. In 1934, the home was opened for tours, and it was an attraction through the 1960s. (Courtesy State Archives of Florida.)

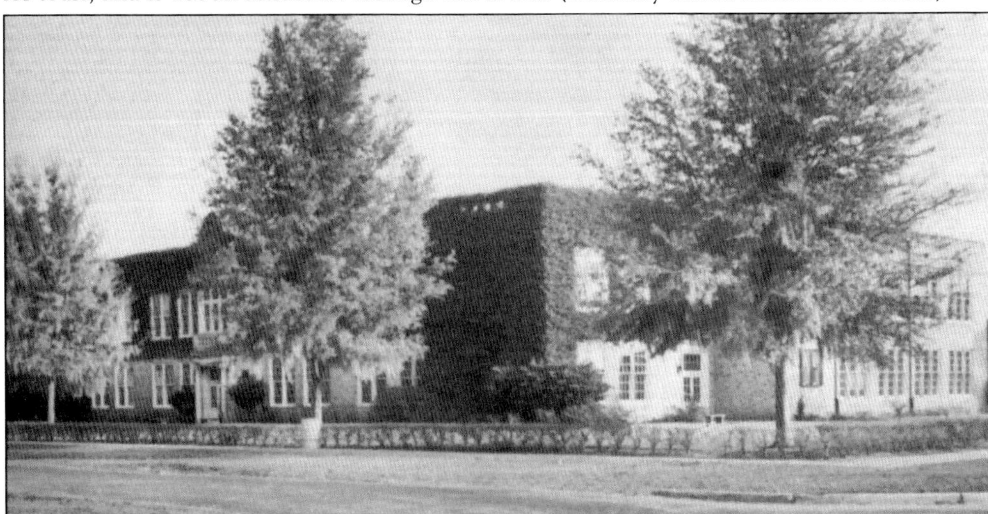

This 1940s photograph shows the ivy-covered Summerlin Institute, located on Tharp Street. It was Bartow's fourth high school building since 1887. Its unique Mediterranean Revival architectural style was popular during the 1920s. The school was built in 1929 and occupied the southern grounds of the former South Florida Military College, which closed in 1905. The name was changed to Bartow High School in 1971. (Courtesy Bartow High School collection.)

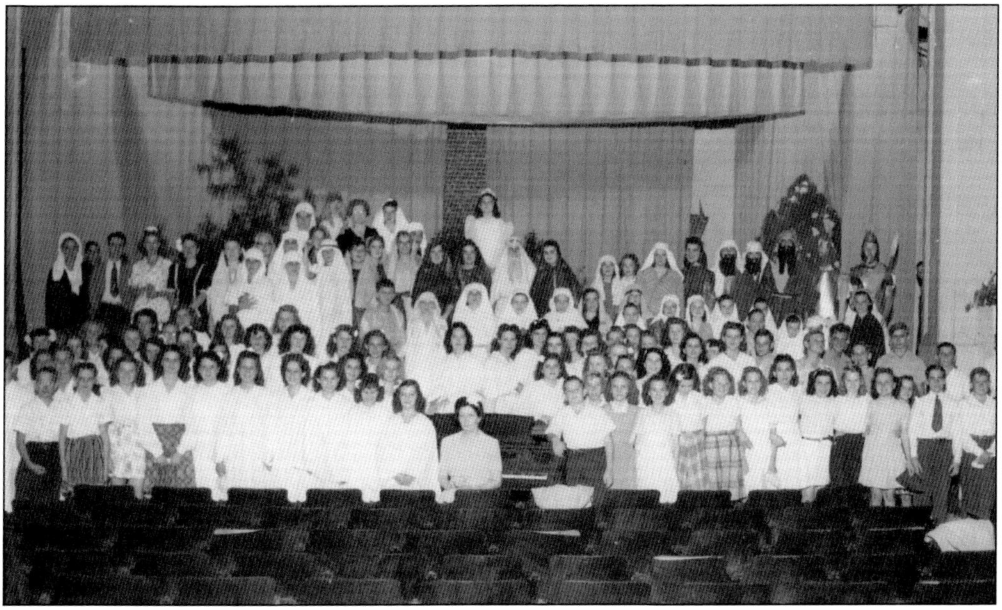

Margaret Clark, seated at the piano, filled the city auditorium with young singers and actors for a 1940s Christmas pageant. Clark was a 1916 graduate of Summerlin Institute and held degrees in music from Erskine College and from Florida Southern College. She was acclaimed for her productions of operettas and citywide musical programs. The Bartow High School auditorium bears her name. (Courtesy State Archives of Florida, Frisbie Collection.)

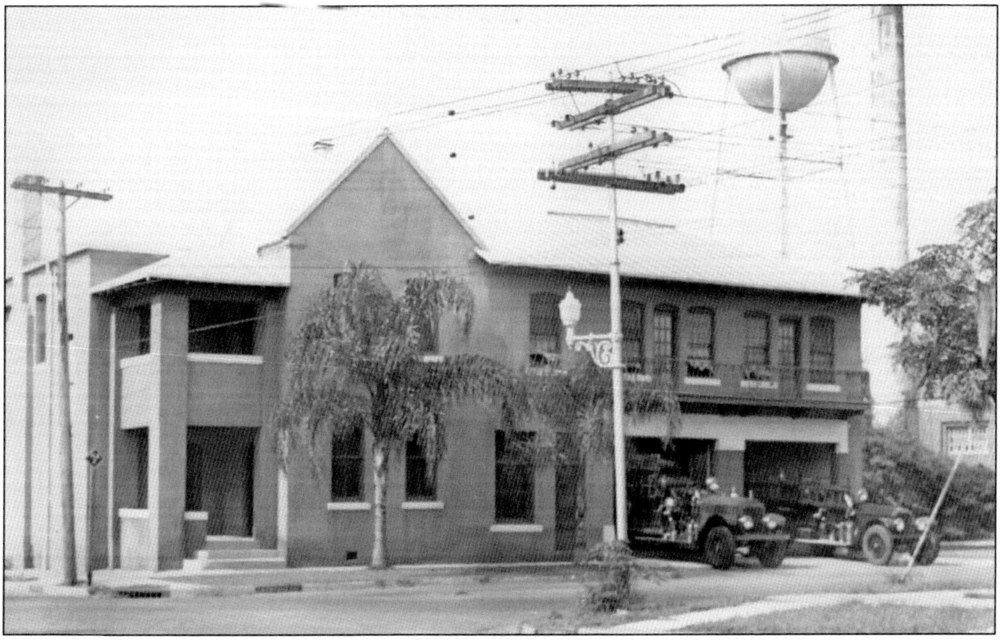

The fire department moved into its new station in 1914. Afterward, it was expanded and remodeled to include a stuccoed exterior. The second floor on the right consisted of a kitchen, meeting room, bedroom, and bath. An indoor swimming pool and gym were located to the left rear of the building for use of the volunteers. Broadway Avenue is marked on the curb in the foreground. (Courtesy State Archives of Florida, Frisbie Collection.)

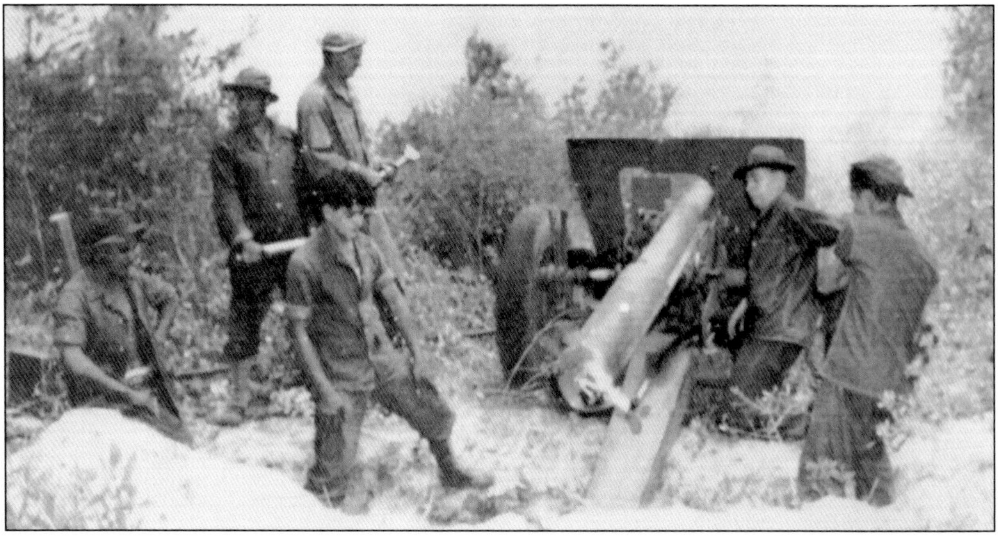

A Bartow gun crew fires a 75-millimeter cannon at Camp Blanding (named for Bartow's Gen. Albert H. Blanding) near Starke, Florida. The Bartow unit of the 116th Field Artillery, 31st Division was mobilized for active duty on November 25, 1940, a full year before America's entry into World War II. Its men would serve in the Pacific and European theaters to the end of the war. (Courtesy State Archives of Florida, Frisbie Collection.)

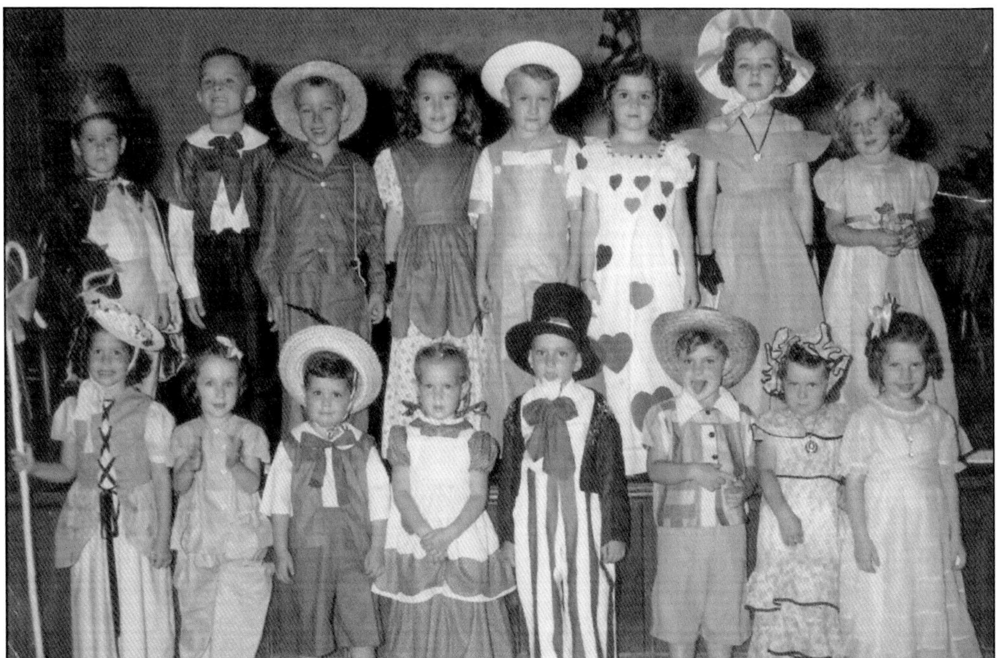

Martha Hunter's Mother Goose kindergarten presented a costumed play on May 28, 1942. *Uncle Sam's Helpers*, performed at the Civic Center, was highlighted by songs and the presentation of diplomas. Shown are, from left to right, (first row) Betty Gustafson, Carol Piowaty, Jay Hunter, Pat Mills, Joe Phillips, George Mann Jr., Carolyn Haas, and Charlene Overton; (second row) Lanier Pearce, Charles Hughes, Billy Stuart, Kay Brook, Joe Hamm, Lynda Belle Hunter, Lady Margaret Phillips, and Kay Jordan. (Courtesy Lynda Belle and David Black.)

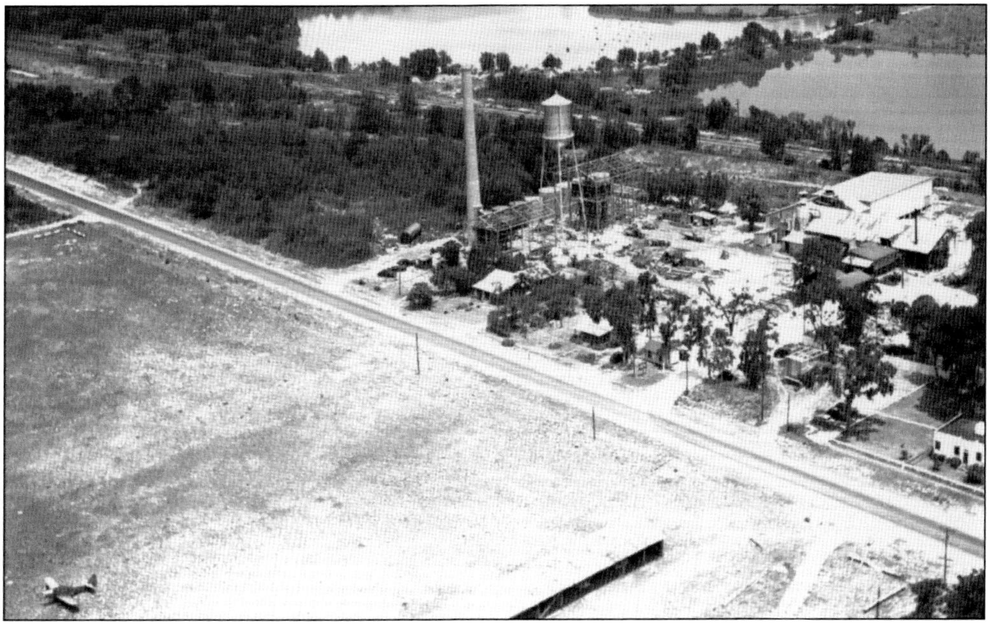

Armour Field, seen in this 1940s wartime photograph, was the city airport from 1931 to 1946 and was the site of horse races, cane grinding, circuses, and medicine shows. It was located on Highway 60 West, south of Hills Brothers Dromedary Foods (a war industry plant) and Kuder Citrus Feed Company, seen here under construction between the smokestack and water tower. Note the airplane and hangar. (Courtesy State Archives of Florida, Frisbie Collection.)

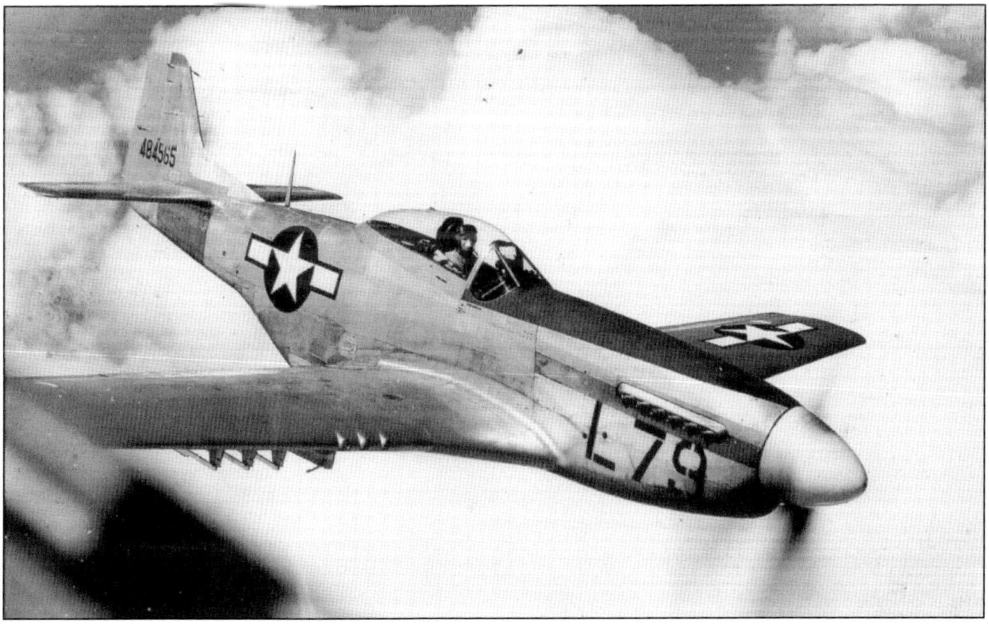

A P-51D Mustang flies over Bartow Army Airfield during World War II. The Third Air Force began training pilots at the airfield in 1942. Noteworthy fliers included Urban Drew (World War II) and James Jabara (Korean War), both of whom became aces. The field was deactivated in 1946 and turned over to the city. Bartow pilot-photographer Donald Robertson was the first civilian to land at the newly designated Bartow Airport. (Courtesy George McClelland.)

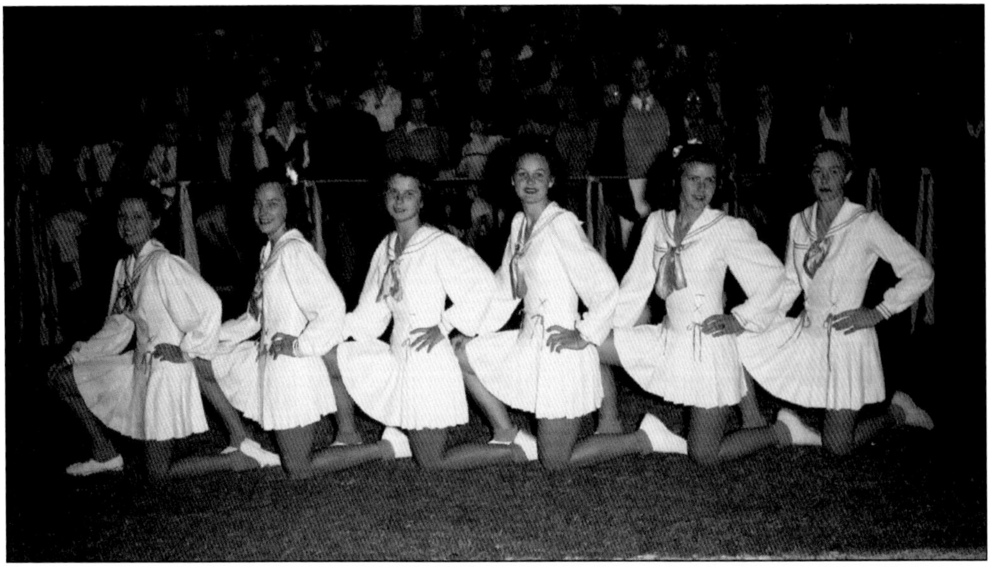

Summerlin cheerleaders pose on the field during a night game about 1944. Their uniforms present a "Cracker Jack" appearance, in keeping with wartime motif. Teen activities took place at the Nut Hut, located upstairs on the northwest corner of Main and Wilson Avenue, while the civic center was being used for USO functions. Many students served as young Aircraft Warning Service volunteers in the dome of the courthouse. (Courtesy State Archives of Florida, Frisbie Collection.)

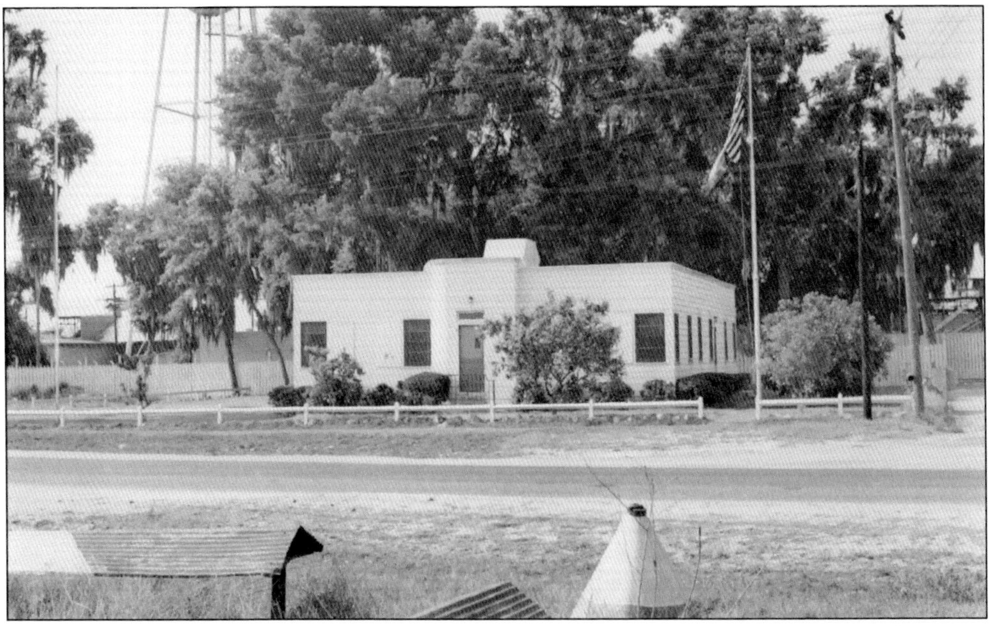

Hills Brothers Dromedary Foods, located west of Crown Avenue on present-day Highway 60, geared up for wartime industry production, canning foods incorporating citrus and fruit bases. Its exceptional production won the company the highly acclaimed Army Navy "E" flag for the processing plant and "E" pins for the employees. The red and blue flag for Defense Industry Excellence flies beneath the Stars and Stripes in this photograph. (Courtesy State Archives of Florida, Frisbie Collection.)

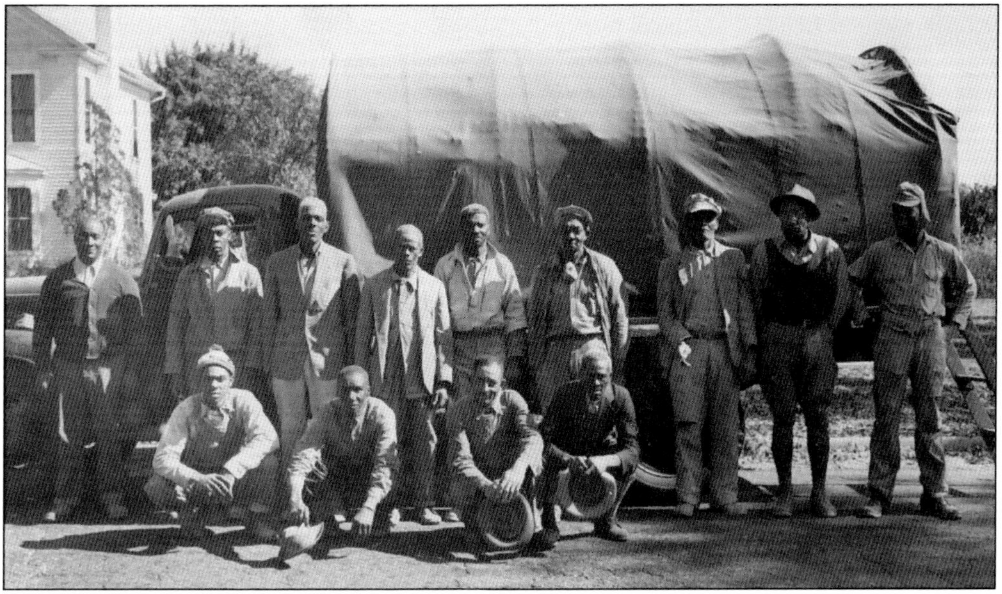

Hitching a ride was commonplace during World War II; gas rationing and shortages on the home front prompted Swift & Company to shuttle its workers. Swift operated a food-processing plant and phosphate mining operation in nearby Agricola. Employees in war industries also carpooled to the Tampa Shipbuilding Company in Tampa and the Food Machinery Corporation in Lakeland, building amphibious, tracked landing vehicles. (Courtesy State Archives of Florida, Frisbie Collection.)

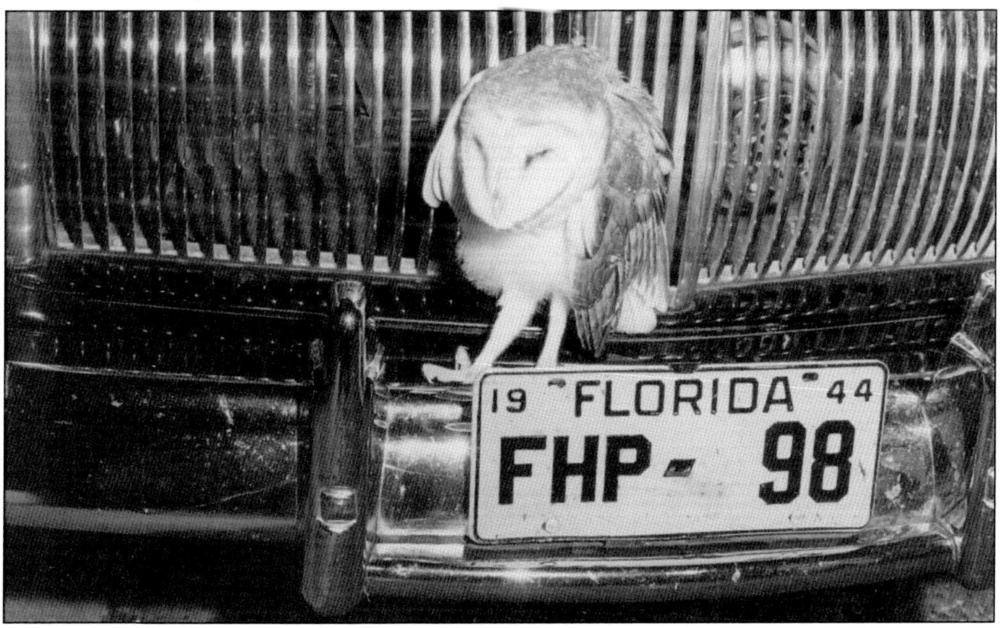

A May 1944 hitchhiker turned heads as highway patrolman C.W. Keith drove from Mulberry to Bartow before discovering he had a barn owl on the front bumper. The 1941 state legislature organized the Florida Highway Patrol and named Bartow its central district headquarters. Wartime highway patrol duties included assisting military police, escorting convoys, tracking prisoners of war, and patrolling beaches and highways. (Courtesy State Archives of Florida, Frisbie Collection.)

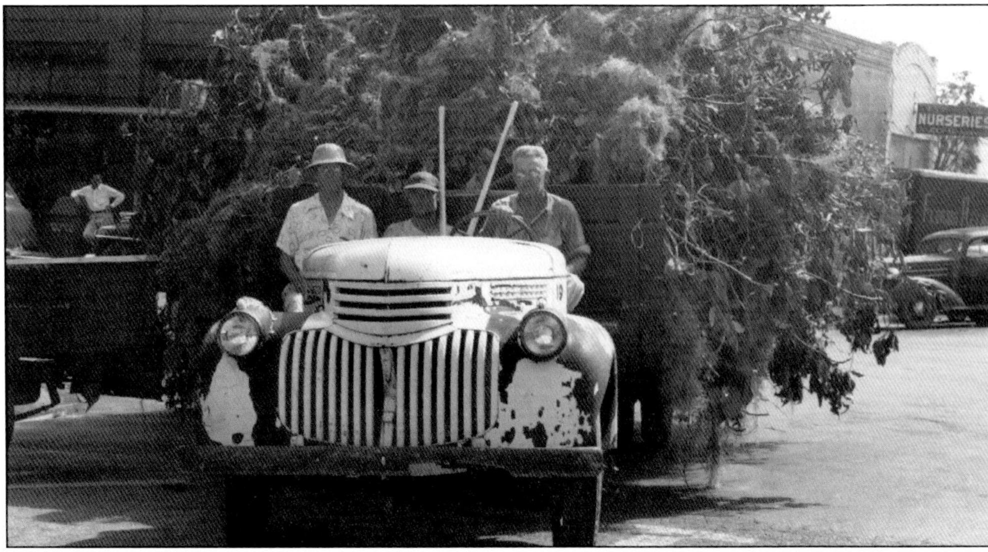

Barnell Stewart, longtime City of Bartow public works employee, drives a 1941 Chevrolet truck through the intersection of Central Avenue and Summerlin Street. The massive load is the result of the October 19, 1944, hurricane that swept through the city, felling uncounted oaks and other trees. German prisoners of war from the camp at Winter Haven assisted in the cleanup. (Courtesy Martha "Marcie" Stewart and the late Eugene Miller.)

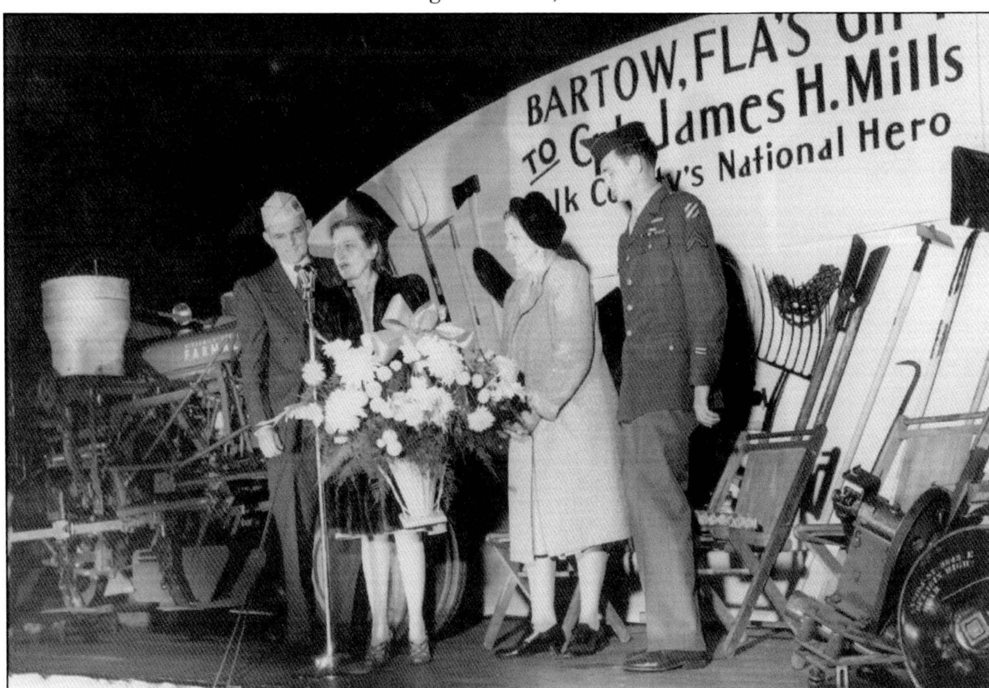

Bartow honors Cpl. James Henry Mills (right), a recipient of America's highest award for valor, the Medal of Honor, at a November 1944 football game. Gov. Spessard Holland (left) and his wife, Mary (at microphone), James's mother, Lessie Mills, and the city pay tribute to the shy hero. Bartow businessmen presented Mills with a truckload of farm equipment during the halftime celebration. (Courtesy State Archives of Florida, Frisbie Collection.)

Bartow's one-room police station, topped with a flagpole, was located north of Main Street at Central Avenue. Previously, a telephone bolted to an oak tree at this location served the three-man force. In the absence of a policeman, citizens answered calls and reported them to the fire department two blocks north. By the late 1940s, city police vacated the small Central Avenue office to share facilities with the fire department. This photograph is from 1946. (Courtesy State Archives of Florida, Frisbie Collection.)

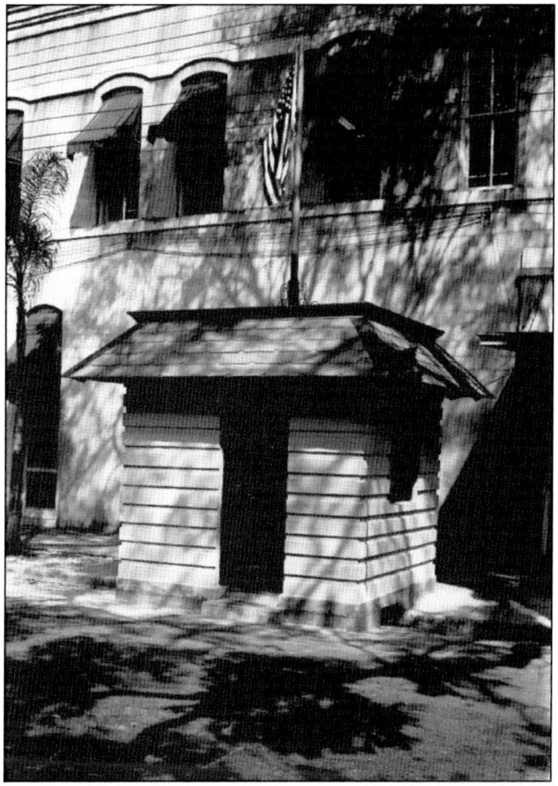

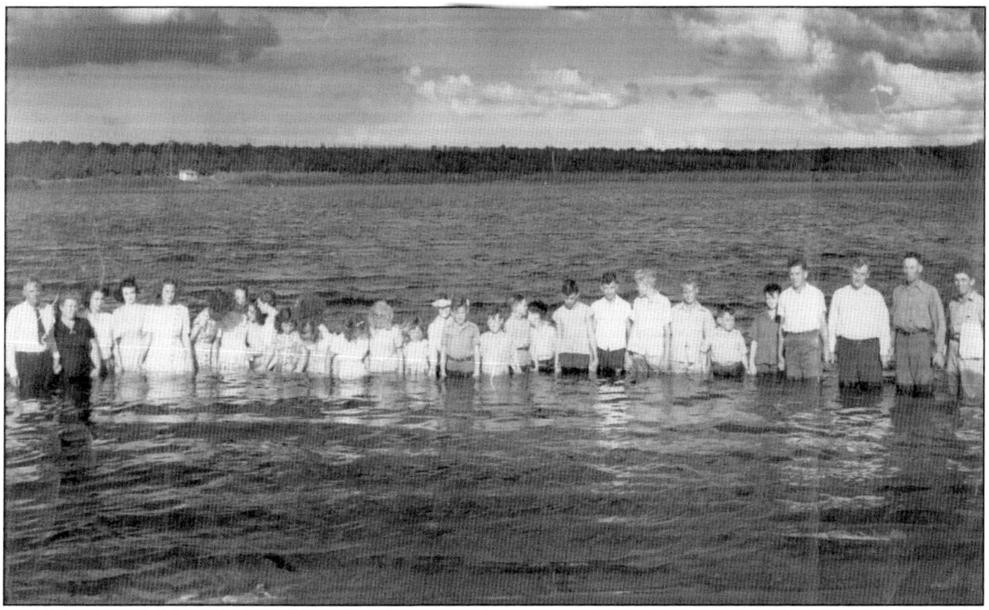

Flora Lake, south of Lake Garfield on Cox Road, was the site of this 1943 baptism by the Lake Garfield Baptist Church. Rev. Linton Mills, pastor, is seen to the left of the baptismal candidates. The traditional service was preceded by prayer and hymns. Many churches observing a tradition of baptism by immersion utilized nearby lakes for the sacrament, most notably Polk Lake and Eagle Lake. (Courtesy Shirley Padgett Johnson.)

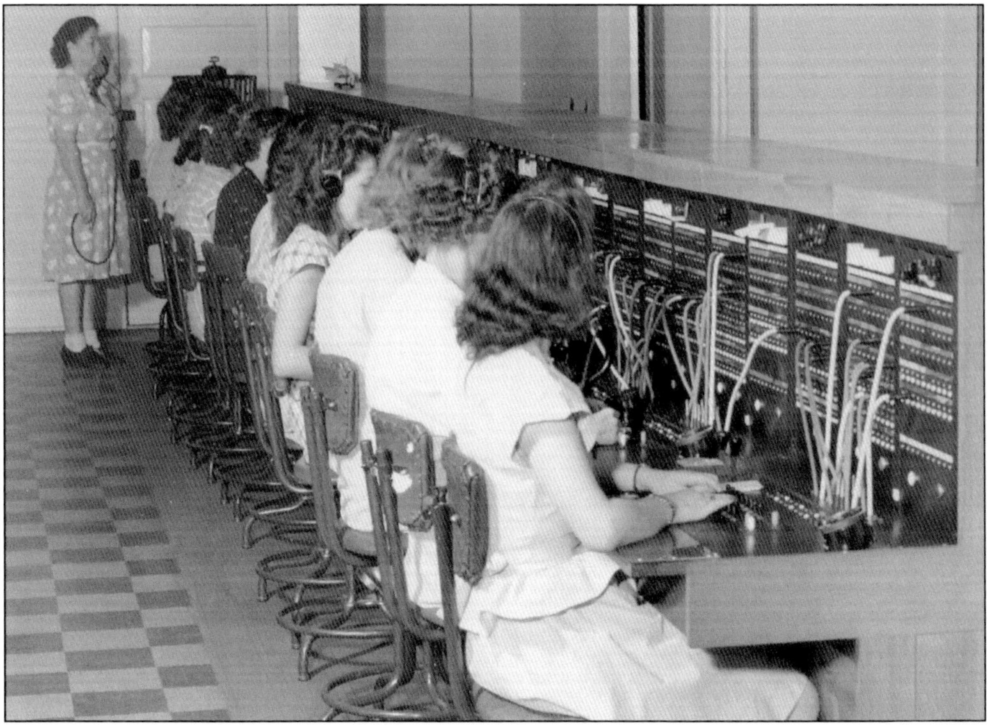

Peninsular Telephone operators in the 1940s keep the 10 switchboards at work, servicing approximately 2,000 rotary phones and multiple-access party lines. The fire and police department numbers were 333 and 666, respectively. Additional fees were charged for long-distance calls outside the city, and telephone guidelines requested a wait of 12 rings for completion of a call. Peninsular installed the first phone in Bartow in 1899. (Courtesy State Archives of Florida, Frisbie Collection.)

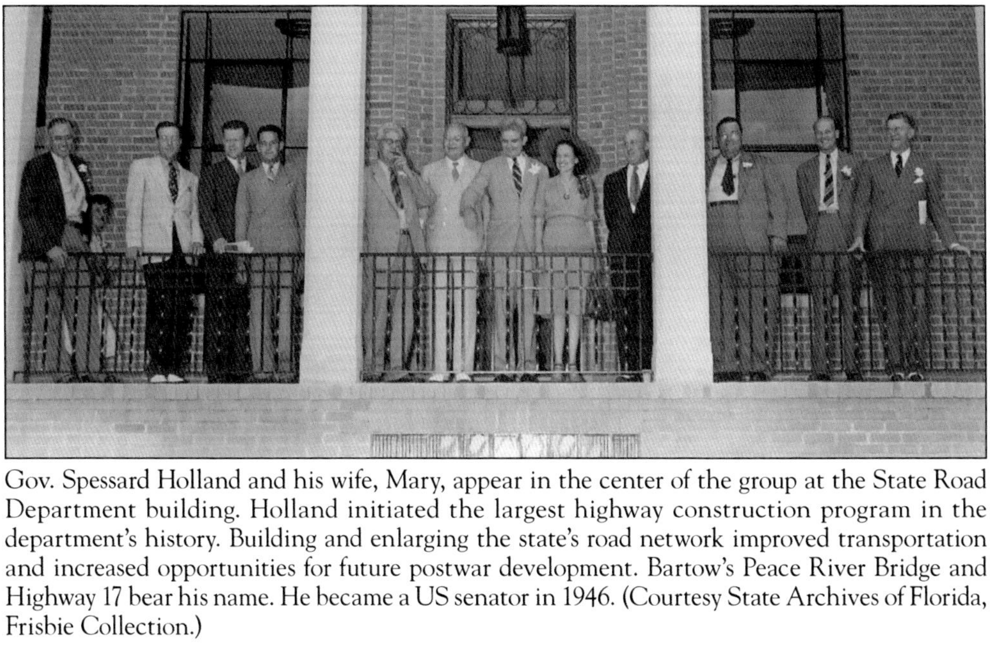

Gov. Spessard Holland and his wife, Mary, appear in the center of the group at the State Road Department building. Holland initiated the largest highway construction program in the department's history. Building and enlarging the state's road network improved transportation and increased opportunities for future postwar development. Bartow's Peace River Bridge and Highway 17 bear his name. He became a US senator in 1946. (Courtesy State Archives of Florida, Frisbie Collection.)

Lt. Gen. Albert Hazen Blanding, chief of the National Guard Bureau and military advisor to Governor Holland during World War II, served in the military for 41 years. He commanded Florida's troops on the Mexican border, the 53rd Infantry Brigade in World War I, and the 31st Division, bringing its headquarters to Bartow from 1933 to 1940. Camp Blanding, Florida, was named in his honor. (Courtesy State Archives of Florida.)

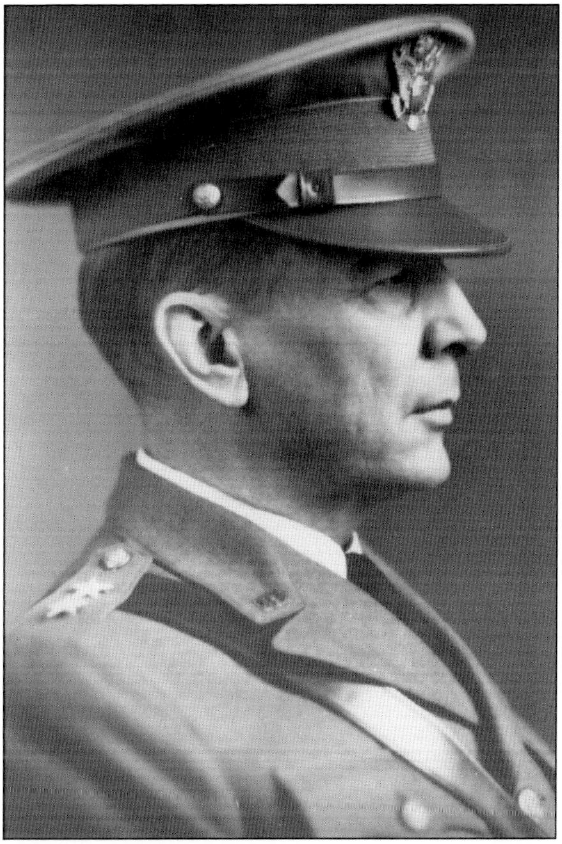

In this 1940s photograph, a worker affixes hooks to Eger baits at the manufacturing plant, located on the corner of US Highway 17 and Gibbons Street. William F. Eger's company manufactured lures from the early 1930s to 1960. Some lures were covered with actual frog skin harvested at Ballard's frog farm on West Pearl Street. The Dillinger was another famous Eger lure. (Courtesy State Archives of Florida, Frisbie Collection.)

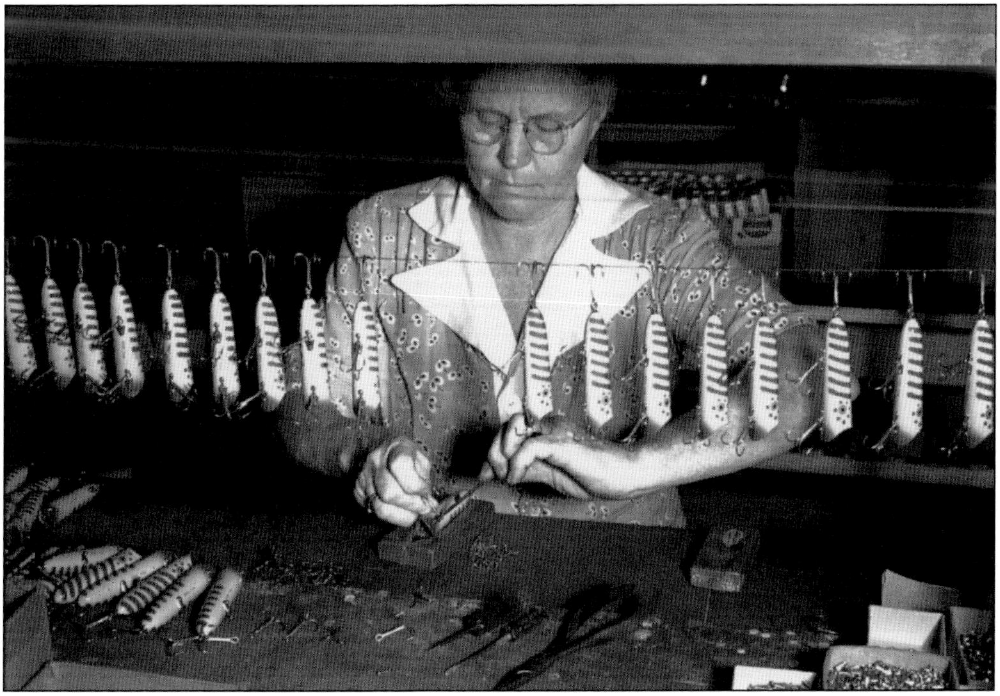

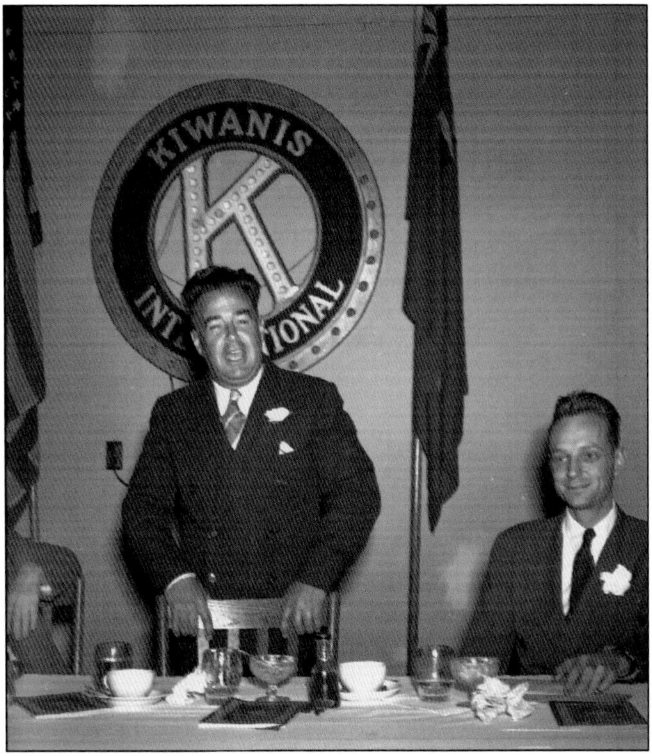

Cypress Gardens founder Dick Pope (left) was honored by the Kiwanis after his promotion of "Bartow Day" in 1944. Bartowans were admitted free, and 13 girls were trained and costumed as "Southern Belles." Water-skiing pageantry and the gardens ensured a great day for all. Leonard Blankner is seated at right. The Kiwanis Club was organized in 1922 and held meetings at the Masonic Temple until the new civic center was completed in 1967. (Courtesy State Archives of Florida, Frisbie Collection.)

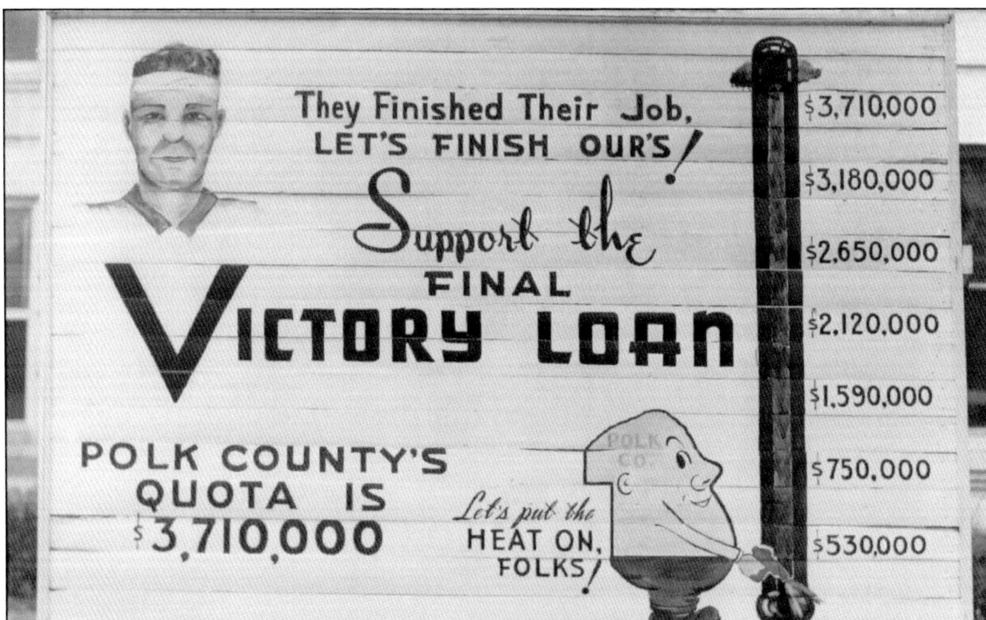

The Victory Loan signaled that the war had ended. Bartow and Polk County's support to offset the national war debt was achieved between October 29 and December 8, 1945. During the war, eight national loan drives were held, and the Victory Loan drive was the most successful. This sign at the courthouse proclaims the county's part in the drive. (Courtesy State Archives of Florida, Frisbie Collection.)

Eight

Moving Forward
1946–1976

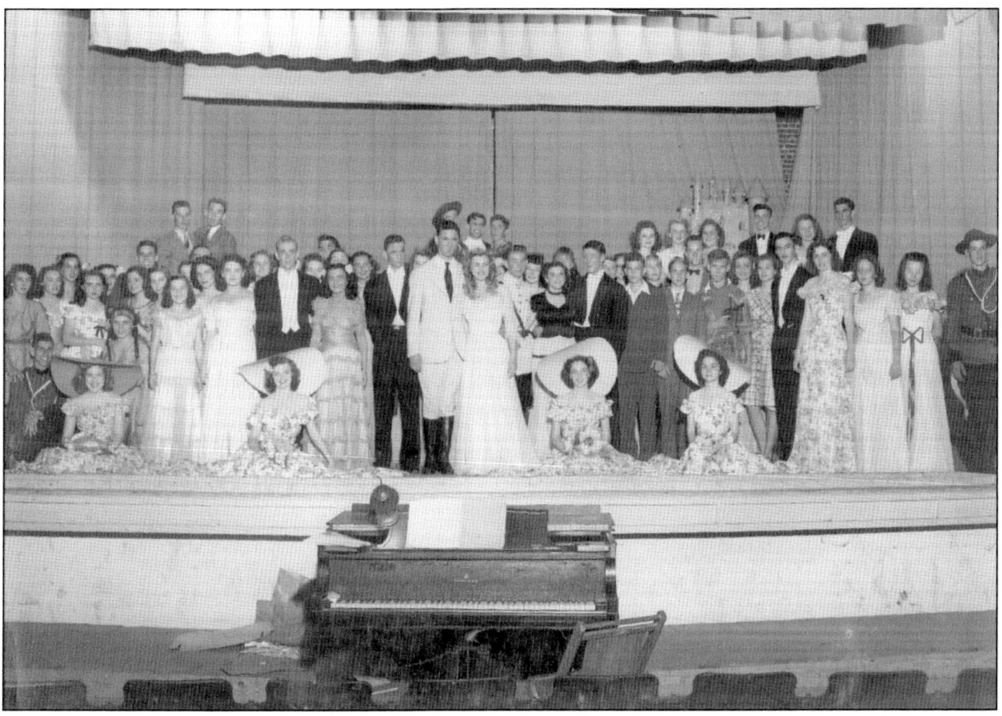

Margaret Clark's 1944 Summerlin Institute glee club poses at its performance of Victor Herbert's operetta *Sweethearts*. The operetta was the highlight of the year. At this performance, the lead roles were performed by Bill Jones and Jeanne Harris (center). Jones became a famous baritone for the Marines and performed for several presidents. The Southern belle kneeling on the right is Barbara Hunter. (Courtesy Barbara and Wallace Orr.)

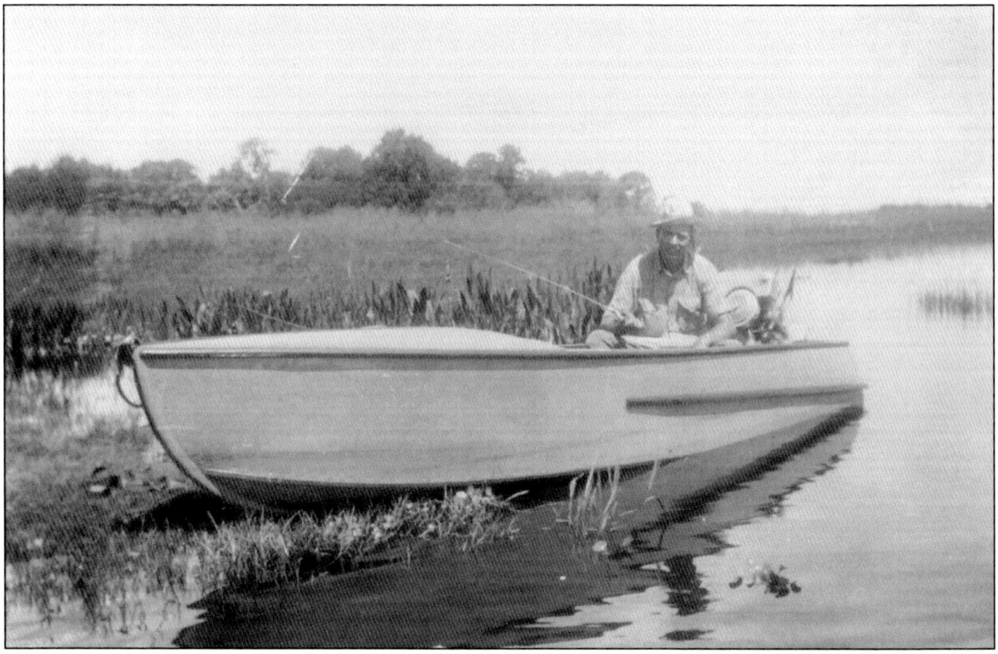

Elmer Wheeler fishes in a cedar boat built by his father, Marion W. Wheeler, owner of a boat and cabinet shop located on West Pearl Street. Kitchen cabinets, interior carpentry, and built-in furniture were specialties of the master carpenter. His large shop included a pond for forming wood planks. Boats were built to order, and his proficiency ranged from johnboats to runabouts. (Courtesy Marion E. Wheeler.)

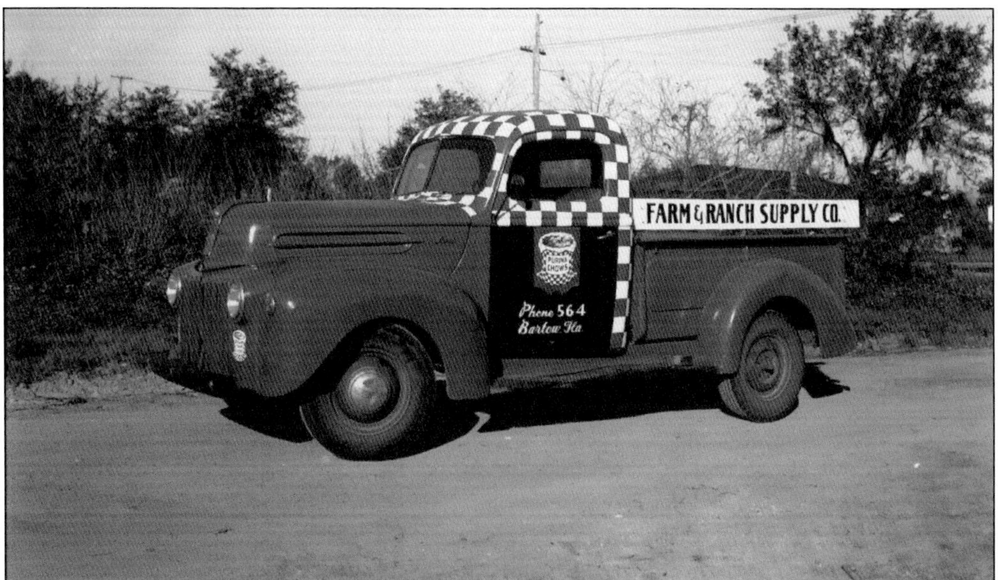

Grover C. Howell's Farm & Ranch Supply sports a new 1947 Ford delivery truck, painted in Purina's iconic checkerboard pattern. The new business, located on West Main Street, was indicative of the postwar economic boom. Farm & Ranch Supply provided garden and poultry supplies, animal feed, seeds, fertilizers, insecticides, and quality baby chicks to the agricultural community. (Courtesy State Archives of Florida, Frisbie Collection.)

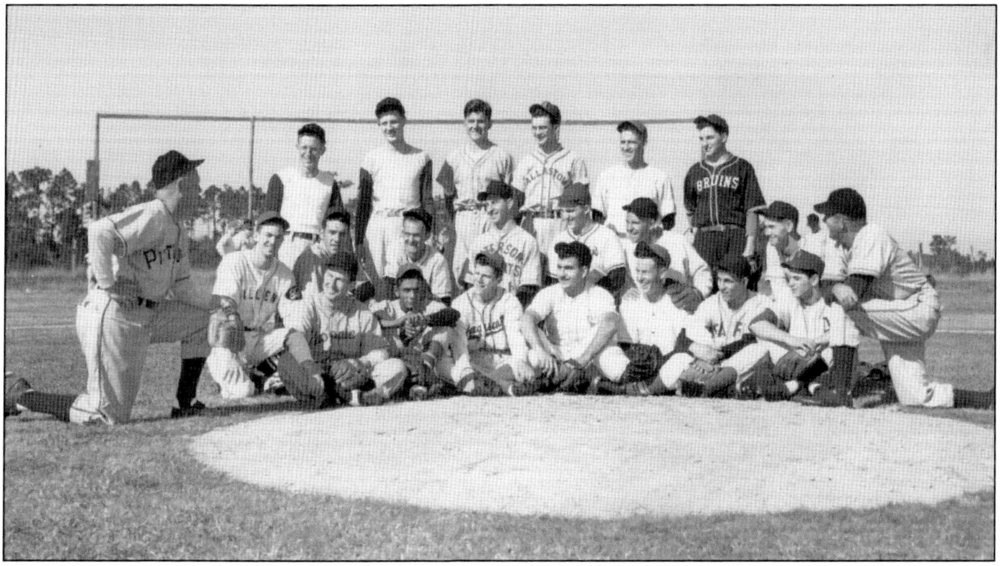

Pittsburgh Pirate "Rip" Sewell (far left) and Washington Senator Bill Phebus (far right) instruct students training at the Bartow Baseball School. Started by New York Yankee George Steinweiss and recreational director Bob Doty, the school fielded 144 major-league players in its first two years. Vacant facilities at the Bartow airfield provided a readymade campus from 1947 to 1949. Korean War reactivation of the airbase forced the school's closing. (*Sporting News* photograph, courtesy W.L. Harris collection.)

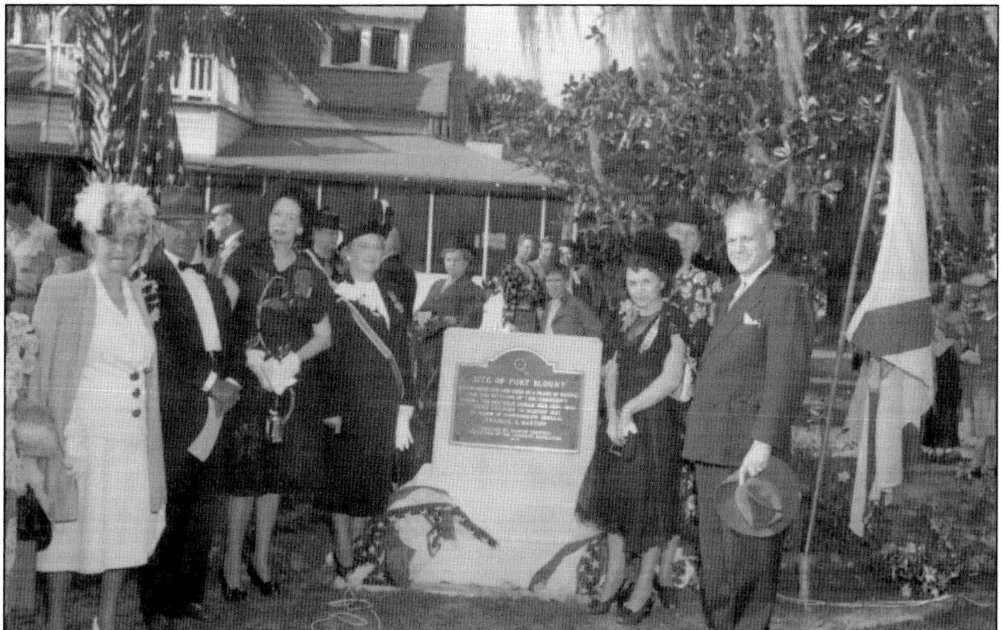

The site of Fort Blount was marked with a monument at the northwest corner of Floral Avenue and Main Street. The dedication ceremony, on February 20, 1948, was a project of the Bartow Chapter of the Daughters of the American Revolution. In 2001, the monument was moved a block east, incorporating it into the new Fort Blount Park. (Courtesy State Archives of Florida, Frisbie Collection.)

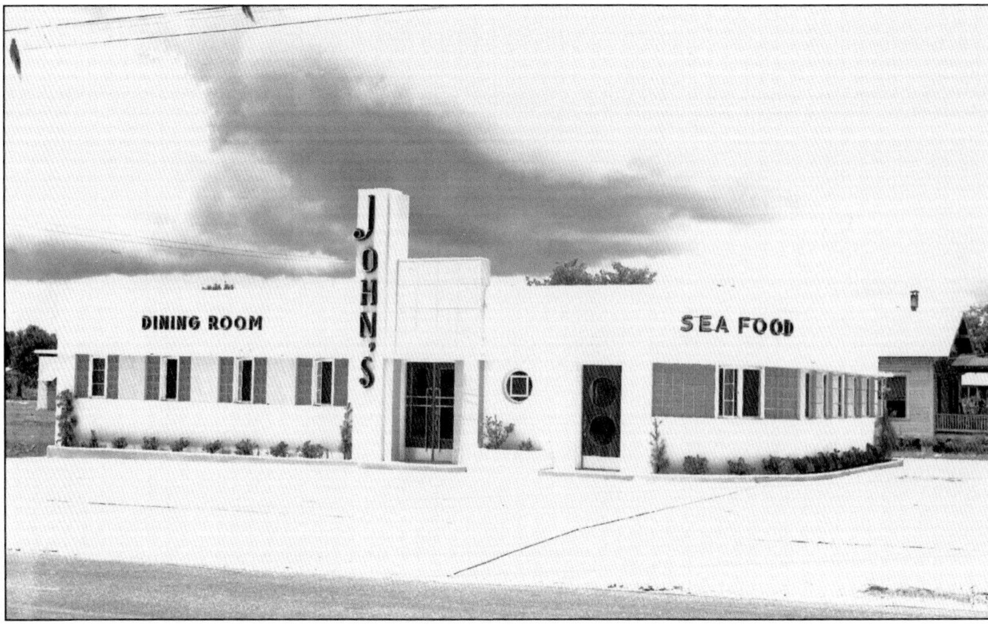

For decades, John's Restaurant, seen here in the 1940s, served "fine food" at the southwest corner of US Highway 17 and Main Street. John Pittas opened his first restaurant in 1926. His brother George Pittas was involved in the family business as well and is honored as the founder of the Little League and Dixie Youth baseball program in the city. (Courtesy State Archives of Florida, Frisbie Collection.)

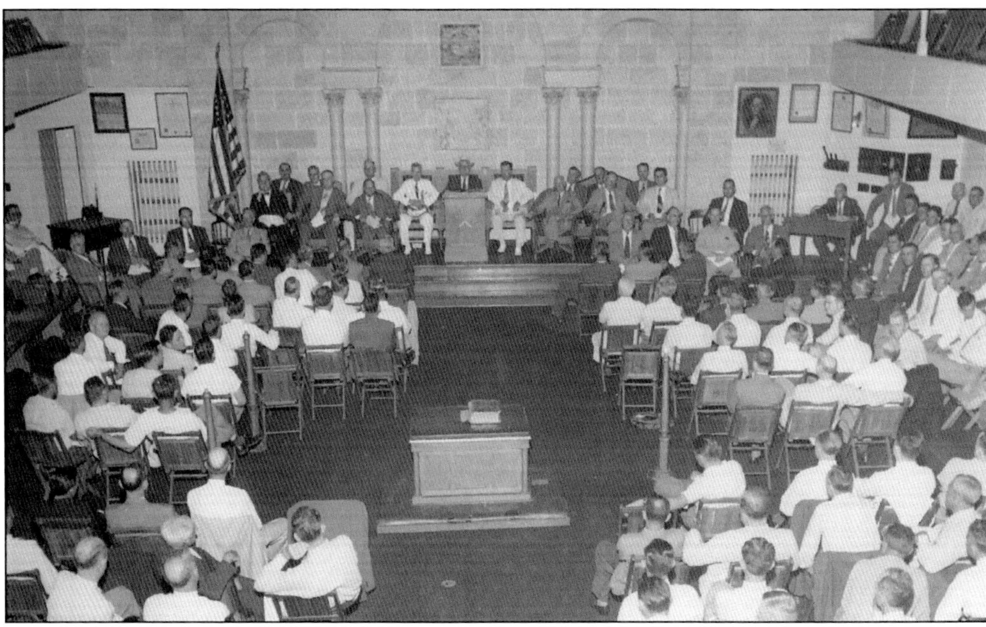

Shown here is a gathering of the Grand Lodge of Florida at Bartow's Masonic Temple in the 1940s. Two Bartowans previously served as Grand Master of Florida, and Gov. Spessard Holland was a member of Tuscan Lodge. The square cenotaph, above the rostrum between the columns, is a memorial to Dr. 1st Lt. Knowles G. Oglesby, the first Bartow combat casualty of World War I. (Courtesy State Archives of Florida, Frisbie Collection.)

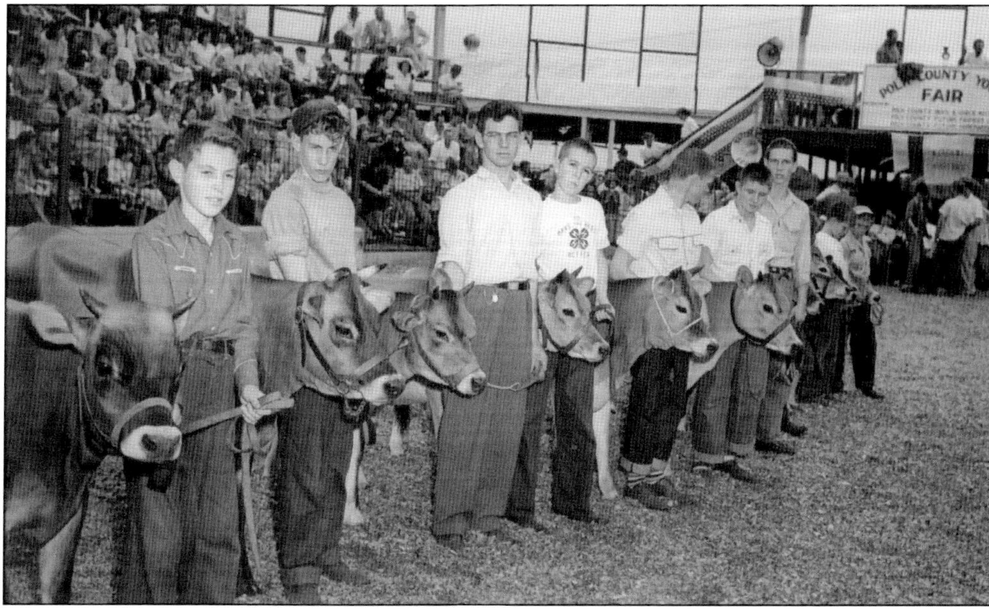

Several students exhibit calves at the 1948 Polk County Youth Fair. The event was envisioned by agriculture teacher Grover C. Howell and sparked the Rotary Club's sponsorship of the creation of the Polk County Youth Fair Association. Achievements of agricultural students, Future Farmers of America, and 4-H Clubs are showcased annually. The fair was first held at the armory in 1947 and subsequently at the agricultural pavilion on south US Highway 17. (Courtesy State Archives of Florida, Frisbie Collection.)

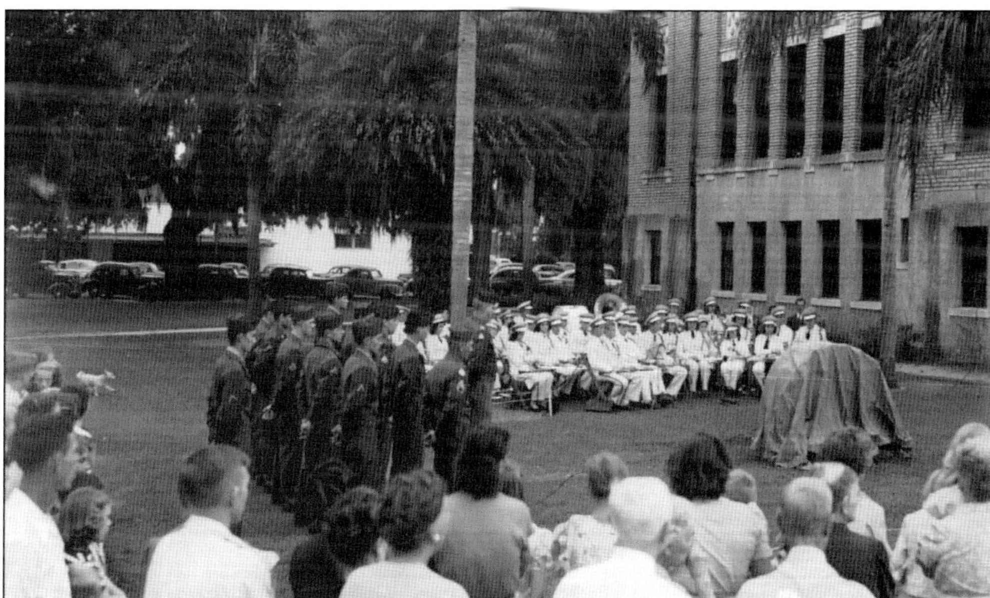

Sen. Spessard Holland was the keynote speaker at the 1948 dedication of the Veterans Monument, located between the post office and city hall. Citizens, National Guardsmen, veterans, a band, civic leaders, clergy, and a dog paid tribute to veterans of World Wars I and II. When the post office expanded south, the marker was moved and updated to include the Korean and Vietnam Wars. (Courtesy State Archives of Florida, Frisbie Collection.)

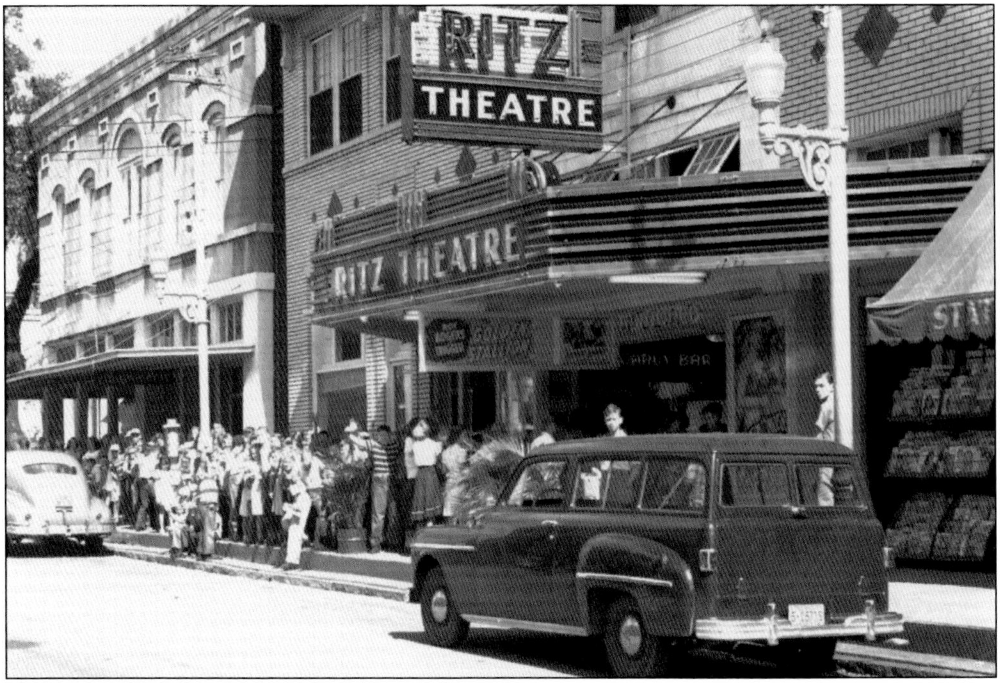

This photograph shows young people in line to see Roy Rogers and Trigger in *The Golden Stallion* at the Ritz Theatre. The cinema held Saturday matinees in the summer for the youth of Bartow. Admission was six Royal Crown Cola bottle caps, which provided entertainment and air-conditioning. The Ritz opened in the 1930s and closed on December 13, 1965. (Courtesy State Archives of Florida, Frisbie Collection.)

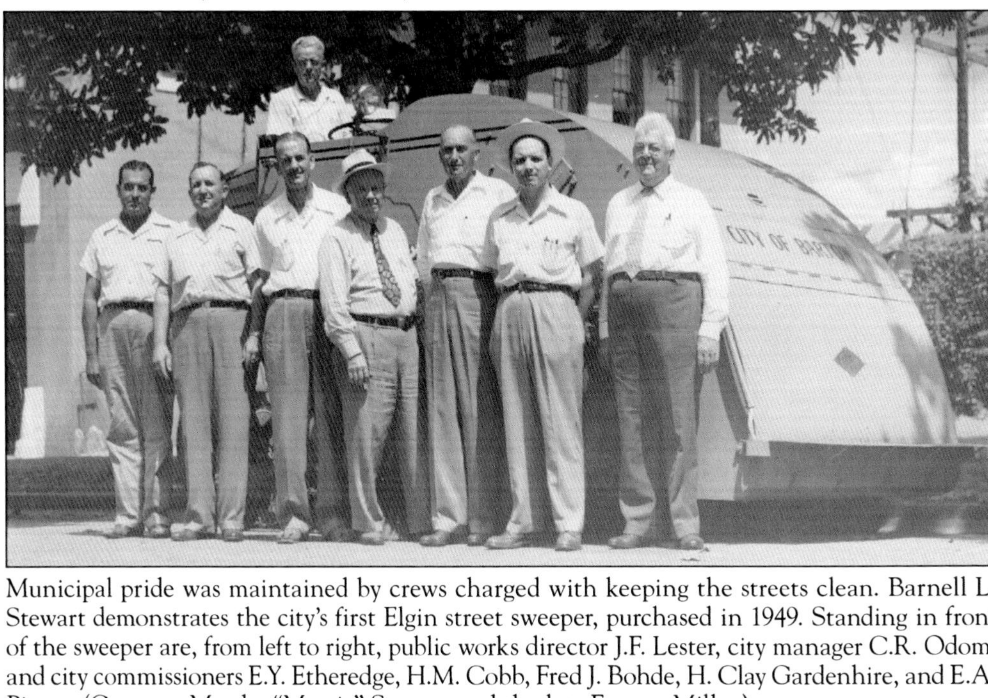

Municipal pride was maintained by crews charged with keeping the streets clean. Barnell L. Stewart demonstrates the city's first Elgin street sweeper, purchased in 1949. Standing in front of the sweeper are, from left to right, public works director J.F. Lester, city manager C.R. Odom, and city commissioners E.Y. Etheredge, H.M. Cobb, Fred J. Bohde, H. Clay Gardenhire, and E.A. Pierce. (Courtesy Martha "Marcie" Stewart and the late Eugene Miller.)

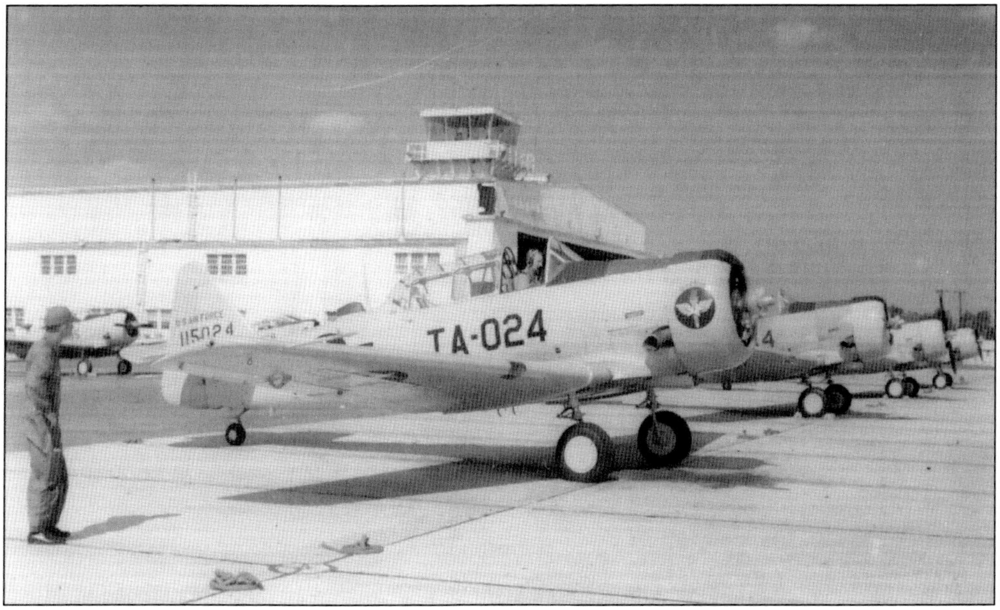

A T-6 Texan, a single-engine advanced trainer aircraft, is on line in front of the tower at Bartow Air Base. The World War II Army airfield was reactivated in 1950 by the Air Force as Bartow Air Base to train pilots for the Korean War. The base remained active for a decade and trained future astronauts Buzz Aldrin, Edward White II, and Karol Bobko. (Courtesy State Archives of Florida, Frisbie Collection.)

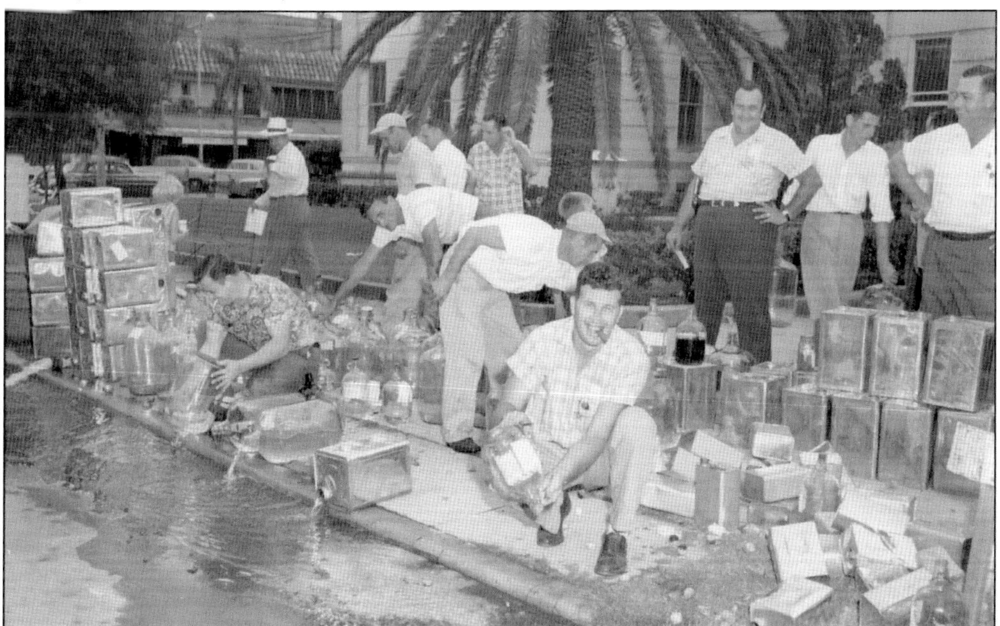

Dep. Sheriff George Gurley (wearing pistol) monitors the dispensing of spirits at the courthouse. Over 500 gallons of moonshine confiscated in a raid west of Bartow provided this publicity photograph. Before 1963, the sale of alcoholic beverages was illegal in Polk County. Bootleggers found a ready source of profit in neighboring counties, and local distilling of liquor strained law enforcement assets. (Courtesy State Archives of Florida, Frisbie Collection.)

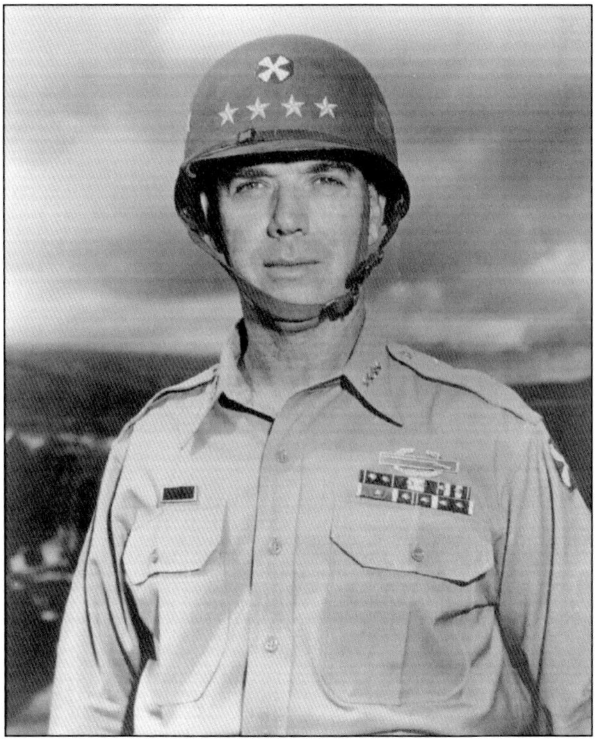

James A. Van Fleet is shown wearing his fourth star after promotion to general and overall commander of UN forces in Korea. He left Bartow in 1911 for the US Military Academy and graduated in the West Point class of 1915—"the class the stars fell on." Van Fleet served his nation for more than four decades and retired in 1953 to pursue ranching and business interests. He died in 1992, shortly after reaching his 100th birthday. Van Fleet Drive is named in his honor. (Courtesy US Army.)

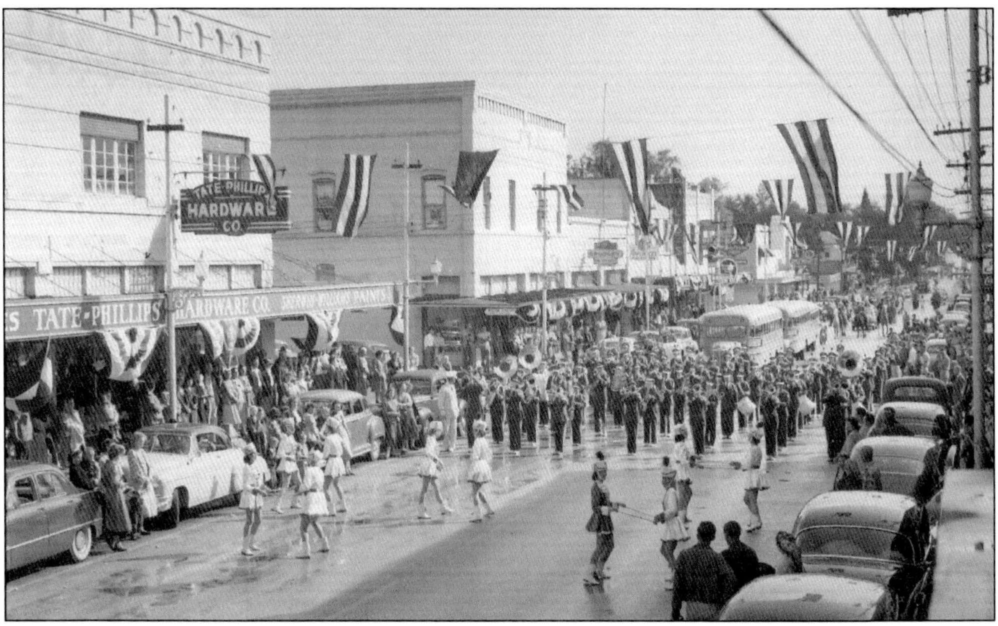

February 1951 witnessed Bartow's centennial celebration of the pioneer Blount party's arrival, which established the community. A weeklong observance was abbreviated to one day due to Korean War austerity. The event was highlighted by a grand parade with contingents and bands from neighboring towns, free barbecue, and a speech by "favorite son" Sen. Spessard Holland. Seen here on Main Street, the parade is in full progress. (Courtesy State Archives of Florida, Frisbie Collection.)

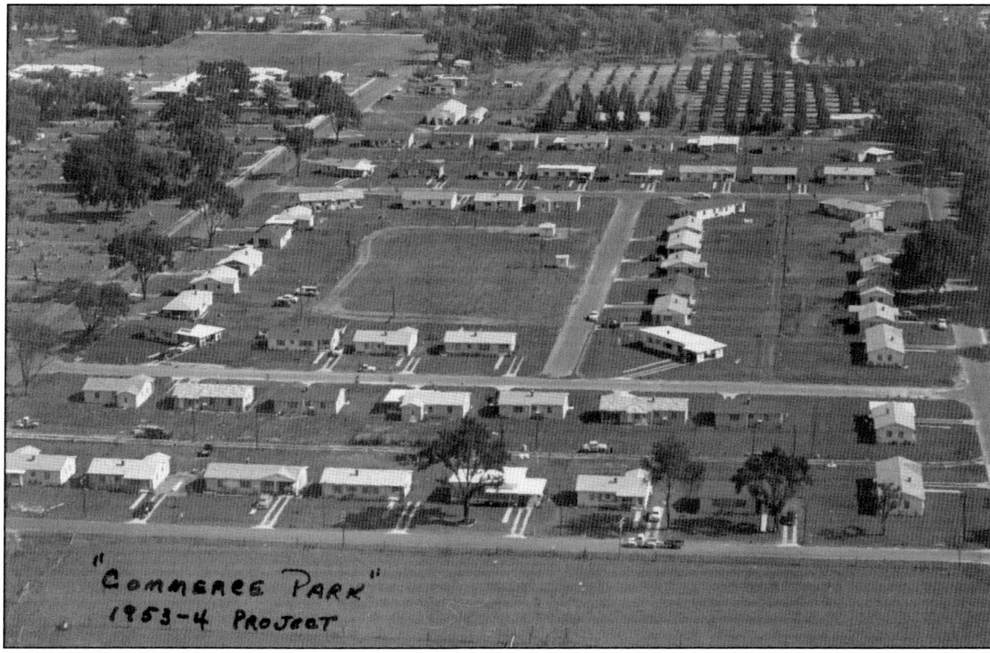

In the postwar boom, the town saw the creation of many subdivisions. Commerce Park south of Wildwood Cemetery, seen here in the early 1950s, was one of the first. The chamber of commerce encouraged the development, hence the name. Wildwood Baptist Church's first sanctuary can be seen to the left of the orange grove. (Courtesy State Archives of Florida, Frisbie Collection.)

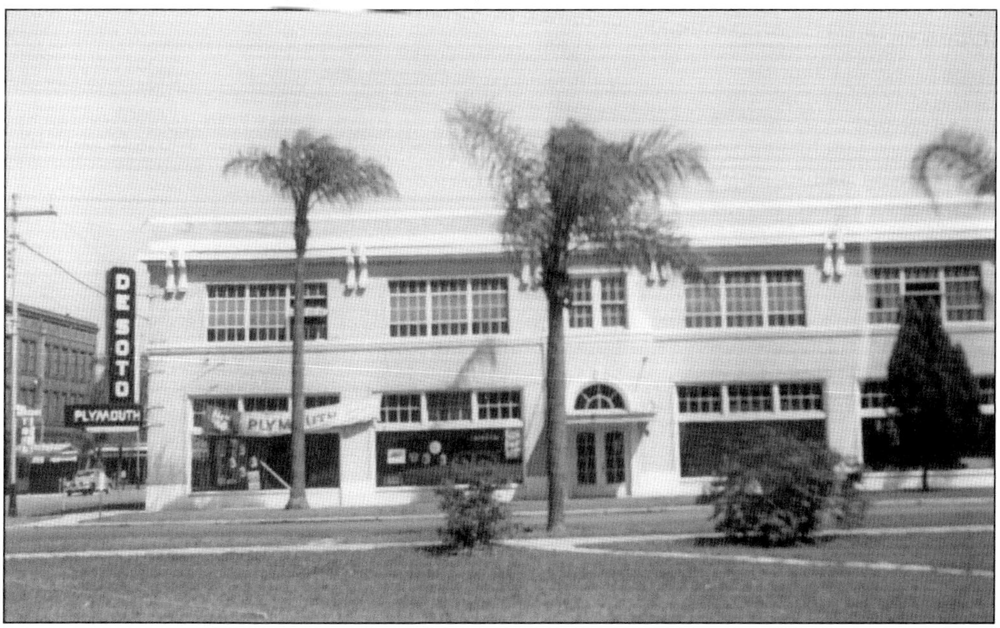

Gentry Brothers DeSoto and Plymouth automobile sales, on the corner of Summerlin Street and Broadway Avenue, advertises the new 1956 Plymouth. The building, of yellow brick with white facings, today houses the supervisor of elections offices. Shawnee brick was the signature of 1920s buildings by businessman Hugh Wear. The Toy Terminal can be seen at the far left. (Courtesy State Archives of Florida, Frisbie Collection.)

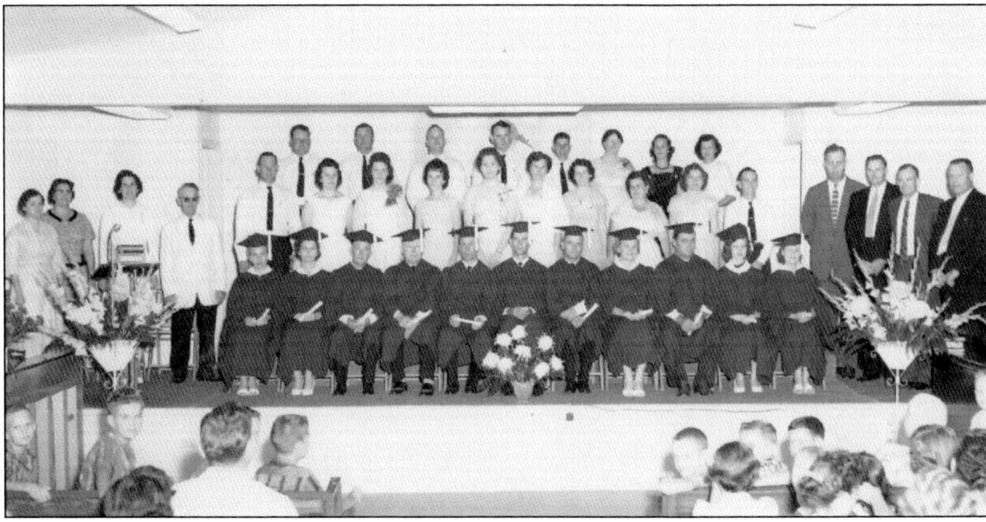

Inaugurated in 1956, the Bartow Bible Institute was founded in association with an evangelical apostolic denomination and existed through 1961. The school was located on the campus of Victory Tabernacle. Completion of the three-year course of study was marked by a graduation ceremony in which diplomas and certificates of ordination were presented. The class of 1959 consisted of 11 graduates. Underclassmen stand to the rear, surrounded by the faculty. (Courtesy W.L. Harris collection.)

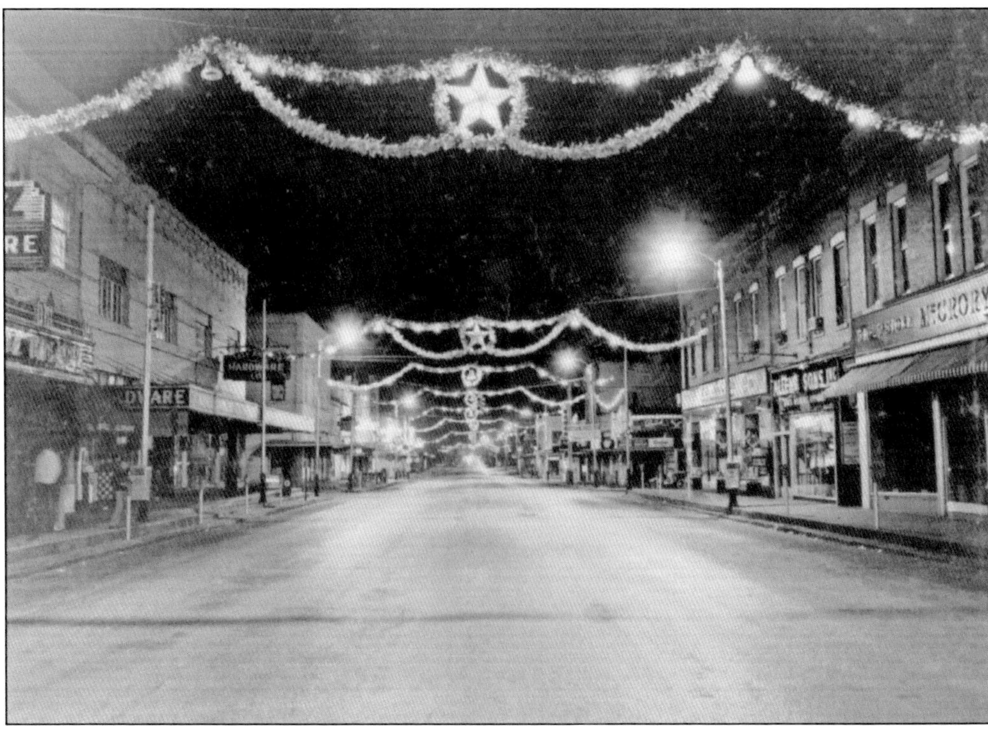

Main Street is fully decorated for Christmas in the early 1960s. This photograph was taken at night, when the thoroughfare was devoid of traffic. At left, moviegoers appear in front of the Ritz Theatre. For many years, the heavy silver garlands, red bells, and glittering lights suspended over the streets commemorated the holiday season. (Courtesy State Archives of Florida, Frisbie Collection.)

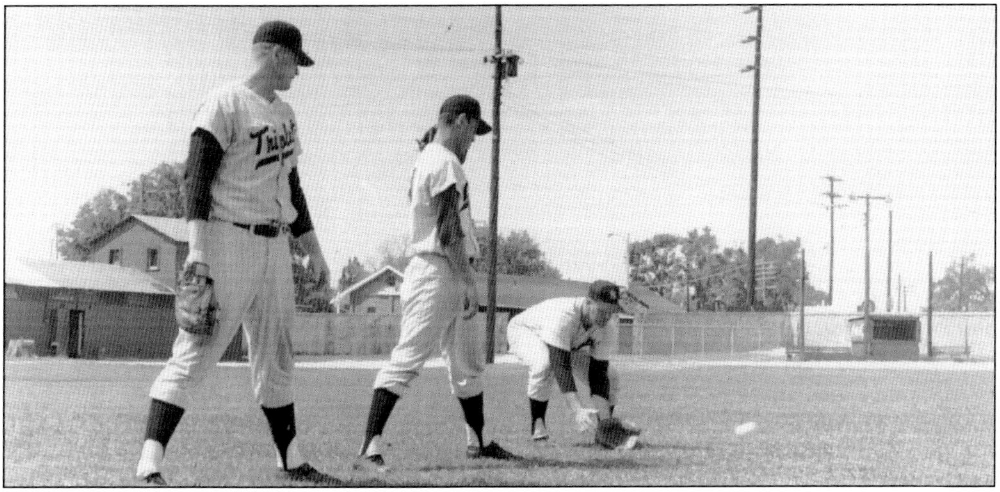

Three players of the Binghamton Triplets, a minor-league affiliate of the New York Yankees, hone their skills at Bartow Athletic Field. Bartow hosted minor-league teams from 1919 through the early 1960s, including the Bartow Polkers, Buffalo Bisons, Denver Bears, and Indianapolis Indians. In addition, the Polk County All Stars, a Negro League team owned and managed by Bartow's Benjamin Williams, played there. (Courtesy State Archives of Florida, Frisbie Collection.)

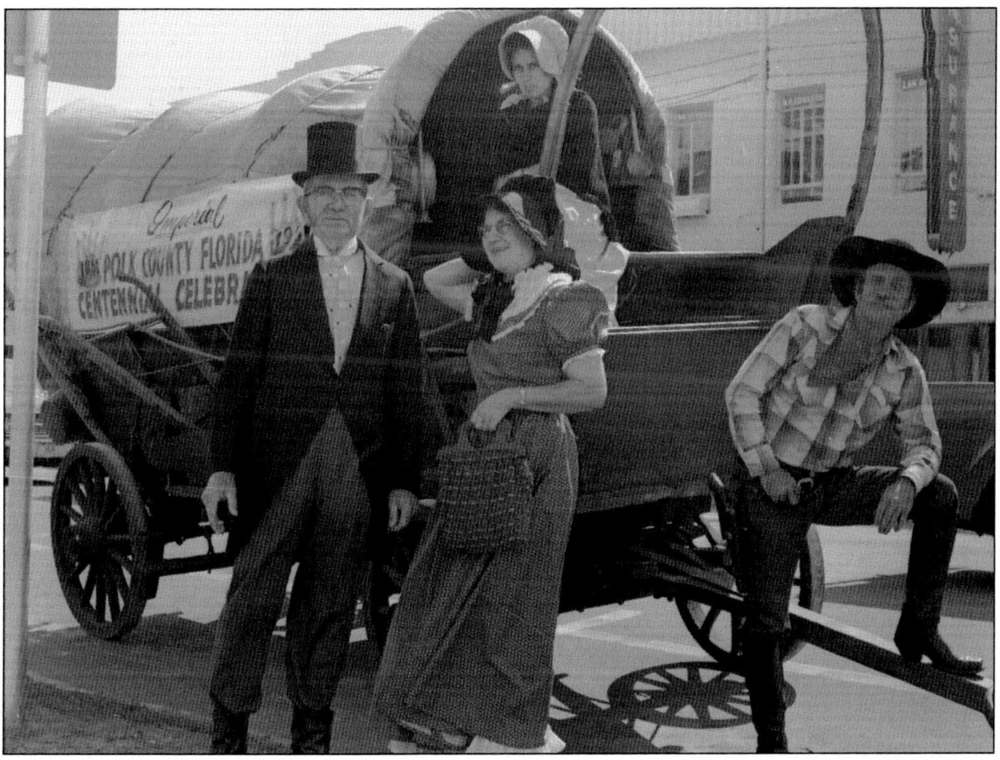

Bartow was the kickoff site of the yearlong celebration of the Polk County Centennial in 1961. The covered wagon carries the banner "Imperial Polk County Florida Centennial Celebration 1861–1961," marking it as the official parade vehicle for the Polk County Historical Commission. The Gibson Insurance sign to the right was Bartow's first neon sign. (Courtesy State Archives of Florida, Frisbie Collection.)

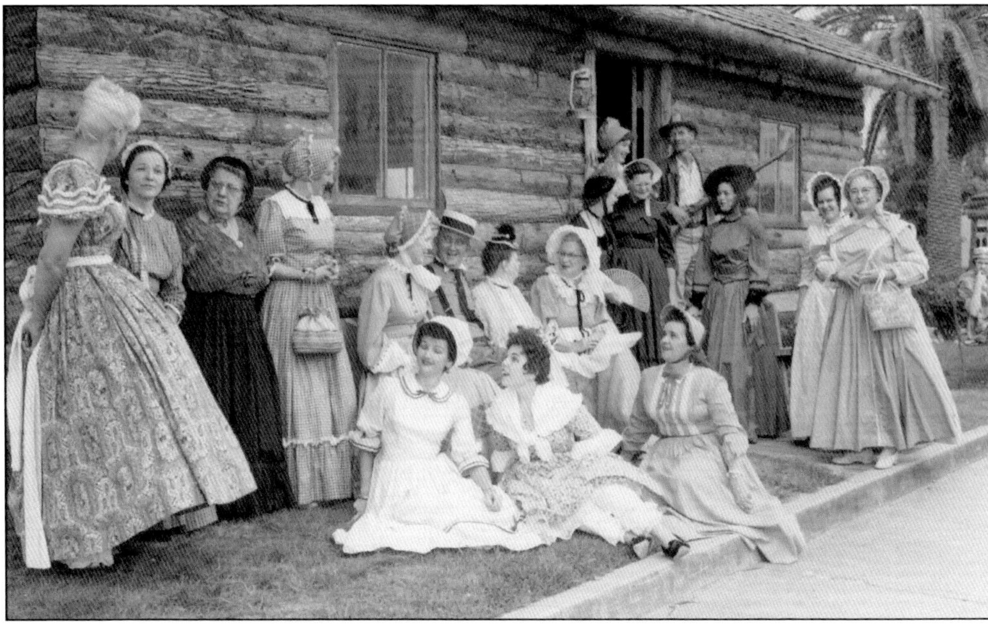

The Polk County Centennial headquarters was a replica of the 1860s courthouse and was situated on the courthouse lawn. Souvenirs, ties, booklets, bonnets, hats, and Civil War centennial items were available for purchase in the log courtroom. The yard boasted a calaboose for clean-shaven gents disregarding the centennial spirit. After the centennial, the replica was moved to Mulberry's civic center. (Courtesy State Archives of Florida, Frisbie Collection.)

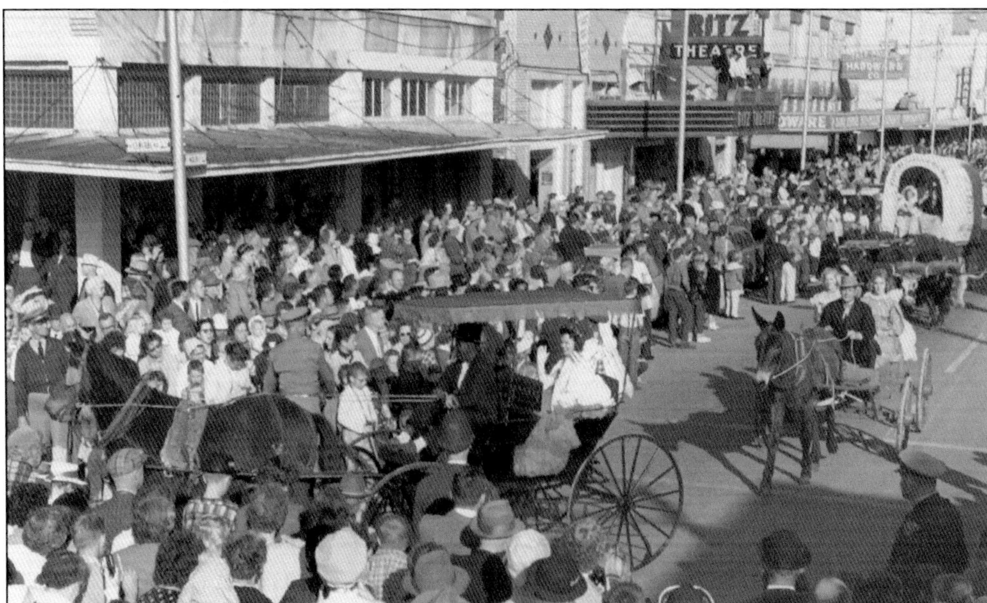

Horses, mules, and oxen provide power for wagons in the February 8, 1961, Polk County Centennial parade, which commenced the celebration of the county's birth. Calico, buttons, and bows for the ladies and whiskers, mustaches, and buckskin for the gents were the styles of the day. The event drew 6,000 people, who lined the county seat's parade route. (Courtesy State Archives of Florida, Frisbie Collection.)

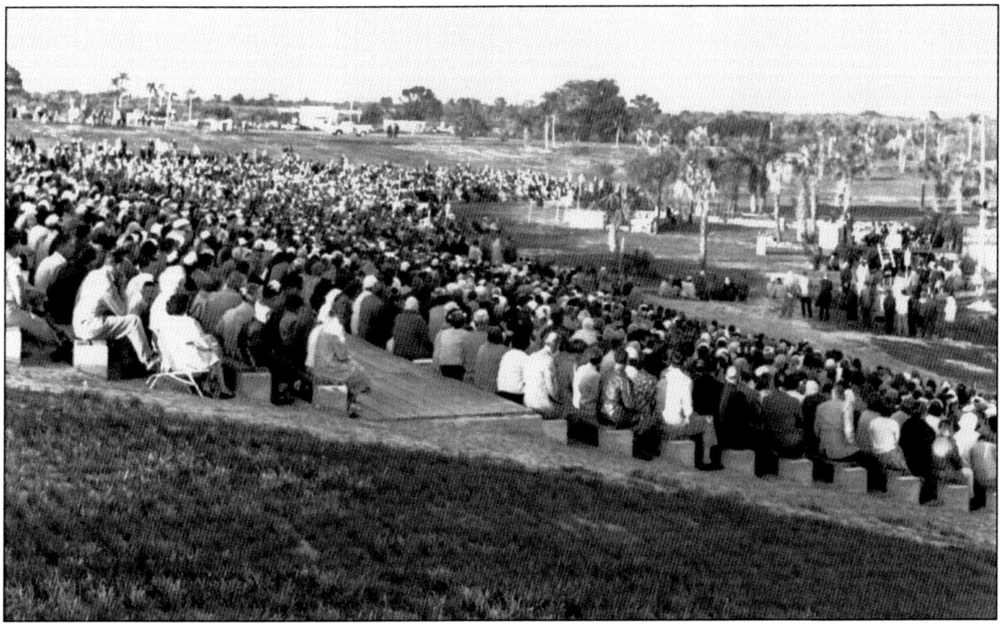

Evangelist Rev. Billy Graham conducted the 1961 celebration of Easter at a sunrise service at Bartow's Peace River Park. The centennial celebratory event was attended by Sen. Spessard Holland and a host of dignitaries. Over 35,000 people arrived to hear the gospel message. The amphitheater was used for the Polk County Centennial's final event and musical extravaganza, *Century in the Sun*, the following November. (Courtesy State Archives of Florida, Frisbie Collection.)

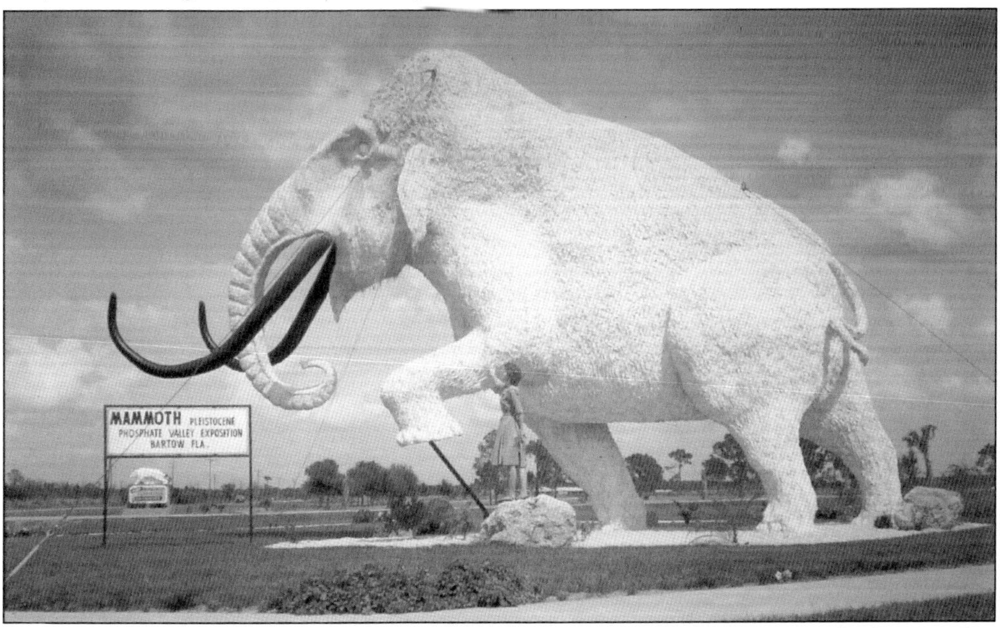

A giant mastodon towers at the entrance to the Phosphate Valley Exposition, which opened in 1959. For a decade, the attraction showcased the phosphate industry. An extensive fossil collection, models, and dioramas served to educate visitors about phosphate's importance to agriculture and commerce. In 1970, the Florida Sheriffs Youth Ranches developed the adjoining Peace River Park and museum into the Girls Villa. (Courtesy State Archives of Florida, Frisbie Collection.)

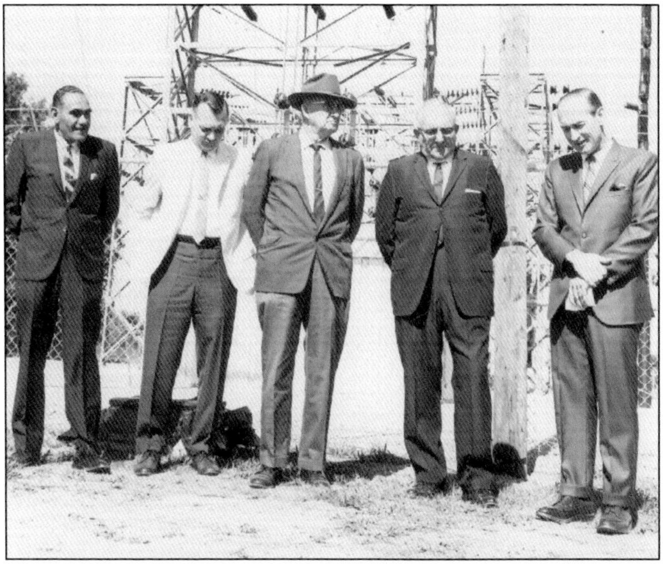

From left to right, commissioners George H. Gause, Charles A. Richardson, and Francis B. Lawrence; city manager Charlie Odom; and Mayor Dr. Webster B. Geiger gather to unveil a bronze marker at the 1970 dedication of the Odom electrical substation. The next year, Gause became Bartow's first black mayor and the first in Florida since Reconstruction. An annual parade, monument, and school honor his memory as a leader in the community. (Courtesy State Archives of Florida, Frisbie Collection.)

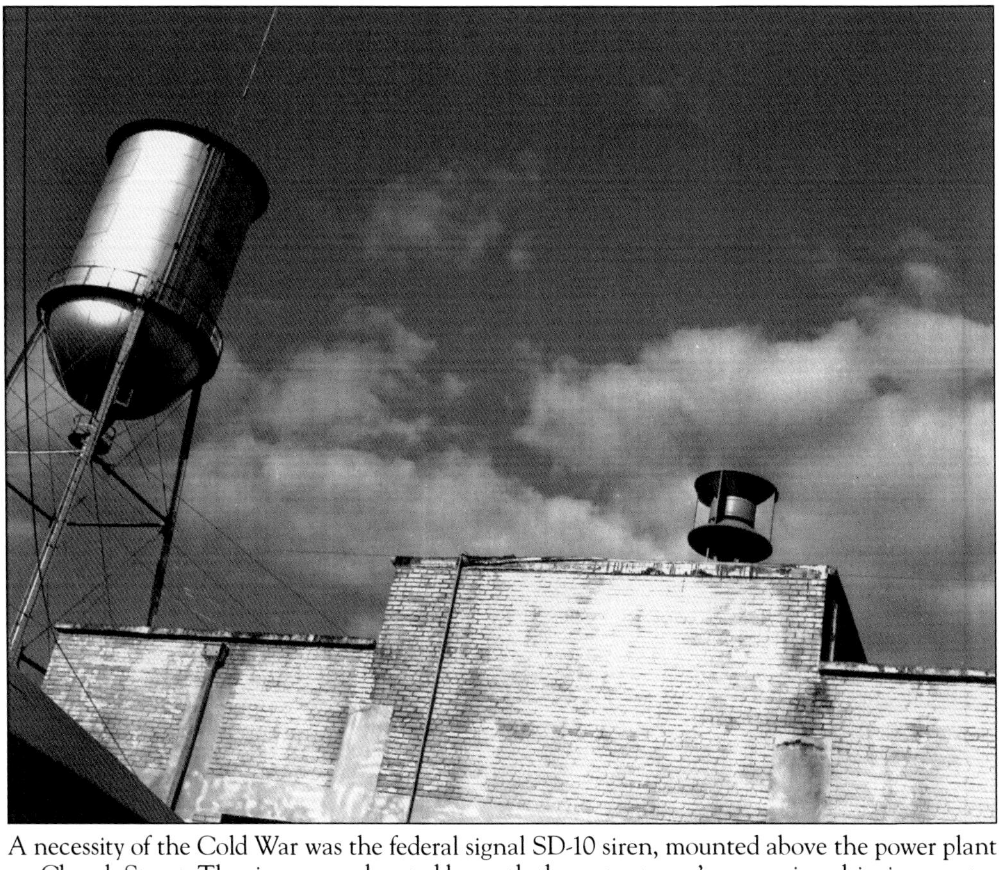

A necessity of the Cold War was the federal signal SD-10 siren, mounted above the power plant on Church Street. The siren was relocated beneath the water tower's reservoir, achieving greater range over the city. Practice drills, signaled by a three-minute blast, and shelters at the courthouse, post office, schools, phosphate mines, and homes were stark reminders of the threat of nuclear war. (Courtesy State Archives of Florida, Frisbie Collection.)

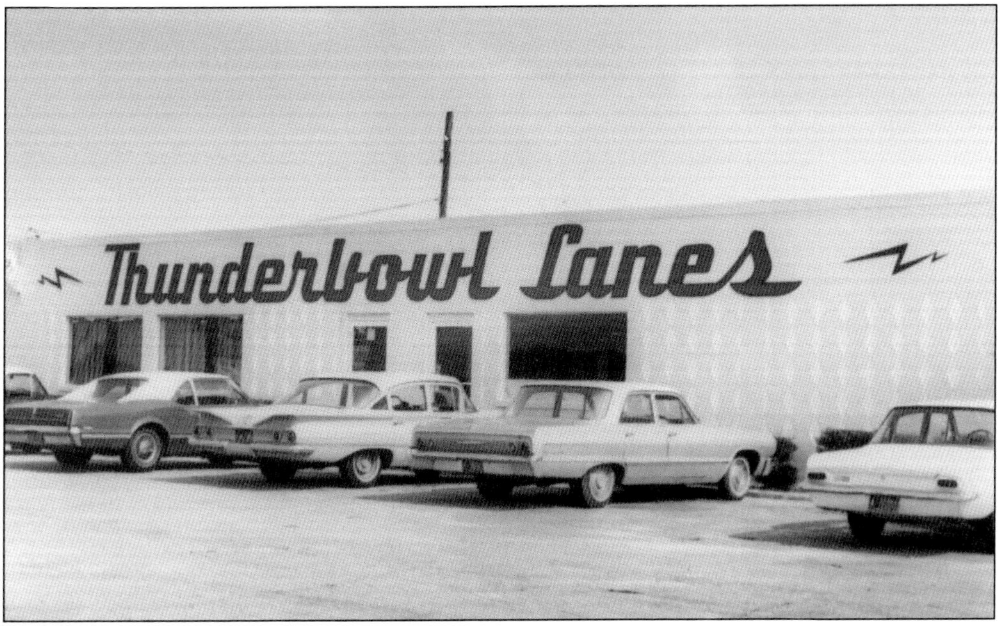

Cars line up at Thunderbowl Lanes located on East Highway 60, which offered bowling, league competitions, billiards, and recreation for many years. Inside, the business maintained a restaurant, which offered meals and snacks and served movie star Dorothy Lamour in 1962 while she was starring in the Florida Living Exposition. Previously known as the Bartow Bowling Lanes, the business closed its doors in 1968. (Courtesy State Archives of Florida, Frisbie Collection.)

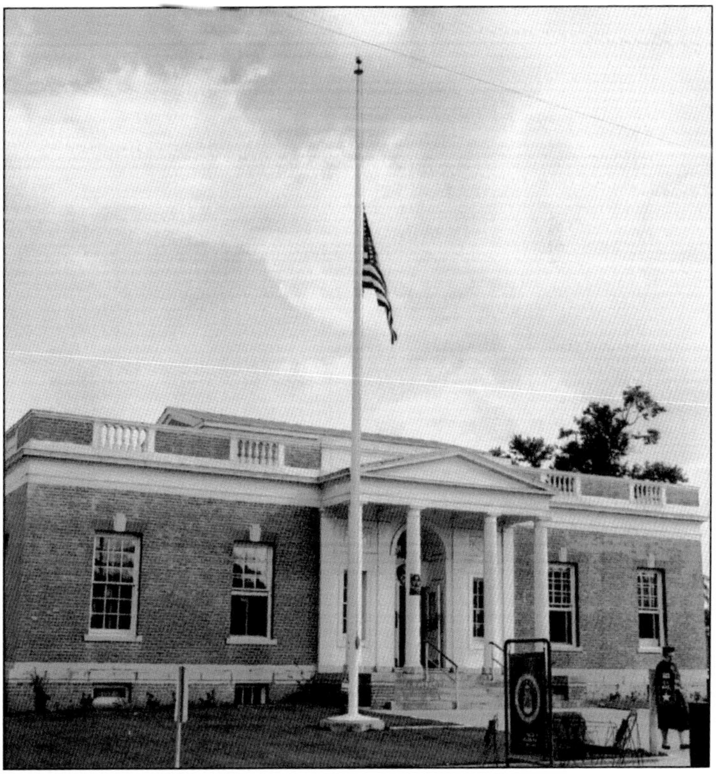

A sad day was experienced throughout the nation when Pres. John F. Kennedy was assassinated on Friday, November 23, 1963. Two days later, Bartow's outward expression of mourning was noted as the post office flag was lowered to half-staff for a period of 30 days. A wreath is affixed above the doors behind the column displaying the civil defense fallout shelter sign. (Courtesy State Archives of Florida, Frisbie Collection.)

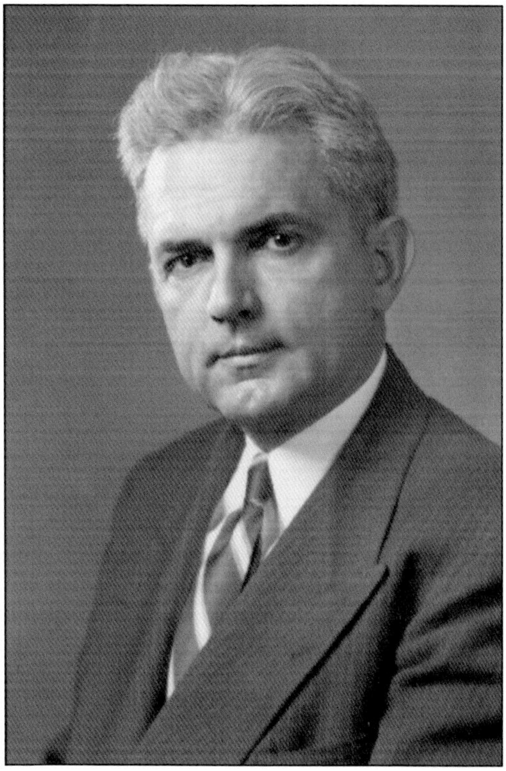

Spessard Holland served as a US senator representing Florida from 1946 to 1971. He was the sponsor of the Twenty-fourth Amendment to the Constitution, which abolished the poll tax in federal elections. As a senator, he championed statehood for Alaska and Hawaii, agriculture, interstate highways, Medicare, flood control, forestry, agriculture, and the space program. He died on November 6, 1971, and is buried in Bartow. (Courtesy State Archives of Florida.)

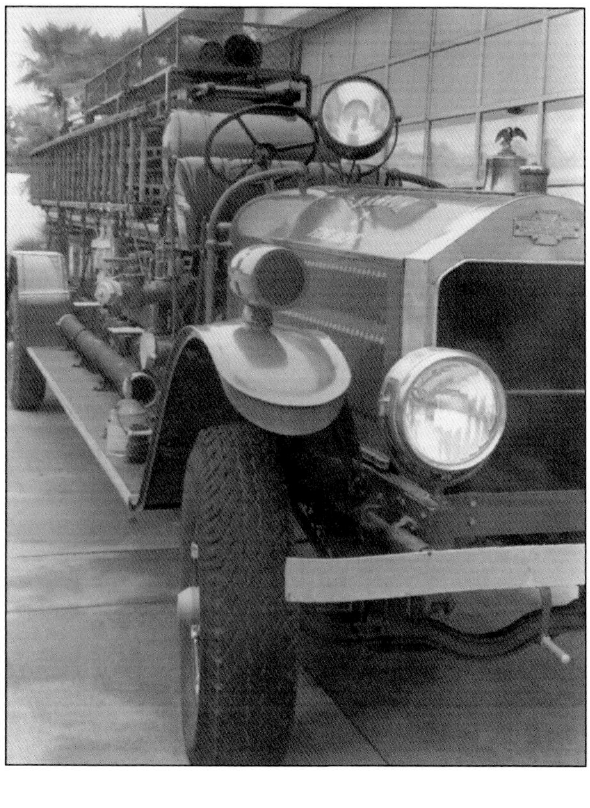

Bartow Fire Department's showpiece, American LaFrance Engine No. 3, awaits parade duty in front of the fire station. The engine was delivered by rail to the city on November 7, 1927. It was equipped with pumps, extension ladders, hoses, hooks, axes, pikes, prying tools, lanterns, a searchlight, and a brass bell. The fire engine served the community for several decades and was retired from active service in the 1950s. (Courtesy State Archives of Florida, Frisbie Collection.)

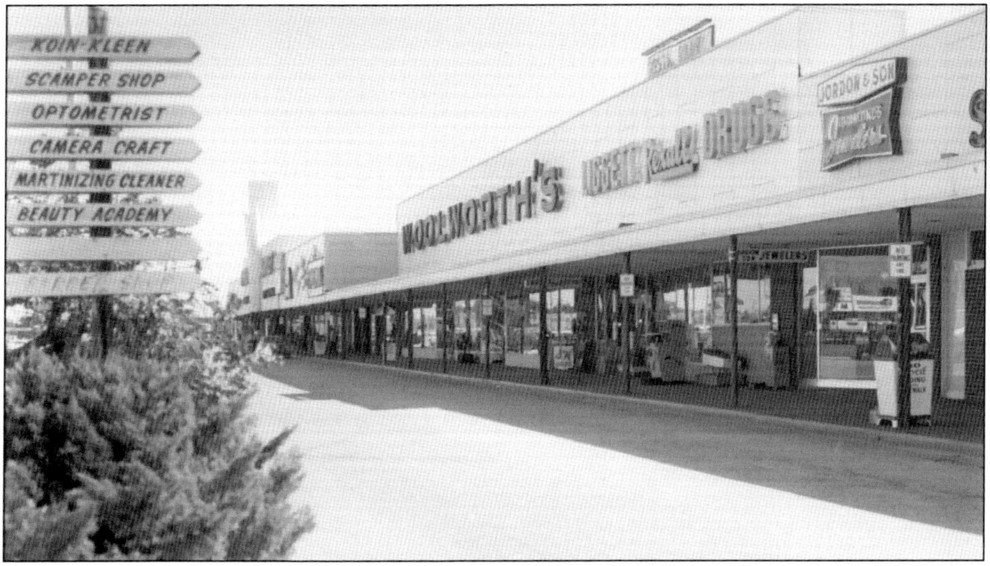

The Golden Gate Shopping Center, built in 1960, was one of many shopping centers anchored by Publix supermarkets. The first businesses were W.T. Grant, Tyree's Appliances, Leeds Shoes, Seven D's Gifts, Toy Nook, Wilson Pipes men's clothing, Colony Shops, Woolworth's, Liggett Drug, Bartow Jewelers, Sun Finance, Koin Clean Laundrette, Scamper Shop children's clothing, an optometrist, Camera Craft, Martinizing Cleaner, Beauty Academy, and Whitaker's Barber Shop. (Courtesy State Archives of Florida, Frisbie Collection.)

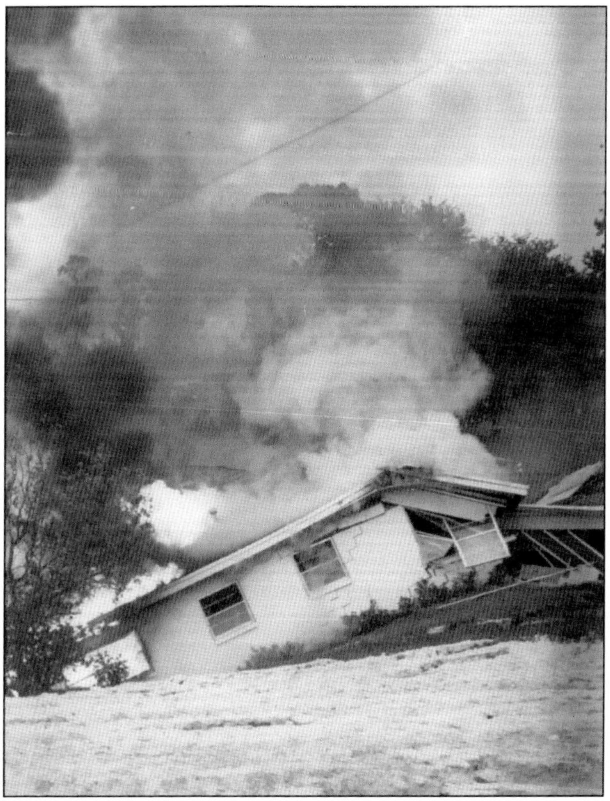

The mid-1960s was a time of extreme drought and falling water tables, which resulted in sinkholes opening up in and around the city. This sinkhole occurred in July 1967 and captured national attention when two houses in Richland Manor were swallowed into the earth. Other sinkholes opened on Main Street, Woodlawn Avenue, Bartow Elementary, West Bartow, and Kincaid Dairy Road. (Courtesy State Archives of Florida, Frisbie Collection.)

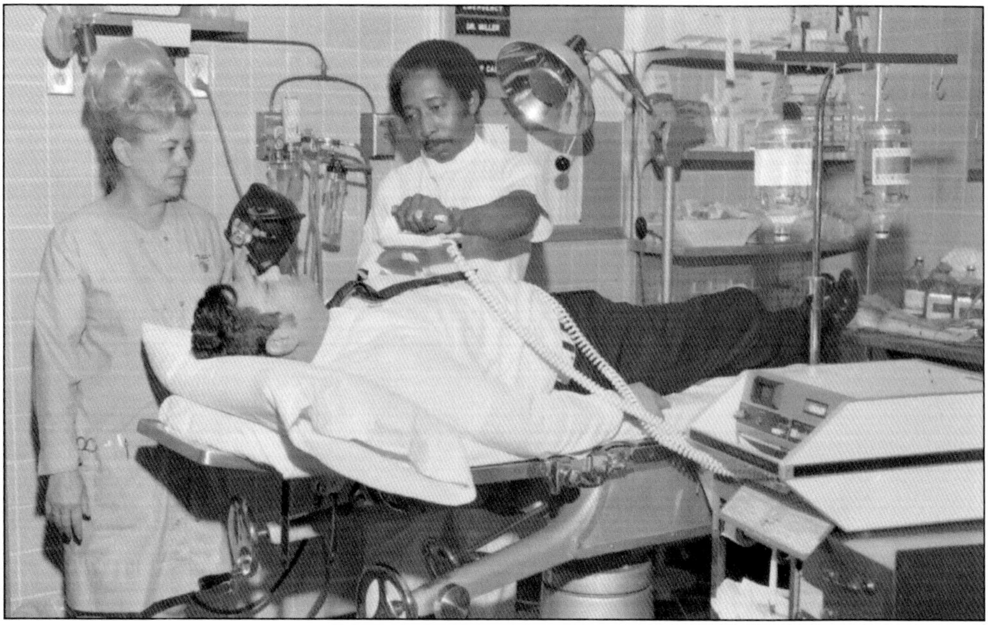

An advance in modern medicine was marked with the purchase and employment of Bartow Memorial Hospital's first defibrillator in the early 1960s. In a staged photograph, hospital employees Patricia Hutson and Willis Bennett exhibit the newest technology on administrator John Turner, posing as a patient. The hospital was opened in 1926. (Courtesy Brian Hinton, Bartow Community Health Care Foundation.)

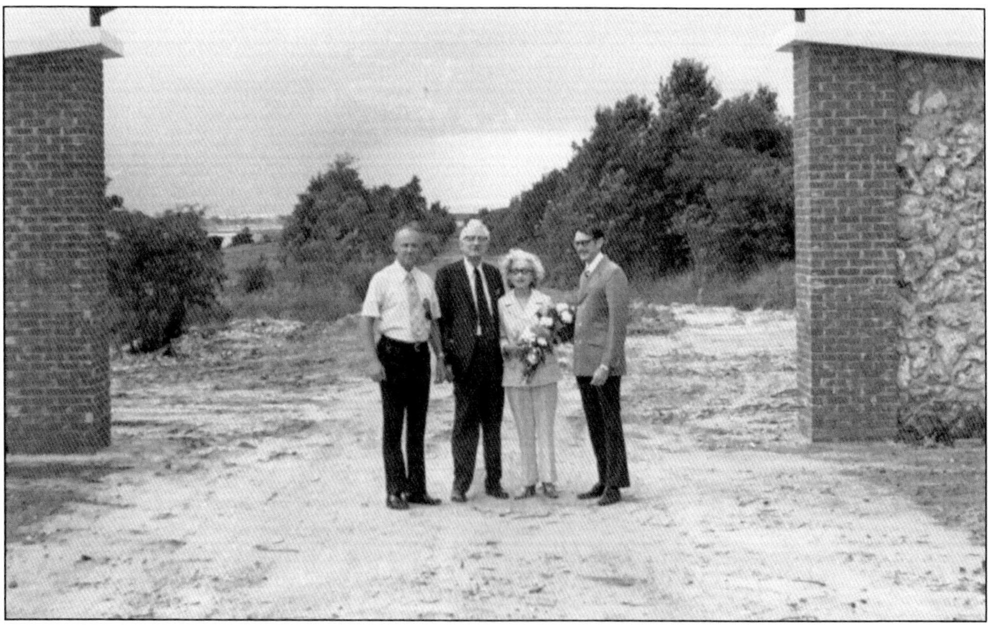

Shown here from left to right, city manager Charles T. Clark, Rep. James Haley, Mary Holland (wife of the late senator Spessard Holland), and newspaper editor S.L. Frisbie IV stand at the entrance to the new Mary Holland Park during its dedication on July 4, 1974. The lakes were named Heron, Cardinal, and Purple Martin in respect to the Hollands' love of bird-watching. (Courtesy State Archives of Florida, Frisbie Collection.)

Charlie Smith, recognized by the Social Security Administration as the oldest living American, at 134 years, was honored as the parade marshal for the celebration of the nation's bicentennial in 1976. Sporting red, white, and blue western attire, he led the grand parade and received national acclaim. Smith celebrated July Fourth as his own birthday, in keeping with his patriotic nature. Smith's claims to longevity have since been disputed based on a 1910 marriage record. It is believed he would have been about 102 at the time of this photograph. (Peggy Kehoe photograph, courtesy *Polk County Democrat.*)

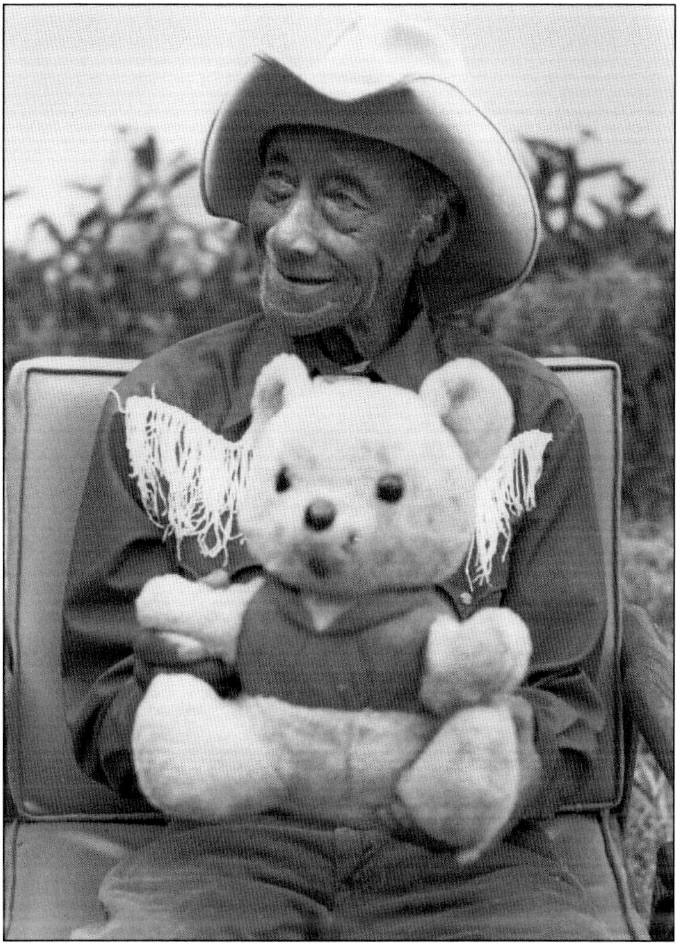

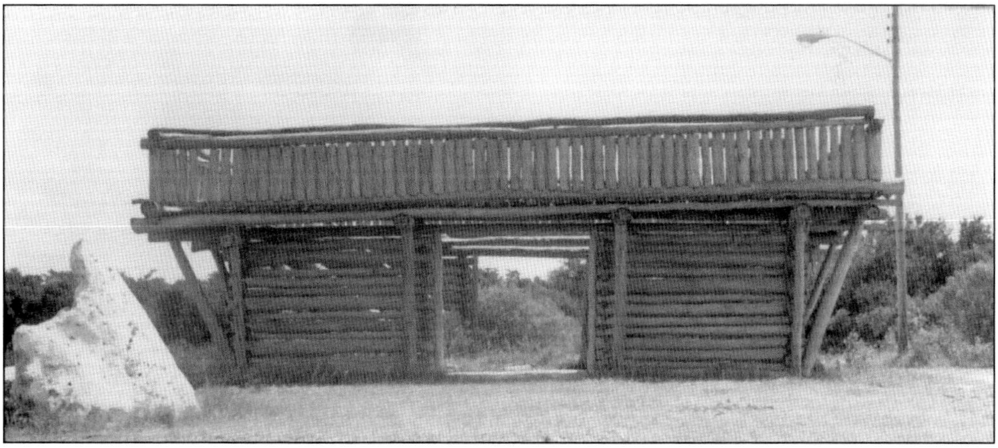

Bartow's celebration of the nation's bicentennial culminated in the completion of the bicentennial committee's 1976 project, a replica of Fort Blount, which was erected on the grounds of the Civic Center. Located south of the present public library, the fort was the product of a two-year effort to provide a glimpse of the city's historic beginning. (Courtesy State Archives of Florida, Frisbie Collection.)